THE SUNDAY ASSEMBLY

THE SUNDAY ASSEMBLY

Using *Evangelical Lutheran Worship*
Volume One

Lorraine S. Brugh
Gordon W. Lathrop

Augsburg Fortress

The Sunday Assembly: Using *Evangelical Lutheran Worship*, Volume One
Copyright © 2008 Augsburg Fortress

Using *Evangelical Lutheran Worship*
  Volume 1, *The Sunday Assembly*
  Volume 2, *The Christian Life: Baptism and Life Passages*
  Volume 3, *Keeping Time: The Church's Years*

Other *Evangelical Lutheran Worship* Leader Guides
  Indexes to Evangelical Lutheran Worship
  Musicians Guide to Evangelical Lutheran Worship
  Hymnal Companion to Evangelical Lutheran Worship

Cover art: Nicholas T. Markell, Markell Studios, Inc. Copyright © 2006 Augsburg Fortress.

Manufactured in the U.S.A.

ISBN 978-0-8066-7013-3

15   14   13   12   11   3   4   5   6   7   8   9   10

CONTENTS

Preface to the *Evangelical Lutheran Worship* Leader Guides

*E*vangelical Lutheran Worship includes a number of related print editions and other resources developed to support the worship life of the Evangelical Lutheran Church in America and the Evangelical Lutheran Church in Canada. The core print editions of *Evangelical Lutheran Worship*, released in late 2006, include the following:

Pew (Assembly) Edition

Leaders Edition and Leaders Desk Edition

Accompaniment Edition: Liturgies

Accompaniment Edition: Service Music and Hymns.

An encounter with these core editions and their introductions is important to an understanding of the goals and principles embodied in *Evangelical Lutheran Worship*.

In addition to the core materials, *Evangelical Lutheran Worship* includes other published resources that extend the usefulness of the core editions and respond to the developing needs of the church in mission. The Evangelical Lutheran Worship leader guides, which include the present volume, supplement the core editions in a variety of ways.

These resources are intended to provide worship leaders and planners with support for *Evangelical Lutheran Worship* in ways that would not be possible within the core editions themselves. Although the assembly edition includes more interpretive material than its predecessors, such as the annotated patterns for worship that complement the notes within the services, it provides only minimal guidance for leading worship in a variety of settings. Although the leaders edition includes a more extensive section titled Notes on the Services, it is not designed to accommodate deeper historical context, theological reflection, or extensive practical counsel for those who want to lead worship with understanding and confidence.

The leader guides include a set of three volumes, Using *Evangelical Lutheran Worship*. This set addresses as its primary audience pastors, seminarians, and church musicians—people who together take the lead in preparing the assembly's worship week by week. In a time when many congregations have implemented a broader sharing in worship leadership and planning, however, the contents of these three volumes will be valuable also for assisting ministers with various roles, altar guilds and sacristans, worship committees, and worshipers who are seeking deeper understanding.

The Sunday Assembly, first in this set of three volumes, includes a general introduction to worship that is evangelical, Lutheran, and ecumenical. This is followed by in-depth historical, theological, and practical reflections on the service of Holy Communion and the Service of the Word. *The Christian Life: Baptism and Life Passages,* the second volume in this set of three, takes up the service of Holy Baptism and related services such as Affirmation of Baptism, together with the services of Healing, Funeral, and Marriage. *Keeping Time: The Church's Years,* the third volume in this set, addresses the church's calendar of Sundays, festivals, and seasons; the place of the lectionary and other propers; and the cycle of daily prayer.

The leader guides also include two volumes focused on assembly song. *Musicians Guide to Evangelical Lutheran Worship* presents essays on the musical leadership of assembly song in a variety of styles and genres, and offers music performance helps for each piece of liturgical music and every hymn in *Evangelical Lutheran Worship.* The *Hymnal Companion to Evangelical Lutheran Worship* includes detailed background on the words and music of the hymns, together with an overview of the role of hymnody in the church's worship. Both of these volumes, while having particular appeal to church musicians, will be useful also to pastors, seminarians, worship committees, choir members, and other worshipers.

Other reference and interpretive resources will be included among the leader guides as needed. *Indexes for Worship Planning* is one such volume, with an extensive list of suggested hymns for the church year and an expanded set of other indexes.

Many of the church's gifted teachers have contributed to the writing and assembling of the leader guides. They have sought to discern and give additional focus to the vision for worship among Lutherans that emerged from the five-year Renewing Worship process (2001-2005), which engaged thousands of people across the Evangelical Lutheran Church in America and the Evangelical Lutheran Church in Canada in encountering provisional materials, in sharing creative gifts, and in evaluating various stages of the proposal. To be sure, this vision is one marked by a great diversity of thought and practice, a diversity the contributors seek to reflect in these volumes. Yet these gifted teachers also bring to this work their own distinctive points of view, shaped by their own experiences and by their encounters with other teachers, rostered leaders, and worshiping communities around the world.

The *Evangelical Lutheran Worship* leader guides thus do not intend to provide definitive answers or official positions in matters related to worship among Lutherans. In these volumes, however, we are invited to engage in conversation with teachers of the church, to consider how their insights and guidance may best inform and inspire the many different contexts in which local leaders guide the worship life of their communities. In so doing, these leader guides in their own ways seek to do what also the core editions set out to do: "to make more transparent the principle of fostering unity without imposing uniformity," so that ultimately all these resources might "be servants through which the Holy Spirit will call out the church, gather us around Jesus Christ in word and sacrament, and send us, enlivened, to share the good news of life in God" (*Evangelical Lutheran Worship,* Introduction, p. 8).

PART ONE

The Assembly on Sunday: Foundational Reflections

CHAPTER ONE

Evangelical Lutheran Worship and the Assembly on Sunday

Evangelical Lutheran Worship, a book bound in a deep-red color, lies open on the desk. Its contents can be surveyed on page 5. The red tabs on the outside edges of the first third of its pages correspond to sections of worship materials: The Church Year, Holy Communion, Holy Baptism, Lent and the Three Days, Life Passages, Daily Prayer. Where those tabs stop, the Assembly Song begins: first the 150 Psalms, then Service Music, beginning with a Kyrie at #151 and ending with the Great Litany at #238, then Hymns and National Songs, #239–893. The Additional Resources at the end of the book include a Daily Lectionary, notes on Scripture and Worship, the Small Catechism of Martin Luther, and various indexes. The important Introduction and General Notes on pages 6–9 can be read. The Leaders Edition, with yet further expansions, resources, and Notes on the Services, offers support for the congregation's use of the book itself. The whole complex of materials is ready to be studied, understood, and used.

This book, *The Sunday Assembly*, is about that deep-red resource as it may come to be employed in your congregation, especially on Sunday, but also at other times when you are gathered. We will explore the contents of *Evangelical Lutheran Worship* (AE, for assembly/pew edition) and its Leaders Edition (LE), with an accent on the materials for the Holy Communion and for the related Service of the Word. In this volume we seek to engage readers about the ways those services in particular may be used by worshiping communities. This chapter and the three immediately following are introductory. Chapter 2 is about the centrality of the Holy Communion in Lutheran practice. Chapter 3 is about the basic structure of the service. Chapter 4 is about music and the arts in worship. Chapter 5 is about leaders in the assembly. In chapters 6–10 we examine each part of the liturgy, exploring its meanings and its options for actual practice. Additional volumes in this series address such topics as the relationship between *Evangelical Lutheran Worship* and baptismal life, the church's year and daily prayer, helps for leading the church's song, and a variety of reference resources.

But while this book and the series are about the red book, in a larger sense, this book—especially in this chapter—is about the *title* of the red book. We need to think about worship that is evangelical and Lutheran in the present time. We need to think about how that worship may be taking place regularly in Sunday assemblies. And we need to think about how that worship is not only evangelical and Lutheran but also *ecumenical*—how it is related to what other Christians around the world are doing, as *all* of our worship is gathered by the Spirit into God's mission of life-giving mercy for the world.

Evangelical, Lutheran, Ecumenical

Evangelical Lutheran Worship is intended, in the first place, as a resource for communities of people in North America and the Caribbean to do worship that is both evangelical and Lutheran in this first part of the twenty-first century. Through formal denominational action, *Evangelical Lutheran Worship* has been "commended for use" in the Evangelical Lutheran Church in America and "approved for use" and "commended . . . as its primary worship resource" in the Evangelical Lutheran Church in Canada. The book inherits much of the tradition and many of the insights that marked other worship books used before it among those churches and their predecessor bodies—especially *The Lutheran Hymnal* of 1941, *Service Book and Hymnal* of 1958, *Lutheran Book of Worship* of 1978, and the supplementary *With One Voice* of 1995. It is the result of a widely participatory process of reflection, composition, review, and editing that sought to inquire how those insights and that tradition might best be continued, refreshed, and enlarged now, in the practice of current Lutheran worshiping communities.

But the book intends also to welcome any community that wishes to use it. Its resources are not only evangelical and Lutheran, not confined to the church bodies that span the United States, Canada, and the Caribbean region. They are also ecumenical. By being faithfully Lutheran and evangelical, these resources also offer gifts that are deeply ecumenical and widely global in their resonance. Note that on the book's spine is a single word: *Worship*. That is all. Perhaps the book will be picked up by communities in other parts of the world. Perhaps it will assist gatherings that are not specifically called Lutheran. Certainly, it will be used by assemblies—in homes and schools and hospitals, but also in large meetings—that are not formally constituted as congregations. *Evangelical Lutheran Worship* seeks to be a resource for worship that is evangelical, Lutheran, and ecumenical, offering its assistance to any assembly that is interested in those characteristics.

But what are those characteristics? What is it to be evangelical? Or Lutheran? And what do we mean by ecumenical in this context?

Evangelical, Lutheran, Ecumenical

Worship can be called *evangelical* when it is centered on the gospel of Jesus Christ—the *evangel*, the good news of his life-giving death and resurrection—and when it is genuinely interested in continually welcoming people into this gospel. Currently, the word evangelical has a number of connotations throughout the world. American English has especially applied the word to those Christians who are inheritors of the practices of American frontier revivals, with their accent on experiences of emotional response, individual conversion, and individual salvation. "Evangelical" has come to be synonymous with this theological emphasis on personal decision, and even with certain political emphases that have come to be related to this individualism.

Lutherans generally do not use the word in this way. Rather than religious individualism, they mean by *evangelical* their own deep interest in communities that gather together around the gospel of Jesus Christ—around the gospel-books that tell the story of Jesus, around all the scriptures that bear witness to God's judgment and mercy, around preaching that speaks God's gift of forgiveness and life in Christ, and around the sacraments of baptism and the Lord's supper that proclaim and give this same gospel in visible and tangible ways. For Lutherans, it is the presence of these things that makes worship evangelical, not the quality of our response. Lutherans believe that the Holy Spirit brings people to gather around this gospel-gift, and—by enlivening the word and the sacraments, the "means of grace"—brings them to trust and believe in God again. Lutherans think that the people who gather are thus formed together by the Spirit to embody and give away to others the very gospel that they celebrate. Interestingly, in many other countries throughout the world and in many other languages, the Lutheran churches are usually called not by the name of Martin Luther, but by the word evangelical. For example, in Germany they are the *evangelische Kirchen,* the evangelical churches—that is, churches that understand themselves to be centered in the gospel, the *euaggelion,* the *evangel.*

In any case, for Lutherans, worship is *evangelical* when—
- it is worship in word and sacrament,
- the gospel of Jesus Christ stands forth in clarity as a gift of God in that word and those sacraments, in preaching and singing, baptizing and forgiving and communing,
- everyone is welcome to this life-giving, faith-making gospel-gift, and
- the assembly is sent to bear witness to this gift in the world.

Evangelical worship, by this understanding, does not so much focus on what we do or decide as on what God has done, is doing, and will do. Evangelical worship knows that all people—young and old, insiders and outsiders, old-timers and newcomers alike—are in need of this gift, this word of forgiveness, this taste of mercy and life, bringing us again and again to faith. Lutherans hope that this gospel in word and sacraments and this open accessibility to all people mark their own gatherings for worship. But they rejoice whenever and wherever accessible, gospel-centered worship in word and sacraments is found. A community does not need to call itself Lutheran to be evangelical.

Evangelical Lutheran Worship intends to help worship be evangelical in exactly this sense. It serves best not simply as a resource for any kind of worship—but for worship that finds its center in the gospel of Jesus Christ. *Evangelical Lutheran Worship's* accents on—
- the word and the sacraments as the heart of worship;
- the presence and gift of Jesus Christ in the assembly;
- the need we all have for God's forgiveness and grace;
- the importance of the preaching of God's word of law and gospel;
- prayers that reflect the wideness of God's mercy for the whole world;
- the normal practice of the holy communion every Sunday;
- baptism enacted within the assembly and remembered with thanksgiving;
- accessible, biblically-formed language that embraces all; and
- the sending of the assembly in mission and witness

—are *evangelical* accents!

Evangelical, *Lutheran,* Ecumenical

These evangelical accents, however, are also classic *Lutheran* accents, for all the Lutheran churches understand themselves to be evangelical churches, whether or not that term is in their official title. More may be said about Lutheran worship, however. Lutherans confess that the God they trust and praise is a *triune* God. They believe that this God has created and continues to sustain all things. They believe that this same God has acted in Jesus Christ to save sinners and justify the ungodly, giving both the word and the sacraments so that the assembly that is called "the church" will be centered in Jesus Christ. And they believe that this same God has sent the Spirit to bring us all to faith through this word and these sacraments and so to bring us to faith-active-in-love, turned toward our neighbor and toward the whole world in its deepest needs.

Furthermore, Lutherans confess that the use of the gift of word and sacrament is what unites the church, rather than the required use of uniformly-practiced human ceremonies, whether new or old. Among Lutherans, pastors are appointed to serve this word and these sacraments in local assemblies. And Lutherans confess that the whole participating assembly—not just the clergy—makes up the church. These articles of Lutheran confession come to expression in worship. A Lutheran service of worship is not at its heart something we intend to do for God, but something we believe that God is doing for us and for the world. Faithful *Lutheran* worship is thus marked by—

- trinitarian faith;
- trust that God's gift of the world is good and is to be cared for;
- the knowledge that all of us are sinners but that God has acted in Christ to save us;
- the reliable centrality of the word and sacraments that proclaim these things;
- a diversity of local ceremonial practice;
- a strong willingness to receive the patterns of worship that have been used by the church down through the ages;
- the use of song, richly varied in forms and genres, as one principal way that all the people are invited to participate in the whole service; and thus by
- a participating, singing assembly drawn together by the Spirit of Christ in the word and the sacraments and sent into the world to serve.

The word *assembly* recurs again and again in the pages of *Evangelical Lutheran Worship*. This too is a Lutheran accent, though not exclusively. The use of this word rehearses the basic Lutheran confession concerning the church: "It is also taught that at all times there must be and remain one, holy Christian church. It is the assembly of all believers among whom the gospel is purely preached and the sacraments are administered according to the gospel" (Augsburg Confession 7:1).

More deeply, however, this usage recalls *biblical* language, namely the New Testament word for church—*ekklesia*, a called-out gathering, a new assembly around Christ like that around the word of God in Deuteronomy 18:16 ("on the day of the assembly") or Nehemiah 8:2 ("Ezra brought the law before the assembly"). The usage also points to the communally active involvement of everyone who is so gathered and thus points to the remarkable paradox of any gathering for Christian worship: God acts here, but God acts on, in, and under our coming together as an assembly. Just so, the bread that we break is the body of Christ (1 Cor. 10:16), given by God and not by us. Just so, the man Jesus whom we encounter is our God (John 20:28), coming toward us, full of grace and truth.

What is Lutheran worship? It is—

- a local and open assembly of people in need,
- gathered by the Holy Spirit
- to encounter God's grace in Jesus Christ, the crucified and risen one,
- given by God through word and sacraments,
- so that these people together might signify how much God loves the world,
- might themselves come again to faith in God,
- and might so turn in love and service to their neighbors.

In worship, God gives to us so that we might in turn give to the needy world. This idea is itself a gift, needed in the world.

Evangelical Lutheran Worship means to be a *Lutheran* book by—

- inviting us to be an assembly, actively gathered around word and sacraments;
- its very accent on song as a principal means of assembly participation;
- its strong expression of trinitarian faith;

- its invitation to the trust that God acts in the assembly of worship; and by
- its varied options for a local community to use for these central things.

The evangelical and Lutheran character of the book can be seen in yet other ways. The great tradition of Lutheran hymnody forms the backbone of its hymn collection, while the collection is also fleshed out with a diversity of song from around the world. The evangelical and Lutheran accent on baptism as a gift that gives us an identity and constitutes the church recurs again and again in the services, as in the very beginning of the Sunday services. The words at communion — that twice repeated "for you" — echo the assertions of the Small Catechism of Martin Luther (the Catechism itself is included in the book). The evangelical interest in sharing the gospel and the Lutheran interest in the well-being of the world are echoed by the missional accents of *Evangelical Lutheran Worship*. "Go in peace. Share the good news." Or "Go in peace. Remember the poor." These optional dismissals may conclude its Sunday services. And the important guiding reflections on word and sacrament, made by both the Canadian church and the U.S. church and adopted by their churchwide assemblies — the 1991 *Statement on Sacramental Practices* of the ELCIC and the 1997 statement on *The Use of the Means of Grace* of the ELCA (both printed in the appendixes of this book) — have functioned to shape much of the contents of the book. The very first words of the introduction in *Evangelical Lutheran Worship* are drawn from *The Use of the Means of Grace* (Principle 1):

Jesus Christ is the living and abiding Word of God. By the power of the Spirit, this very Word of God, which is Jesus Christ, is read in the Scriptures, proclaimed in preaching, announced in the forgiveness of sins, eaten and drunk in the Holy Communion, and encountered in the bodily presence of the Christian community.

But there is even more. The Lutheran character of *Evangelical Lutheran Worship* can also be seen in the many ways the book affirms and extends the worship renewal marked out by *Lutheran Book of*

Worship of 1978. That book came to be known for introducing many important characteristics into North American Lutheran worship, characteristics that built on deep Lutheran conviction and well-grounded Lutheran practice as well as on Lutheran commitment to ecumenical developments. Through *Lutheran Book of Worship*, a Lutheran version of the ecumenical three-year lectionary spread widely in North American congregations, becoming the practice of the overwhelming majority of them. Lay assisting ministers were given integral worship leadership roles — leading prayer and other appointed parts of the service, reading scripture, ministering communion, animating song. Still other emphases included the strong celebration of baptism and its regular remembrance, the recovery of psalm singing in the Sunday liturgy, the local composition of Sunday intercessions, the importance of the hymn of the day, the use of current English language forms marked by biblical images and by inclusive words for humankind, the use of ecumenically drafted texts for prayers many churches hold in common, notable examples of evangelical prayers of thanksgiving at the table, the use of a dismissal to service at the end of the liturgy, the recovery of the liturgies of Holy Week and the Vigil of Easter, the use of a light-service and a sung litany in Evening Prayer, the inclusion of Prayer at the Close of the Day among the daily prayer forms available in the congregation's book, the availability of psalm prayers to conclude any psalm used in daily prayer, the commemoration of Christian women and men throughout history who are models of faith, and a widening circle of world hymnody.

All these features and emphases continue to be found in *Evangelical Lutheran Worship*, sometimes with yet further development, sometimes with helpful redirection based on a generation of use. The three-year lectionary, for example, is now the ecumenically shared Revised Common Lectionary, revised partly with significant Lutheran input. The prayers we have in common now include the most recent ecumenical versions of the Nicene and Apostles' creeds, the dialogue of the great thanksgiving, and the canticles in daily prayer. The language of the services includes careful crafting of the ways we speak of God and of humankind. A service that includes musical portions in both English and Spanish is possible with this book. The collection of prayers at the table of the Lord has continued to grow. The list of matters for the preparation of local intercessions includes prayer for the well-being of creation. The psalm prayers have been redrafted and refreshed. The services for Ash Wednesday, the Sunday of the Passion, Maundy Thursday, Good Friday, and the Vigil of Easter are now included in the assembly's book, not only in the Leaders Edition. So is a singing version of all of the psalms. The collection of psalm tones has been revised and expanded. The list of commemorated Christians from the past has been richly reframed. The hymn list draws widely from throughout the world, sometimes making one or more stanzas available in a great variety of original languages. And the evangelical Lutheran accents on lay assisting ministers, on the hymn of the day, on baptism, on sending to witness and service, and on accessible forms of daily prayer all continue in strength. The worship renewal that became familiar to many Lutherans through *Lutheran Book of Worship* is alive — continuing, changing, meeting new needs — in *Evangelical Lutheran Worship*.

The visual art in *Evangelical Lutheran Worship* is another evangelical and Lutheran feature that was present in a limited way in *Lutheran Book of Worship* but is now greatly enriched and integrated with the contents. Unlike some other Christians, Lutherans have never rejected the use of images to celebrate the gospel of Jesus and show forth both the goodness and the need of God's world. The very cover of the book carries a symbolic image of the cross as the tree of life, holding out leaves for the healing of the nations of the world (Rev. 22:2), for the healing of each person who comes into the assembly and picks up the book. It is as if in holding this book and its resources for an assembly around the gospel, we — in our deep need for healing — hold a handful of the leaves of the tree of life. This image is repeated throughout the book. The tree of life that is Jesus Christ and his gospel — the heart of any evangelical assembly — recurs in yet other forms (AE pp. 11, 245, 266, 333, 339), as do many other images: Christ and the disciples at Emmaus; the assembly itself, in realistic and more symbolic forms; a baptism in a great, cross-shaped font; people marking life passages; and several graphic symbols of the elements of worship. While these images are only printed in a book, they may invite you to look again at the images in the room that may now or could sometime in the future surround and interpret your assembly as it gathers around the gospel.

But Lutheran worship has one further characteristic, shared by *Evangelical Lutheran Worship*. It is sometimes challenging and difficult. To plan and lead a service that is participatory and yet accentuates God's activity and not ours takes hard work, considerable skill, self-criticism, communal trust, and a good deal of love on the part of an assembly's leaders. It also takes simple humility and trust in the God who acts in word and sacraments. Something like the same thing can be said of all of the other seemingly contradictory pairs that mark worship that is evangelical and Lutheran: worship that is centered yet welcoming, Lutheran but also ecumenical, local but more than local, traditional but also contemporary, faithfully biblical but honest to the current times, uniting but not required or compelled, free but reliable. It is easy to fall off on one side or the other of any of these important, balanced pairs. In the past, for example, Lutherans were often regarded as impossibly traditional and conservative, never trying anything new. Today, some congregations have fled from tradition, wanting to be marked only by the contemporary. Evangelical Lutheran worship, at its best, is both, finding the sources for authentic tradition and genuine contemporaneity in the gift of the gospel of Jesus Christ, set out today in the faithful word and the accessible sacraments. Some Lutheran Christians long for a central authority to issue the rules of worship that must be followed. Other Lutheran Christians refuse anything they did not create themselves. Neither approach will work. Both seem to assume that there's a single "right way." Instead, Lutherans confess that word and sacraments are the gifts from God that unite us—and they must be made the constantly renewed center of our gatherings by teaching and love, not constraint. The deep-red worship book will not automatically make all this work easier. The book itself will require study and work for us to know its contents, to perceive its reasons, to see its possibilities. But *Evangelical Lutheran Worship* is intended to be a significant resource in each local place for the balancing act that marks faithful worship that is evangelical and Lutheran.

Evangelical, Lutheran, *Ecumenical*

We have already seen that faithful Lutheran worship is, by the best definition, ecumenical. That is, from the start, Lutherans—evangelical Christians of the Lutheran Reformation—never intended to create new forms of worship but rather to try to ensure that the good, received forms of the church of the ages were always filled with the gospel. That initial stance has meant that the ongoing changes and reforms in worldwide ecumenical Christianity—the trinitarian

Christianity that has come to be called "catholic" in the broadest sense of that word—have also gained the attention of Lutherans. The winds of healthful change blowing through various Christian communions in the first two-thirds of the twentieth century influenced *Lutheran Book of Worship*. They are also found in *Evangelical Lutheran Worship*. Furthermore, Lutherans have hoped to urge other Christians to place the gospel in word and sacraments at the heart of their own assemblies. Shared with other Christians, *Evangelical Lutheran Worship* can be such an encouragement, such a proposal.

In describing worship that is ecumenical today, these characteristics, all shared by *Evangelical Lutheran Worship* with wide numbers of Christian communities throughout the world, are worthy of mention:

- the shape of the Sunday service as gathering, word, meal, and sending;
- the recovery of the idea that in worship the assembly is central and active, God's people receiving God's gifts and responding with praise and thanksgiving;
- the ecumenical three-year lectionary and a related lectionary for daily prayer;
- the importance of preaching, intercessions, holy communion, and the ministry of the forgiveness of sins;
- the role of an ordained presiding minister;
- the importance of Sunday and the general shape of the church year;
- the recovery of gospel-focused patterns for thanksgiving at the Lord's table;
- the recovery of the liturgies of the Three Days;
- the centrality of baptism for Christian identity, the celebration of baptism in the Sunday Assembly, and the recovery of a welcoming process for bringing people to the font;
- the shape of daily prayer, especially the recovered congregational forms of morning prayer, evening prayer, and night prayer;
- the texts and prayers held in common among the churches; and
- a long list of hymns shared with many other Christian communities.

But while we may recognize these ecumenical traits of the book, they will serve more profoundly if they actually lead local assemblies to an ecumenical practice. A local assembly, gathered around the gospel in word and sacraments, can long for signs of communion to be exchanged with other such assemblies—in its own neighborhood and around the world. It can seriously and regularly pray for the health and renewal of other churches and their leaders. It can engage in the common work of witness and service together with other congregations. It can recognize and study together with others the shared lectionary and the shared liturgical pattern. It can even explore the possibility of a shared process of baptismal formation for people coming newly to Christian faith. *Evangelical Lutheran Worship* can be a resource for such a vision.

But, in considering the current meaning of the title of the book, there remain yet other balancing acts. Worship that is evangelical and Lutheran must be ecumenical. It must also be both traditional and contemporary and both local and more-than-local. And this worship takes place on Sunday. *Evangelical Lutheran Worship* means to put a book in the hands of the people that can be a resource for these things.

Traditional but Also Contemporary

Evangelical Lutheran Worship stands in the church's long tradition of handing on to contemporary assemblies both the worship of its forebears in the faith and the new songs and expressions of current practice. This is consistent with Martin Luther's own liturgical reforms and the earliest Lutheran practices. Luther retained the structure of the Western catholic form while adding contemporary adaptations. One of the most notable new developments that flourished during that time was encouragement for new musical expressions in familiar language. The emergence of the chorale as the primary congregational song of this period is evidence of that new practice. Luther encouraged poets and musicians to develop new resources and to publish them in hope of making worship accessible and understandable to all the people.

How far back does our own liturgical tradition reach? It reaches fully and deeply back to biblical roots, both Old and New Testaments. Beginning with the biblical witness, our liturgical texts combine words of scripture with other Christian texts to form the tapestry we now hear as the familiar prayers, responses, and songs of worship. For a look at many of the scriptural texts that ground Lutheran liturgy today, see pages AE 1155–1159. They outline the key foundational biblical passages for the services of Holy Communion and Holy Baptism. We can see how scripture weaves its way through the prayers we pray, the texts we say, and the songs we sing. Our worship is scriptural to the core.

As the introduction to these pages notes, scripture's pervasiveness in our worship extends beyond words. "Scripture grounds not only the words but also the patterns and actions of worship" (p. 1154). We derive our worship patterns today from scriptural sources, recounting and remembering early patterns of prayer and worship. In Holy Communion we remember Jesus' words and actions at the supper, and we retain that clear pattern today. In recalling these scriptural events, we bring their meaning into our contemporary assemblies. In our present context, these scriptural words and actions carry truth about God's actions in the past and God's continued actions today. Thus, recalling the scriptural pattern is not reenacting a historical event; rather, it is bringing the truth of the historical event to present Christian gatherings.

Knowing this scriptural center of our worship provides a foundation upon which to build a contemporary expression of Christian worship today. Worship is not simply a tradition we bring with us intact from the past. It is a living and breathing organism, enlivened anew with each faith-seeking generation as we adapt it to our own context while preserving the essential core.

In his generation, Luther breathed new life into existing liturgical forms, reforming the worship practices of his day with contemporary expressions and gospel-centered theology. To support this renewal, Luther used the means at hand, taking great care in choosing and shaping them. He translated texts into German so that the assembly would be able to understand them. He placed emphasis on the Lord's supper as a meal, not a sacrifice, and encouraged more frequent participation. He introduced elements like chorale singing to engage the assembly, making use of musical forms from the current culture in addition to the treasury of plainsong.

In these and other ways, Luther made contextual choices. He selectively introduced things from his contemporary context that were helpful to proclaiming the gospel. Luther believed it was critical that the texts, music, and actions in worship be able to proclaim the gospel in the assembly. In a preface to Georg Rhau's hymnbook *Symphoniae iucundae,* Luther wrote:

> I would certainly like to praise music with all my heart as the excellent gift of God which it is and to commend it to everyone . . . Let this noble, wholesome, and cheerful creation of God be commended to you . . . At the same time you may by this creation accustom yourself to recognize and praise the Creator. [LW 53:321, 324]

God's creation is good, Luther wrote, and thereby nothing is ruled out on the basis of its own substance as having potential for praising God. Rather, the new and contextual choices for each time and place benefit from such guiding principles as their usefulness in context and ability to proclaim the gospel. Principles like these continue to be important in testing worship choices today.

We may ask questions when considering a new hymn, prayer, or response in our liturgy to help us determine usefulness for our present assembly. Can this new element speak to our present assembly? Can it bear repetition over extended use? Does it have the ability to proclaim the gospel in our midst, to clarify the pattern of our gathering? Can this element gain accessibility in our assembly? These questions may help to determine when to introduce something new, something from contemporary culture into our own assembly.

Still more questions may help us be constructively selective in these choices. Is a hymn or prayer able to be voiced by the whole community using it, or does it narrowly describe an individual's experience? Does it give the impression that our works will gain us favor with God? Does it gloss over the reality of the world's suffering? Does it represent only a theology of glory, or is there a theology of the cross? Does it exclude anyone in the assembly? Questions like these help us discern wisely texts that can truly carry the assembly's proclamation, and they help us ensure a healthy balance of emphases in all the expressions that are used on a given day.

Christian assembly is always communal. It includes all who show up that day—members, guests, visitors—as well as those who are absent but held in mind by the present worshipers. No one is too young, too old, too sinful, or too righteous in the assembly. It is different every week, a reminder about the dynamic nature of the body of Christ. The people who show up for a particular service are not the whole gathering, however. Each local context is part of a larger body of Christ: those who have gathered in that place in the past, those who gather in other assemblies that morning, the larger communion of saints throughout the world. Each local gathering is a subset of that larger communion; it is the expression of the body of Christ in that place. In remembering that larger communion, we are drawn out of ourselves and connected to the church in its many other expressions.

Worship becomes contextual as a community grapples with how worship will be enacted in its particular place. How that work occurs, and what elements it contains, will vary from place to place. In fact, it will be distinctly different in each local assembly, reflecting the people, the resources, the physical environment, and many other factors. The large pattern will remain clear; the contextual choices illuminate and enrich that pattern.

Making contextual choices in liturgical practice involves discernment and care. Planning worship together is good work for a worship committee, a staff team, or other regularly-meeting group. To know the congregation well and to determine what will proclaim the gospel in its ongoing life requires thoughtful reflection, diligent planning, and genuine openness. This is mutual work, done best by those who have a love for the worshiping community, expertise for planning, and personal maturity to work for a larger good. No one individual's experience can match the collected wisdom of such a planning group.

Local but Also More-than-Local

Another way to express the character of Christian worship is to say that this worship is "more-than-local." Many of the most important materials of Sunday worship did not come from "here." We did not write the Bible. We did not make the lectionary selections. We did not invent the basic pattern of Sunday worship nor write the creeds. Most of the hymns come from other people and places. Our pastor probably did not originally come from the congregation where she or he presides. Lutherans have taken these facts as symbolic of a very important thing: God's salvation comes to us as a gift, from outside of ourselves. The sent ones of God—the apostles and missionaries of Christian faith—have come also here, bringing to us the good news of God's life-giving mercy. In this sense, all of us belong to "mission" churches, congregations that have been created, at one time or another, by the mission of the gospel reaching throughout the world.

But that gospel has come *here*. On Sunday morning our voices join the song. Our participating bodies form the assembly around the good news. Words in our language are used for preaching and for praying. Our local water is used for baptism, and bread and wine that we have provided are used for the meal of holy communion. These facts also signify an important thing. This local place, with all its concrete reality and actual people, is beloved by God. This local place, in all of its sorrow and sin and death, is being saved in Christ. Through this local place the Spirit blows.

Locality and *more-than-locality* are both characteristics of worship that is evangelical, Lutheran, and ecumenical. *Evangelical Lutheran Worship* is a resource for both.

The local assembly — your assembly — has its own ethos, its own way of doing things, its own gifts. The local pastor and the local lay assisting ministers bring particular voices and particular skills to the practice of the Sunday Assembly. The many options available in *Evangelical Lutheran Worship* should be regarded as supporting this constantly local character of Christian worship. In what follows in chapters six through ten of this manual, diverse proposals for enacting parts of the liturgy should also be seen as supporting the many diverse gifts of local pastors and lay leaders and the wonderfully diverse ways that Christian assemblies gather. There are yet other ways of enacting locality. Local hymn choices need to be made — according to the context and ability of your congregation. Local readers and communion ministers and ushers need to be found and trained. The local choir needs to be rehearsed. The local room-for-the-assembly — the local "house for the church" — needs to be arranged. *Evangelical Lutheran Worship* commends the practice of local composition of the intercessions each Sunday, by someone skilled and trained for such praying, someone with a heart for both local and more-than-local needs, rather than reading prayers verbatim from a pre-written resource. Similarly, many congregations are finding value (and flavor!) in locally provided communion bread — perhaps baked by someone in the congregation with a skill for such baking or acquired from a nearby bakery — in place of boxed wafers from a church supplier. In any case, evangelical Lutheran worship is preeminently local.

But evangelical Lutheran worship is equally more-than-local. For all the local choices, it is the Bible we read, the church's lectionary we follow, a basic pattern of worship we faithfully use, the whole worldwide assembly of Christians with which we join. *Evangelical Lutheran Worship* is a tool for these things coming to us. The lectionary is used by Lutherans, for example, because it is a way to join with a wider church than simply our own local assembly, because it gives a richer and more challenging set of readings than we would choose ourselves, because it enables everyone in the assembly — not only the pastor—to know what we will be reading, and because it symbolizes how the scripture comes to us as a gift from God. We are not in control of that gift. For Sundays and festivals—but also for every day of the year between those Sundays and echoing them—*Evangelical Lutheran Worship* contains the gift of that lectionary, connecting our local reality with a more-than-local pattern for reading the scripture. Similarly, while *Evangelical Lutheran Worship* does not contain the intercessions in either Holy Communion or the Service of the Word and encourages that these prayers be prepared locally, it does contain a list of matters that should be present in the prayers. As *Evangelical Lutheran Worship* says, "prayers reflect the wideness of God's mercy for the whole world." That encouragement invites a local assembly to pray for others, beyond its own concerns and its own members—to pray genuinely for other churches, for the well-being of creation, for peace and justice in the world, for the poor, the oppressed, the sick, the bereaved, the lonely, the suffering, and to remember those who have died. This list is a more-than-local list, and it encourages a practice of prayer that reaches beyond only local concerns and celebrates that a genuine Christian sense of locality knows that every local place is connected to every other.

A Book in the Hands of the People

Most Lutheran worshipers are accustomed to using a book. Worship books have sustained generations of faithful persons both in public worship and in other settings, including the home. During the development of this generation of worship resources, it became critical to consider a book's ongoing importance in the assembly's hands. Indeed, electronic media, offering the potential for projection and for service folders that include all the materials needed by worshipers, raised the question of the need for any new worship book. Would a new generation still find a book important and benefit from its use?

Among the purposes of a worship book are to—

- Provide continuity for our worship. We see that we are not an isolated gathering each week, but part of a larger church gathering in many places and various settings. We sing hymns and speak words that others also use in worship. We are indeed part of a larger church.
- Serve as a tangible sign of the treasury of Lutheran contributions to the worship of the whole church through time and across space.

At a glance we see Reformation chorales, newer hymns and songs from Lutheran sources worldwide, and prayers passed on to us by our forebears. The book carries our Lutheran heritage, placing it before us today.

- Lead us into the future of our worship together. New hymns and songs from around the globe, a range of musical styles both well-established and currently popular, and new worship texts from many sources are waiting to be discovered. *Evangelical Lutheran Worship* draws upon thousands of newer hymns and songs, as well as resources in use in other denominations and around the world. New materials were added with care: congregational testing, the experience of other denominations, and an evaluation of suitability for Lutheran assemblies were some of the factors influencing decisions about inclusion in the book.
- Empower the whole people of God to own their worship. An extensive collection of resources is visible and accessible to all who open the pages of the book, not only to leaders who choose what their assemblies will see and use.

Evangelical Lutheran Worship can support worship in a variety of ways. It can be used independently in the hands of the people, perhaps aided only by an outline of the service. It can be used in combination with other printed or projected resources. When used with a folder in which the service, or most of it, is printed out, it can serve as a book of hymns and songs. It can serve as a prayer book when used for Bible studies, church meetings, and other gatherings. Hymns and worship texts from other traditions and denominations may enrich those present in this book. Although this book offers more content than its predecessors, it is nevertheless a core rather than a comprehensive resource. Although many worshiping communities will find that its contents are sufficient for most of their needs, other assemblies will seek to supplement its resources in a variety of ways appropriate to their contexts.

Evangelical Lutheran Worship may also be used in the home. The hymns can be sung at home. The services of daily prayer, especially Night Prayer, are easily adapted for use by a family or an individual. A treasury of collected prayers under titles such as Daily Life and Spiritual Life (AE pp. 82–83, 86–87), such as prayers for daily renewal, for a peaceful night, for those who live alone, and for the care of children, are usable at home or in church. The Small Catechism is also useful in multiple contexts. Although designed primarily for assembly worship, this core volume's usefulness in other settings demonstrates the continuity of worship in all of our public and private life.

Books and Service Folders

The many possible uses for worship service folders merit consideration in determining their use for any given assembly. From a simple listing of parish announcements to printing the entire worship service, worship folders can be used for many purposes. There are often competing values at work in decisions about service folders, including hospitality, economics, and environmental concerns. A priority on user-friendly materials may be at odds with a desire to use the worship book in the pew. These values have different emphases, and none of them are necessarily poor choices in and of themselves. Considering their impact over the long term may help an assembly determine which values they rank highest. Once those values have been clarified, an assembly's best use of the service folder may be clearer.

Some assemblies print the entire contents of their services each week in a service folder. These offer the obvious advantage of putting an entire service in one printed piece. Hymns and songs can be inserted, so that the entire service unfolds in order, eliminating shifting from one place to another in the worship book. In some cases, books are not used at all, and worshipers rely entirely on the worship folders.

In other cases, a service folder provides a brief guideline for using the worship book as the primary worship resource. Here, more emphasis is placed on the worship book itself as the resource, with the service folder as the guide. The service folder may announce upcoming parish events, prayer requests, and other information for worshipers to take home.

Intermediate choices include printing everything except the hymns and songs, printing only words but not music, printing only parts that change with the day or season, or other permutations that may suit various communities.

Consideration of a more extensive worship folder's advantages and disadvantages will assist people in deciding on the merits in their context. Advantages include an easier entry point for visitors, simplicity of following the service, having all worship material in one place, and the easy inclusion of resources beyond those in the worship book. Disadvantages include staff time for preparation, cost of additional paper and printing, copyright management, ecological considerations, and—if books are unavailable—loss of tangible connection to the church beyond and its collected repertoire of resources.

Assemblies with particular worship emphases, such as bilingual liturgy, ethnic-specific hymnody, or popular musical idioms, will find more choices for worship beyond the primary books in this unfolding family of resources. These additional resources will be delivered in ways that make them available to assemblies who weekly use the book as well as to those who print extensive service folders each week.

Evangelical Lutheran Worship Continues

The primary editions of *Evangelical Lutheran Worship*—assembly edition and leaders edition—are complemented by a variety of resources, some more closely integrated with these editions than others. Accompaniment editions for various keyboard and other instruments, resources for additional services and occasions, additional psalm settings, and more hymns, songs, and liturgical music are examples of the contents of these further resources. Understanding that renewal of the church's worship life is an ongoing process, these resources will continue to make available new compositions and wider expressions of the church's praises in future years and in changing contexts.

For example, many assemblies regularly sing psalms within the services. *Evangelical Lutheran Worship* provides all 150 psalms in a version simply laid out for singing to psalm tones. Additional resources, such as *Psalm Settings for the Church Year* (2008) and *Psalter for Worship* (2006–2008), provide a variety of other ways of singing the psalms, including more ways for choirs to participate.

Other volumes in this unfolding family include resources for occasional services, additional materials for Lent and the Three Days, and expanded resources for daily prayer. Over time, new hymns and liturgical music will become available to enrich the core collection in *Evangelical Lutheran Worship*. It is expected that wider use of musical materials from a variety of contexts around the world will continue to recognize the changing nature of the church's song and the global nature of the body of Christ.

These and other resources support and extend the core editions of *Evangelical Lutheran Worship*, allowing an assembly to explore a fuller range of particular types of material, while still maintaining a center in the core resources. They offer opportunity to connect with other assemblies, ecumenical partners, global communities, and others beyond the borders of any local assembly, while remaining solidly Lutheran in theology and practice.

Assembling on Sunday

Worship that is evangelical, Lutheran, and ecumenical, using the resources of *Evangelical Lutheran Worship*, finds its primary home in the gathered assembly. That gathering takes place principally on Sunday. There are other great festivals in the church. And there are gatherings for prayer and for funerals and weddings and seasonal services at other times than Sunday. But the principal festival of Christian faith is Sunday. *The Use of the Means of Grace* counsels:

> Sunday, the day of Christ's resurrection and of the appearances to the disciples by the crucified and risen Christ, is the primary day on which Christians gather to worship. Within this assembly, the Word is read and preached and the sacraments are celebrated. . . . Sunday is the principal festival day of Christians. [6 and 6a]

Some congregations, for pastoral reasons, may find it important to have celebrations of word and sacrament at other times. Perhaps they do so in order that Christians who are engaged in work for the good of the community on Sunday morning—emergency workers, for example—may also join a communal gathering around the gospel. Certainly some school and seminary communities cannot meet together on Sunday. In such cases, Saturday evening, taken to be the arrival of Sunday as Christmas Eve is taken to be the arrival of Christmas, may be one alternate time. Wednesdays or Thursdays, traditional midweek meeting times in some communities, may be another. Other congregations may take the creative step of holding midweek services on days that are designated as lesser festivals or commemorations. Still, such decisions should be made with great care. A proliferation of, or a preference for, alternate times can minimize the communal meaning of Sunday and reinforce an unhealthy characteristic of contemporary culture, namely that individual convenience or stylistic choice is of higher value than nurturing a lively, caring community that participates in diverse gifts of worship.

At any rate, in the view of the larger Christian church, the meeting on Sunday remains the great Christian festival: the Lord's Day, the Day of Light and the Eighth Day, to use old Christian names. Worship that is evangelical and Lutheran is a gathering around the presence of the life-giving gospel of the risen Christ. The meaning of Sunday is part of that good news.

What follows in this book is primarily reflection on using *Evangelical Lutheran Worship* whenever Holy Communion or the Service of the Word is celebrated. Despite the emphasis in these pages on how the services take shape, the most important thing to remember about the work of worship is this continual surprise: when the assembly comes to the living Word, Jesus Christ, and to the gifts of baptism and the Lord's supper, it discovers that the assembly itself is not doing the most important work at all. God is the one who above all is present and active in worship, working wonders among us and in us. According to the Holy Communion Pattern for Worship in *Evangelical Lutheran Worship* (AE pp. 92–93):

The Holy Spirit calls us together as the people of God.
God speaks to us in scripture reading, preaching, and song.
God feeds us with the presence of Jesus Christ.
God blesses us and sends us in mission to the world.

This is the basic pattern for the work of God that takes place in worship. Within this pattern, as we carry out and respond to what God is doing, the worship book proposes various leadership roles. It outlines options and provides materials for what the assembly makes their own. It commends actions and words and songs that intend to make visible the mighty works of God in worship. After all the study and the planning, this deep-red book and its companions are most fittingly at home not on the shelf or on the desk but in the hands of the Sunday assembly, the people of God gathered around the gifts of God, especially on the day of resurrection.

CHAPTER TWO

The Holy Communion on Sunday

Jesus teaches us the importance of assembling for worship. "Where two or three are gathered in my name, I am there among them" (Matt. 18:20). We can eat and pray alone, but we must come together in order to be and experience the body of Christ. That is, our coming together is more than functional or efficient; it is *necessary*. It is how we find out and know who we are in relation to Christ. We are diverse individuals, but when we gather in Jesus' name, we are gathered into one by the Holy Spirit. As Martin Luther put it in the Small Catechism, the Holy Spirit "calls, gathers, enlightens, and makes holy the whole Christian church on earth and keeps it with Jesus Christ in the one common, true faith" (Explanation to the Third Article of the Creed). That is most certainly true of the whole church and of our local assembly.

Not only did the Jesus we encounter in the gospels *talk* about the benefits of gathering in assemblies; it was his own daily practice. This was true to such an extent that when he withdrew to be by himself, it was a noteworthy event. As a regular practice, Jesus wasn't content with issuing oracular pronouncements or writing a book of teachings. Rather, the Jesus of the four gospels surrounded himself with *assemblies*, people from many different backgrounds—young and old, rich and poor, educated and not, of good and ill repute. Once they were gathered, he interacted with them in worship and teaching.

So when we come together on Sunday, we are following Jesus' lead, confident that he will be present in our gathering. Will we know him among us? Probably yes, in the gospel reading, the sermon, the holy communion. But Christ is with the gathered assembly in other ways that we may easily miss. Just as the disciples at times didn't recognize Jesus in their midst, today's disciples often miss Jesus' presence as well. We often fail to recognize our Lord in the assembly's song, in the peace, in the faces of our fellow communicants. Yet Jesus' promise here is that he is with us anyway, recognized or not. So we come together, forming our assemblies, and trusting Jesus to be present in those gatherings.

This is especially good news for present-day cultures that emphasize individualism. The Sunday assembly is different from the world of the Internet, computers, individualized programs, self-help books, and entertainment. Although a person may come into the assembly feeling isolated, knowing deep personal need, or looking for a particular individual experience, the assembly's gift is that this gathering is not merely a collection of isolated persons, not simply individuals seeking personal fulfillment in a public place. It is a *community*, forming the body of Christ from each person who joins the assembly. Each person has a unique set of gifts and skills, which together build up the whole assembly. This gift of the assembly is a somewhat countercultural gift, a counterpoint especially to the consumerist dynamic that thrives on creating perceived individual needs. In the Christian community, each individual contributes, out of their weaknesses and strengths, to a larger, communal whole. This community is an assembly of persons contributing talents and gifts, people who discover that, paradoxically, by attending to the needs of the corporate body of Christ, their individual hopes and needs are addressed in life-giving ways they had not even imagined.

Jesus teaches that we are not sufficient in and of ourselves. We need one another to complete our basic identity as members of the body of Christ. There are many things we can do alone, but becoming Christ's body is not one of them.

The Body of Christ, in Both Senses

One way we can recognize worship's communal nature is to think about what God is doing here with us, the body of Christ. A common criterion for evaluating worship is, "What did I get out of the service?" How much more constructive it is to ask, "What did God (yet again) do for us—and with us—in this time of worship?" What is it we are doing together in worship as the body of Christ in light of God's gracious work, and how are we taking that out into the world as we are sent from worship? Worship in community demonstrates that our salvation is not only an individual matter. It is our encounter with God's saving work for all of creation. When we enter into worship, we join with those around us, and with the whole church, in being surrounded by God's gracious acts in all of history.

One service in the church year in which we encounter this salvation story most dramatically is at the Vigil of Easter, an ancient liturgy observed by a growing number of congregations on Saturday night just preceding Easter Day. In this liturgy we hear of God's salvation from the beginning of creation, through the exodus from slavery and then the prophets' visions, to the very death and resurrection of Jesus, and then that salvation is enacted and celebrated in baptism and holy communion. We are caught up in this grand sweep of salvation history, which God is still accomplishing in each of us, in each local place where Christ's salvation is still proclaimed and celebrated. So our weekly gatherings, modest though they may be, are a participation in this larger narrative of God's great salvation history. Individuals gather to form the local assembly, which in turn is wrapped up in the larger reality of the whole church, and in God's gracious action for all.

Once we understand this larger context for each of our local gatherings, we can see that our individual faith and its expressions are part of a larger whole. Our gathering is no longer merely about individuals, with their solitary requests and needs—important though each of those is. Much more, it is about our joining in a long communal procession, with those around us and with the whole body of Christ, in God's saving actions among us. The proclamation of the word in which we join through the scriptures and preaching, song and prayer, and the sharing of the holy meal—these actions testify to that communal nature, our interdependence with one another, and our participation in the body of Christ. "Now you are the body of Christ and individually members of it" (1 Cor. 12:27). The body of Christ extends from one person to another in the local gathering; from one local gathering to others around the neighborhood and around the globe; and to Christians who have preceded us in many times and places.

So in one sense Jesus is present among the gathered assembly because we are, collectively, "the body of Christ." But of course there is another sense in which the body of Christ is present. "This is my body, which is given for you . . . This cup that is poured out for you is the new covenant in my blood" (Luke 22:19-20). In receiving the meal of holy communion, we receive Jesus' presence into our very bodies. In the physical means of bread and wine, the body of Christ is given for us. Luther spoke about this reality as Christ's "real presence," the promise that Jesus Christ is present in the bread and wine we receive each Sunday in communion. The wine remains wine; the bread remains bread. Even so, Jesus Christ is truly present in this meal. The bread is the very body that was born of Mary and that walked in Galilee, a means whereby he still encounters us. This cup is the very blood that was shed at Golgotha, a means through which he still gives us his life. Martin Luther said that Christ is present "in, with, and under" the bread and wine. As we receive these elements, we participate in Christ's body in a tangible way; Christ becomes part of our very bodies. The physical elements are parts of God's creation; they are also the body and blood of Christ.

That this mystery belongs to the realm of faith rather than science does not make it less true. Jesus calls us simply to experience and trust. In faith, we are the beneficiaries of Christ's life given for us, recipients of this wonderful gift. We find our very identity as we hear the words spoken to us, "The body of Christ, given for you"—a formula both simple and beyond our comprehension. It is the body of Christ, our Lord, in our humble Sunday assembly.

And so the circle continues: we gather as the body of Christ; we receive the body of Christ; and in that communion at the table we, the assembly, become still more the body of Christ, ready to be sent out to further Christ's mission. We also join ourselves with others around other tables and recognize that the body of Christ encompasses more Christians than we will ever know. This too is mystery and opens us to seeing Christ's presence in every person we encounter. Though unable to explain it, we can witness to Christ's presence in our lives, pointing to the table where we experience the body of Christ—in both senses.

The Lord's Supper on the Lord's Day

One account of a Christian Sunday meeting in the book of Acts begins simply: "On the first day of the week, when we met to break bread . . ." (Acts 20:7). Recalling that the phrase "the breaking of bread" is used in Acts to indicate what we would call "holy communion" (see Acts 2:42), we will find that this simple passage sounds a great deal like the report of a regular practice. It seems that the communities known by the author of Luke-Acts ordinarily met on the first day of the week to break bread. They ordinarily gathered on Sunday for the meal of Jesus Christ. When we further see that the gathering described by the passage included both something like preaching (20:7b) and the meal itself (20:11), then we may understand that the practice encouraged by *Evangelical Lutheran*

Worship—an every-Sunday gathering for reading and preaching of the word of God and for the celebration of the meal of Christ—is a very old practice indeed.

The Lutheran confessions state that "among us the Mass is celebrated every Lord's day and on other festivals" (Apology 24:1). This has not been universally accurate for many years. The recovery of the Holy Communion as the principal service on every Sunday in each congregation has long been a goal of worship renewal among Lutheran churches throughout the world, a goal that is growing ever closer. Among Lutherans, such a practice is to be realized by teaching and encouragement, not by requirement or law. But this teaching and encouragement does need to take place. We do need to tell each other how much this recovery can mean, how deeply it is rooted in the New Testament, and how profoundly it corresponds to the confession of faith we make as Christians and as Lutherans. So *The Use of the Means of Grace,* adopted by the Evangelical Lutheran Church in America in 1997, urges:

> This confession [from the Apology] remains the norm for our practice . . . All of our congregations are encouraged to celebrate the Lord's Supper weekly . . . [35, 35b]

But this urging—this "norm of our confession"—has a reason beyond simply adhering to confessional wording. Christ has promised to meet us in the supper with forgiveness of sins, life, and salvation. Such meeting with Christ brings us to faith again, makes us to be church, and forms us as the body of Christ for mission in the world.

The Use of the Means of Grace describes the richness of the meaning of holy communion by noting its many names:

> Each name has come to emphasize certain aspects of the sacrament. The *Lord's Supper* speaks of the meal which the risen Lord holds with the Church, the meal of the Lord's Day, a foretaste of the heavenly feast to come. *Holy Communion* accentuates the holy *koinonia* (community) established by the Holy Spirit as we encounter Christ and are formed into one body with him and so with each other. *Eucharist* calls us to see that the whole meal is a great thanksgiving for creation and for creation's redemption in

Jesus Christ. *Divine Liturgy* says the celebration is a public action, carried out by a community of people. Yet, *Divine Service* helps us to see that the primary action of our gathering is God's astonishing service to us; we are called to respond in praise and in service to our neighbor. The term *Mass* is probably derived from the old dismissal of the participants at the end of the service and the sending away of the bread and cup to the absent: it invites us into mission. *Sacrament of the Altar* invites each one to eat and drink from the true altar of God, the body and blood of Christ given and shed "for you." [36a]

These names mirror something of the even greater richness to be found in New Testament texts about the Lord's supper. Of course, the church's practice of the meal is rooted in the narrative of Jesus' last supper in the synoptic gospels (Mark 14:22-25; Matt. 26:26-29; Luke 22:14-20) and in Paul's first letter to the Corinthians (11:23-26). Those texts present any assembly around the table with the mystery of Christ's gift of himself, in body and blood, as the very gift of God in the power of the Spirit. They bear witness to the church constantly rediscovering that the crucified one is present now and that his death is made to be the source of life. But the actual practice of the Lord's supper in the church also has roots in the stories of Jesus' resurrection. According to the New Testament, the church comes into existence as a meal-fellowship (Acts 2:42, 46; 1 Cor. 11:17-22), in which the thanksgiving, eating, and drinking are the very place where the community discovers that the crucified one is risen (Luke 24:28-35, 41-43; Acts 10:41; John 21:1-14). Then the words of Jesus remembered at the last supper can be seen as a testimony to the deepest level of meaning in this meal-practice of the earliest church, intending to criticize and reform any pattern of meal-keeping not in accord with his gift (1 Cor. 11:23-34).

It follows that all the rest of the meals of Jesus and many other images in the gospel stories have been taken by Christians—in the New Testament writings themselves and down through the ages—to interpret the gift of holy communion yet further. Jesus feeds the multitude in the wilderness, forming a company on which he has compassion. His compassion still feeds us in the church today, and many basketsful are left over to be given away in the world. Jesus eats with sinners and welcomes them—as he does still today. Jesus teaches that the coming of the reign of God will be like a marriage feast, or like beggars at last being able to eat, or like a father throwing a banquet for his lost and prodigal son, or like a wounded man brought to an inn to be fed and to recover. This feeding, this banquet, is already spread at the table of the Lord in the church. The risen Christ shows his hands and side to the disciples, breathing the Spirit on them, doing so on two subsequent Sundays in John 20. So the wounds of Christ are held out to us and the Holy Spirit is breathed upon us disciples Sunday after Sunday, that we may come to believe and that we might speak the forgiveness of sins to others in the world. Jesus teaches us to pray, "give us today our daily bread," and that very bread for which we pray—that foretaste of the feast to come—is present now, by the power of the Spirit, in the regular nourishment of this holy meal.

This meal-gift of Jesus Christ, this practice of the earliest church, was continued throughout the ages of church history. Sometimes it was neglected. Sometimes it was obscured. Sometimes it was misunderstood or scorned. But it continued, down to our own day. The scriptural witness about the meaning of the meal of Christ continued to live in the church and to influence year after year of faithful practice and recurring renewal. The church listened to the New Testament and practiced its meal. The great evidence of that long history shows that from the earliest days this meal was especially associated with Sunday, first in the evening, then later, when evening gatherings were forbidden, in the morning when more people could come and when the morning itself could remind them of the resurrection. The Lord's supper was the very center and meaning of the Lord's day, the very place of the encounter with the risen one, the very heartbeat of the churches that came to be called "catholic" because they were the churches throughout the world who held to the orthodox faith in the triune God.

A first- or second-century writing called the Didache, using one of the names of the supper discussed above, said, "On the Lord's day [the people] of the Lord come together, break bread and hold eucharist . . ." (14:1). A second-century writer called Justin described how the Christians of Rome came together on "the day called after the Sun" to hear the word and hold the meal, because that was the day on which God both began to make the world by saying "Let there be light!" and remade the world by raising up Jesus (1 Apology 67). This same Justin demonstrated that Paul's criticism of self-centered meal-practice continued to be heard in the churches. Justin says that the church in Rome used the Sunday gathering—the Sunday eucharist, now become a morning service of scripture, preaching, prayers of intercession, thanksgiving over a simple meal of bread and wine, communion and sending of communion to the absent—as the place to gather food and money for distribution to widows, orphans, the imprisoned, the hungry, and the wretched of every sort. The meal of God's making and remaking of the world was to be echoed in the extension of help to the poor. This meal continued to do its work, especially on Sunday, of bringing people to faith in God, feeding people with Christ, and turning them in love toward their neighbor. It did this work first of all in the Mediterranean world and in North Africa, but then also in Syria and into Asia, in Europe, in all of Africa, in America, and in Australia and Oceania. Listening to the scripture and coming to its meal, a whole host of people—Irenaeus, Augustine, Cyril, Ambrose, Chrysostom, Gregory, Isidore, Mechthild, Julian, Catherine, Thomas Aquinas, Jan Hus, Martin Luther, Philipp Melanchthon, John Wesley, Henry Melchior Muhlenberg, Nikolai Grundtvig, Wilhelm Löhe, Dietrich Bonhoeffer, Dorothy Day, Oscar Romero, to name just a few—testify in diverse ways and in diverse lives, bearing witness to the importance and centrality of holy communion.

The confessional writings of the Lutheran churches join this universal witness. As noted earlier, the Augsburg Confession points to an assembly around word and sacrament, around the gospel in preaching and in the meal, as the place where church is to be found. In case that is not clear, the Apology repeats, "We do not abolish the Mass but religiously retain and defend it. Among us the Mass is celebrated every Lord's day and on other festivals . . ." (24:1; cf. 15:40). And it is not simply celebrated, but eaten and drunk as a gift. In the Small Catechism, Luther admonishes:

> We should preach in such a way that the people make themselves come without our law and just plain compel us pastors to administer the sacrament to them . . . For Christ did not say, "Omit this," or "Despise this," but instead, "Do this, as often as you drink it . . ." He really wants it to be done and not completely omitted or despised. "Do this," he says. [Preface, 22]

The Small Catechism itself has one classic way to say why: "The words 'given for you' and 'shed for you for the forgiveness of sins' show us that forgiveness of sin, life, and salvation are given to us in the sacrament through these words . . ." (Sacrament of the Altar, 5–6).

But in much Lutheran practice through the years, there was a decline in this original Reformation intention to celebrate Holy Communion every Sunday and festival day and to encourage frequent, glad participation in the sacrament. There were many complex reasons for this decline. In Europe, during the eighteenth and nineteenth centuries, a tendency to accentuate our profound unworthiness to receive the body and blood of Christ was one characteristic of the renewal movement called Pietism. Many believers came to commune very seldom and to prepare for that communion with great seriousness. At the same time, the movement called the Enlightenment tended to regard outward, earthly symbols — like eating and drinking bread and wine — as gross, unintelligent, primitive, not "spiritual" enough. Both movements had the effect of reducing the number of communicants who might be ready or willing to receive the sacrament on Sunday morning in a local Lutheran church. Contributing to this effect were the frequent and devastating wars, social tumults, and diseases that swept through large parts of northern Europe. Because Lutherans did not think that the priest or pastor should be the only communicant, the practice developed of not finishing the service — celebrating only the word part of the service — when there were no people in the church who were ready to commune. Increasingly, this liturgy — the service of the word, mass without communion, *missa brevis*, or "the half-mass," to list some of its titles — came to be the standard practice of many of the Lutheran churches in Europe during the eighteenth and nineteenth centuries. This very period in history saw the immigration of many Lutherans and their liturgical practices to North America. And in America the possibility of frequent communion was made even more difficult by the lack of enough pastors to serve every Sunday assembly and — increasingly — by the influence of other Protestant groups in the American Christian environment, in which communion had already been marginalized.

Beginning in the late nineteenth and early twentieth centuries, however, North American Lutheran churches — together with the

Lutheran churches of the world—have been reading their sources again. Lutherans now are more aware of their original confessional commitment to word and sacrament at the heart of the life of the church. They are also newly attentive to the meals of Jesus in the gospels and the "breaking of bread" in Acts.

The Use of the Means of Grace similarly reflects the witness of the New Testament. It joins the Lutheran confessions and the ancient practice of the catholic churches in urging us to recover the Lord's supper every Sunday. And it too says why, this time accenting the communal reasons:

> The Church celebrates the Holy Communion frequently because the Church needs the sacrament, the means by which the Church's fellowship is established and its mission as the baptized people of God is nourished and sustained . . . We continue to need "consistent pastoral encouragement and instruction relating to Holy Communion . . . pointing up Christ's command, his promise, and our deep need." [35a]

Two more New Testament texts may help us as we plan, teach, encourage, preach, and invite our congregations toward Holy Communion as the principal service of every Sunday. The story of the risen Christ and the two disciples at Emmaus (Luke 24:13-35) was likely told, at least in part, to help hearers of the story understand more profoundly a practice they already knew. The communities that first received the Luke-Acts work probably had a practice that this story could interpret. Like the community reflected in Acts 20:7-12, they met on Sunday for scripture reading and its interpretation and for the meal. The Emmaus story helped them to understand what this meeting was for: the scripture is read and interpreted that they may learn what God is doing in the death and resurrection of Jesus—indeed, that they may encounter the risen one himself. The meal is held, next to this scripture, so that this meaning of the scripture may be burningly clear. Or, rather, the scripture is interpreted next to the meal so that the presence and gift of God in the meal may stand out like the burning bush itself. This text and its meaning will be more accessible to us if our Sunday practice also includes the meal of Christ next to the word, the word followed by the meal: "Were not our hearts burning within us . . . while he was opening the scriptures to us?" they said after the meal. And "then they told . . . how he had been made known to them in the breaking of the bread" (Luke 24:32, 35).

In the last book of the New Testament, an exiled Christian also keeps Sunday. He cannot come into the gathered assembly. He cannot join them in the Lord's supper on the Lord's day. But by the power of the Spirit, he does see the Risen One (Rev. 1:9-20), and in seeing him he sees the one who holds all the assemblies—all the churches—in his hand. John, the exiled elder, then is made to connect with seven of these churches by letter, written in the name of Jesus. It is as if John comes into the assembly, even when he cannot. In any case, by the Spirit he sees the heart of any Christian assembly, the risen Christ burning with the light of God. It is fascinating that the final part of the last of these seven letters—the conclusion of the word John speaks to the churches—leads on toward the meal: "Listen! I am standing at the door, knocking," says the risen Christ. "If you hear my voice and open the door, I will come in to you and eat with you, and you with me" (Rev. 3:20). It is as if the elder in exile sees the Sunday assembly, its word and its meal. Several current interpreters of the Revelation to John argue that the book was probably intended to be read in the assembly as part of the community's practice of the word in the eucharist, perhaps as preparation for the meal. Then it is all the more remarkable that in the end of the book, there is the tree of life holding out its fruit and leaves for the healing of the nations (22:2). There is the Lamb (22:3-4), around whom the assembly gathers, whose mark is on their foreheads. There is the call, "Come . . . Come" (22:17a). And there is that amazing drink: "Let everyone who is thirsty come. Let anyone who wishes take the water of life as a gift" (22:17b). The Lamb. The words of the book, on the Lord's day. Then the fruit of the tree of life and the gift of the water of life as food and drink. The book of Revelation can be faithfully read as a very old image of the meaning of the practice of the Lord's supper on the Lord's day.

The practice of the ancient churches reflected in these texts is commended to our twenty-first-century churches: also among us, the amazing gifts of God; also among us, word and sacrament in a community marked with the name of Jesus; also among us, a turning to our neighbors with words of witness and gifts of concrete help; also among us, the Lord's supper on the Lord's day.

Contemporary Culture and the Gathering around Word and Meal

The witness of the Bible, the practice of the ancient churches, and the renewing influence of the Lutheran Reformation are thus some of the factors influencing many Lutherans to recover the centrality of the service of Holy Communion in their primary weekly gatherings. Yet this recovery is not limited to a Lutheran return to roots. Others on this continent—among them Presbyterians, United Methodists, congregations of the United Church of Christ, and others in Reformed traditions—are reclaiming the full service of word and table as the central weekly practice. Increasingly, the churches are influencing and encouraging one another in this recovery—sharing patterns and practices, word and song in mutually beneficial ways.

This widespread recovery may indicate more than mere attention to tradition. Is it possible that the strong, meaningful signs of the service on the Lord's day are a welcome countercultural message in the face of impoverished signs in our day, often created by a consumer-driven culture to stimulate consumption and to identify wants posing as needs? In this environment it is ever more urgent that the church clearly offer its meaningful signs of God's means of grace. Hearing God's word proclaimed in the assembly, sharing in the bread and cup, we experience the presence of Jesus Christ with us in this gathering. In these signs we are given meaning in a life that is rich, full, and free. These are the signs that root and anchor our lives—and that nourish us to serve a world in need as we live in God's free grace.

CHAPTER THREE

The Pattern for Worship

An assembly using *Evangelical Lutheran Worship* will find on pages 91–93 (LE, 163-165) a centrally significant feature of the book. Those pages provide an important interpretive key for thinking about and doing worship. As a foundational preamble to the service of Holy Communion, *Evangelical Lutheran Worship* sets out a "Pattern for Worship" for the Sunday and festival gathering. This pattern is an account of the shape or structure of the event as it happens "on the day of Christ's resurrection, and at other times" in a community committed to worship that is evangelical and Lutheran, a community engaged especially in the Lord's supper on the Lord's day.

What is proposed here is a simple shape for what we do together as a community when we meet for holy communion. But the pattern first of all emphasizes and claims in faith that, according to Christ's promise and the Spirit's gift, *the principal actor here—in all the central parts of the service—is not us but God.* By God's gift, we do indeed gather, sing, read, preach, listen, pray, and commune. We do have things to plan and to do. But in, with, and under our communal activity, God gives us the word and meal of promise. God gathers us and sends us in love to our neighbors in the world.

Extensive and diverse resources are supplied in *Evangelical Lutheran Worship* for what takes place in the assembly, for our singing and reading and praying using the foundational shape of worship. Further materials are available in the family of resources that surrounds *Evangelical Lutheran Worship*. This volume, *The Sunday Assembly*, explores the pattern itself, its range of possibilities and choices, its meanings, and some of the available resources. But through all of this exploration we should remember the image impressed on the cover of *Evangelical Lutheran Worship*: the cross becomes the tree of life, holding out to us its healing leaves. In our gathering, in its pattern, in the resources used to unfold that pattern, and in our communal use of *Evangelical Lutheran Worship*, the most important thing is God's promise to meet us here, with the life-giving gospel of Jesus Christ as the very fruit and leaves of that tree. When we hold and use the materials of worship in word and sacraments, we are holding in our hands some of the leaves of the tree that God uses to heal the nations (Rev. 22:2).

The first paragraph on page 91 (LE, 163) makes clear both the basic flow of the pattern for worship and its claim of faith:

> In the principal service of Christian worship, the Holy Spirit gathers people around the means of grace—the saving Word of God and the sacraments. From the table of communion where Jesus Christ comes with forgiveness, life, and salvation, God sends us out to share the good news and to care for those in need.

This Gathering, Word, Meal, and Sending—a way to summarize the pattern—correspond to the evangelical and Lutheran convictions that worship is centered in the gospel-gift of Jesus Christ, expresses the unity of the church while encouraging and welcoming considerable local flexibility in practice, and gathers the participants again into the mission of the triune God.

This pattern appeared in an earlier form in *With One Voice* (1995), a supplement to *Lutheran Book of Worship*. But Lutherans are not alone in recognizing and using this pattern. Worship that is evangelical and Lutheran, as we have seen, is rightly ecumenical. A glance at the worship books of many other Christian churches will demonstrate the extent to which the structure being discussed here is a common ecumenical inheritance. Presbyterians in their *Book of Common Worship* (1993) speak of the "basic movement of the service of the Lord's Day" and outline it as Gathering, The Word, The Eucharist, and Sending. *The United Methodist Book of Worship* (1992) describes the "basic pattern of worship" as Entrance, Proclamation and Response, Thanksgiving and Communion, and Sending Forth. The Church of England, in Order One of its *Common Worship* (2000), follows a structure articulated as The Gathering, The Liturgy of the Word, The Liturgy of the Sacrament, and The Dismissal. The Episcopal Church USA, in its *Book of Common Prayer* (1979), has long had a similar structure with slightly different accents (pp. 400–401), centrally important to their book and recounted in verbs (Gather in the Lord's Name, Proclaim and Respond to the Word of God, Pray for the World and the Church, Exchange the Peace, Prepare the Table, Make Eucharist, Break the Bread, Share the Gifts of God). The Roman

Catholic Sacramentary (1970, in English 1974), speaks of Introductory Rites, Liturgy of the Word, Liturgy of the Eucharist, and a Concluding Rite. There are many other examples throughout the world.

None of these outlines of structure includes the brief commentary on the flow of events that *Evangelical Lutheran Worship* places on pages 92 and 93, with a characteristic Lutheran interest in theological meaning. But it is clear that they all have drawn from the same sources. These other churches have also reflected upon the scriptural witness, paid attention to the themes of ecumenical liturgical renewal, and considered carefully how the history of worship in the churches informs the present day.

The Pattern in Christian History

The earliest clear account we possess of the actual flow of events in the Sunday meeting of Christians comes from mid-second-century Rome and from the pen of the lay teacher called Justin Martyr. While we cannot know if Justin's report, written as an open letter to the emperor, Antoninus Pius, reflects a wider Christian practice than that of his own community, his text is nonetheless a treasure for us. At the end of his *First Apology*, just after he has described how baptism is done in his community, he writes:

> And for the rest after these things [after baptism is enacted] we continually remind each other of these things [of baptism]. Those who have the means help all those who are in want, and we continually meet together. And over all that we take to eat we bless the creator of all things through God's Son Jesus Christ and through the Holy Spirit. And on the day named after the Sun all, whether they live in the city or the countryside, are gathered together in unity. Then the records of the apostles or the writings of the prophets are read for as long as there is time. When the reader has concluded, the presider in a discourse admonishes and invites us into the pattern of these good things. Then we all stand together and offer prayer. And, as we said before, when we have concluded the prayer, bread is set out to eat, together with wine and water. The presider likewise offers up prayer and thanksgiving, as much as he can, and the people sing out their assent saying the Amen. There is a distribution of the things over which thanks have been said and each person participates, and these things are sent by the deacons

to those who are not present. Those who are prosperous and who desire to do so, give what they wish, according to each one's own choice, and the collection is deposited with the presider. He aids orphans and widows, those who are in want through disease or through another cause, those who are in prison, and foreigners who are sojourning here. In short, the presider is a guardian to all those who are in need. We all hold this meeting together on the day of the Sun since it is the first day, on which day God, having transformed darkness and matter, made the world. On the same day Jesus Christ our savior rose from the dead. For on the day before the day of Saturn they crucified him, and on the day after the day of Saturn, which is the day of the Sun, he appeared to his apostles and disciples and taught them these things, which we have presented also to you for your consideration. (67)

There are many remarkable things about this old text, but one of the most helpful is its outline. Justin seems to tell us this: In Rome, in the mid-second century, Christians met together on Sunday, received as a day of witness to both the creation and the new creation in Jesus' resurrection. They met together, reminding one another that they were baptized. When they met, with a sense that these things had been taught and given them by Jesus, they read the scriptures, heard a sermon, prayed in intercession (and, as is made clear earlier in Justin's *Apology*, shared a kiss of peace), set out bread and wine and joined in assenting to the presider's thanksgiving, ate and drank these gifts as the body and blood of Jesus Christ (also made clear earlier in the text), sending them to the absent members of the church, and took a collection for the poor and hungry. There was a reader. There were table servers called deacons. There were probably leaders of prayer and people who helped with the distribution to the poor. There was also a presider, whose task was especially to preach on the biblical texts that had been read, to give thanks to the best of his or her ability at the table, and to see to it that the collection for the poor was received and fairly distributed.

After nearly nineteen centuries, this list is still recognizable to us. It is close to our own sense of what happens in church or of what we are trying to recover in church, even if the sequence of things (such as the collection—or "offering," as we call it) is slightly different. In many ways, the text also can serve as a tool for looking at the rest of Christian liturgical history.

With this ancient text in mind, we recognize its points of significant continuity with the churches mirrored in the passages from Luke-Acts—the Emmaus story (Luke 24) and the gathering at Troas for the breaking of bread (Acts 20)—in which a Sunday meeting for word and meal seems to have been the regular practice. As we have seen, this same pattern—gathering on Sunday, scripture reading and interpretation followed by the meal of Christ—may also be recognized in the Revelation to John. The idea of a collection for the poor on Sunday was also known and encouraged by Paul (1 Cor. 16:2), presumably because that was the day of Christian assembly for the word and the meal.

Furthermore, it may well be that some Christians of the earliest period recognized the continuity of this pattern of their meeting with one of the Old Testament stories of an "assembly" before God, the story in Nehemiah 8:1-12 of the great gathering at the Water Gate after the exile. There, on the first day of the seventh month, all the people—men and women and children, the text stresses—gather to hear the word of God read and interpreted. Then, weeping, they are comforted by Ezra, who tells them to eat a meal of fat food and rich wine and to send portions of these to those who have none. Gathering, word, meal, and sending are already present in the text from Nehemiah.

But the outline recorded by Justin can be recognized also in the centuries-long history of worship that follows this report. All the matters Justin notes continued to be basic matters in Christian liturgy: assembly; various leadership roles including especially readers, communion ministers, and a presider; gathering together; remembering baptism; reading scripture of both Old and New Testaments; preaching; intercessions followed by a kiss of peace; table setting; a great prayer of thanksgiving; communion; a sending to the absent; and a collection for the poor.

Sometimes the elements of worship might be moved around—as when the kiss of peace came to be placed just before communion in some communities. Sometimes they might be lost altogether—as when the intercessions or the collection for the poor or the reading from the Old Testament disappeared—only to be recovered at a later time in history. Not uncommonly, some very basic matters could be obscured—as when the prayer of thanksgiving at the table came to be regarded as the priest's "sacrifice" or when the language of the whole service was no longer comprehensible to the participants. And sometimes—as in the Reformation and again in the twentieth-century recovery of the liturgy—the very matters mentioned in Justin's outline are taken up again and brought to the fore, such as assembly participation, full reading of scripture, preaching at every Sunday service, intercessions for a needy world, strong thanksgiving, everyone communing, a collection taken and sent.

In Christian history, this pattern was made available to leaders of worship in a variety of ways. In some places in the early centuries, "church orders" were written that described the ways Christians should worship. The Didache, the Didascalia, the so-called Apostolic Tradition, and the Apostolic Constitutions of the second through the fourth centuries are examples of this genre. Later, especially in regional churches, an *ordo* or order of worship was presumed, and varieties of books were prepared with texts that were to be inserted at appropriate places in the ordo. Commonly, this *ordo* was thought about as a "liturgy of the word" joined with a "liturgy of the eucharist." In places where there was a memory of the catechumens being present for scripture and preaching but being dismissed from the assembly before the eucharist, this order could also be called "mass of the catechumens" (for the word service) and "mass of the faithful" (for the meal).

But sometimes, with a forgetfulness of the pattern, the liturgy seems to have become simply a list of the texts that should be sung or recited in the proper sequence, one thing after another, to get the job done correctly. In the middle ages, commentators on the liturgy worked to make sense of these lists again, and *ordines*, or orders, were once again written, describing the shape and flow of liturgical actions.

The Pattern among Lutherans

With the Lutheran Reformation, "church orders" began to be written again. Usually these books set out in descriptive prose the order that local churches should follow in worship, sometimes also including some of the texts or music that might be employed in following this order, sometimes simply referring to available resources. Interestingly, these Reformation church orders, or *Kirchenordnungen*, also usually included proposals about church leadership, about the care for the poor, and about education.

Luther himself exercised a significant influence on the directions for worship in these *Kirchenordnungen*, having himself written two essays about the pattern to be followed in a reformed mass and the resources that could be employed in this pattern. It is important to note that these essays of Luther—called *Formula Missae* and *Deutsche Messe*, or the Formula for Mass at Wittenberg and the German Mass—were not themselves liturgies, but rather descriptions of liturgical pattern. Furthermore, there were two of them, spelling out two different ways that the local church in Wittenberg was trying to enact the ancient pattern for the service. These two ways shared a single overarching outline—very like the pattern of worship in *Evangelical Lutheran Worship*—and thereby underscored the unity of worship, its traditional or more-than-local character. But their very diversity also sought to avoid uniformity and compulsion, spelling out the pastoral and local decisions that always had to be made.

However, when single worship books began to be printed in considerable number—when printing made possible the inclusion, within an available single volume, of all of the needed liturgical texts and at least some of the needed song—the great shape or *ordo* of the service could be easily forgotten. Some people certainly remembered and taught the shape of the event. The nineteenth-century Bavarian Lutheran pastor Wilhelm Löhe—a figure of great importance to American Lutheranism—was one. His writings traced the flow of the event of worship, likening it to a double-peaked mountain, the two peaks being word and sacrament. Earlier, Henry Melchior Muhlenberg in eighteenth-century Pennsylvania could be considered another, since his important "liturgy" was, like Luther's work, a handwritten guide and essay about how to use the diverse available resources for an evangelical Holy Communion service in colonial America. But for many people, the "liturgy" was simply a long text in a book, a text that was primarily the concern of the clergy and was primarily recited and performed by the clergy and, perhaps, the choir.

In the twentieth century the old pattern, or *ordo*, was rediscovered. Among various Christian churches a worship renewal movement awakened a widespread interest in such emphases as a participating assembly, a balance of strong preaching and vibrant celebration of the Lord's supper, an expanded use of the Bible through the lectionary, intercessory praying, diverse leadership roles, and a new sense of sending.

By the 1970s, *Lutheran Book of Worship* could introduce both the idea of a "presiding minister" and the idea of a "shape" or pattern of the liturgy, an idea underscored by the few required central things in the service and the several optional matters. The idea of the "presiding minister" won wide resonance and acceptance in Lutheran circles, along with its strong implication of many assisting ministries. The "shape" idea, however, was not clearly outlined, except for important passages in the book's introduction, passages many people did not realize were there:

> The services of the *Lutheran Book of Worship* embody the tradition of worship which received its characteristic shape during the early centuries of the Church's existence and was reaffirmed during the Reformation era. As such, they are an emblem of continuity with the whole Church and of particular unity with Lutherans throughout the world. At the same time, the services are adaptable to various circumstances and situations. Freedom and flexibility in worship is a Lutheran inheritance, and there is room for ample variety in ceremony, music, and liturgical form.

> Having considered their resources and their customs, congregations will find their own balance between fully using the ritual and musical possibilities of the liturgy, and a more modest practice. A full service should not allow secondary ceremonies to eclipse central elements of the liturgy, nor should a simple service omit essential or important parts. Every service, whether elaborate or spare, sung or said, should be within the framework of the common rite of the Church. . . . [*LBW*, p. 8]

Like *Lutheran Book of Worship* and the ecumenical sources noted earlier, *Evangelical Lutheran Worship* draws from Luke 24, Acts 20, and Nehemiah 8, as well as from the early presence and recent rediscovery of the pattern in Christian history. But by making the pattern for worship more clear and primary—by putting the pattern up front—it stands as well in continuity with Luther's essays on worship, with the old Lutheran church orders, with Löhe's description, and with Muhlenberg's liturgy. In an evangelical and Lutheran way, this pattern seeks to be theologically responsible, liturgically traditional or more-than-local, and yet open and encouraging to local responsibility and local diversity.

Evangelical Lutheran Worship Pattern for Worship

Gathering

The Holy Spirit calls us together as the people of God.

Confession and Forgiveness
OR
Thanksgiving for Baptism

On the day of Christ's resurrection, and at other times, God gathers us in Christian assembly. We confess our sin and hear God's word of forgiveness. We give thanks for God's mercy in the gift of baptism.

Gathering Song
    Hymn or Psalm
    Kyrie
    Canticle of Praise

Singing at the gathering may include hymns old and new; a prayer for God's mercy to fill the church and the world; a canticle of praise to God's glory revealed in Jesus Christ.

Greeting
Prayer of the Day

During the gathering, the presiding minister and the assembly greet each other in the name of the triune God. The presiding minister gathers the assembly into prayer.

Word

God speaks to us in scripture reading, preaching, and song.

First Reading
Psalm
Second Reading
Gospel Acclamation
Gospel
Sermon

The word of God is proclaimed within and by the gathered assembly. The first Bible reading, usually from the Old Testament, is followed by a psalm sung in response. The second reading, usually from the New Testament letters, bears the witness of the early church. We acclaim the living Word, Jesus Christ, present in the gospel reading. Preaching brings God's word of law and gospel into our time and place to awaken and nourish faith.

Hymn of the Day
Creed
Prayers of Intercession
Peace

God's word is further proclaimed as we sing and as we confess our faith with the whole church. After praying for the whole world, we receive and extend to one another the gift of Christ's peace.

Central elements of the liturgy are noted in bold type; other elements support the essential shape of Christian worship.

Meal

God feeds us with the presence of Jesus Christ.

Offering
Setting the Table
Offering Prayer

A collection of material goods for the church's mission, including the care of those in need, is a sign of the giving of our whole selves in grateful response for all God's gifts. The table is set with bread and wine.

Great Thanksgiving
   Dialogue and Preface
   Holy, Holy, Holy

Before the Lord's supper is shared, the presiding minister leads us into thanksgiving. With the whole creation, we join the angels' song.

   Thanksgiving at the Table
   with **Words of Institution**
   OR
   Words of Institution

   Lord's Prayer

The grace of God's gift is always proclaimed in Jesus' own words of command and promise at the table. A full thanksgiving also includes praise to God for creation and salvation; remembrance of the crucified and risen Christ; and prayer for the Holy Spirit in this meal. The thanksgiving concludes with the prayer our Lord Jesus taught us.

Communion
   Communion Song
   Prayer after Communion

In Christ's body and blood given to us, God forgives us and nourishes us for mission. We sing as the bread is broken and as the meal is shared. We ask God to send us in witness to the world.

Sending

God blesses us and sends us in mission to the world.

Sending of Communion
Blessing
Sending Song
Dismissal

God's mission includes the gifts of grace that we share in worship and take also to the absent; now, we are sent to continue our participation in God's mission. With the blessing of God, we go out to live as Christ's body in the world.

Four Parts, Sometimes Five, Flowing Together

There are a variety of ways to think about this pattern. One is clear in the printing itself. The central elements of the liturgy are noted in bold type. They are:

- *the greeting* and the *prayer of the day* in the Gathering section;
- all the scripture *readings*, with the *psalm* and *gospel acclamation*, the *sermon*, the *hymn of the day*, the *prayers of intercession* and the *peace* in the Word section;
- *offering, setting the table*, the *great thanksgiving* with its diverse parts, and *communion* in the Meal section; and
- the *blessing* in the Sending.

The other elements support this essential shape. One could imagine that the matters marked by bold type are the weight-bearing walls in an open and welcoming building, with room for us all. Then the other matters of the liturgy—hymns or actions or prayers or songs listed in lighter type—could be regarded as significant pieces of furniture or works of art or rich carpets that unfold the meaning of each space in the liturgy and help us to live and to move around there, within that building. Or we could consider that this short list of bold-type matters is what would be needed in a simple and spare service, with little ceremony. Or one could consider that these are the matters that unite two congregations that otherwise do the Sunday service in very dissimilar ways. It is certainly not that the other things, the elements not in bold print, are unimportant. Though some of these latter things may sometimes be omitted or done in quite varied ways, the songs and prayers so indicated do significantly unfold the flow of the service and engage us all in Gathering, Word, Meal, and Sending.

Note that there are few of these "weight-bearing" matters in the Gathering and the Sending. The greeting and the prayer of the day are indeed important parts of the pattern, but they themselves, together with other parts of the Gathering, are supportively secondary to the reason we gather, namely to hear the word of God and to share in the meal of Christ. So also, the blessing, together with other parts of the Sending, is secondary to these same central things that form us and send us in mission. Neither the Gathering nor the Sending should become so protracted and important as to dwarf the Word and the Meal in an assembly's practice. As the Notes on the Services (LE, 17) say of the Gathering:

Whatever elements are included, it is important that the gathering rite not overshadow the principal parts of the primary service of the Christian assembly, namely, the proclamation of the word of God and the sharing of the meal of the Lord's supper.

Still, such a way of considering the pattern for worship runs the risk of again seeming like a mere list: one thing after another. The flow of communal action is missed. It might be better to state the pattern in this way: Christian worship is made up of God's gift of the word set next to God's gift of the meal. Each of these central matters is itself two-fold: reading is followed by proclaiming; thanksgiving at the table is followed by communion. But each of these central matters is also manifold. Reading is made up of several scriptures and their responding songs. Proclamation is made up of preaching together with communal hymn singing and often the communal declaration of the creed. Thanksgiving at table is a combination of prayer, song, proclamation of Christ's promise, and the Lord's Prayer. Communion includes both eating and drinking as well as sending communion to the absent. Further, all of these things are not static but part of a movement. Each of the basic pairs—reading and proclaiming followed by thanksgiving and communing—leads to a third thing. Reading and preaching leads us to prayer for the world. Or, said in faith, God uses the means of the scripture and proclamation to bring us to faith in Christ and in all of God's promises. Such faith comes to expression in prayer to God for those promises to be known and fulfilled in places of need throughout the world. Then the word next to the meal—and the proclamation of the thanksgiving next to the eating and drinking of the gift of Christ—bring us again to a third thing: mission. Or, said in faith, God uses this holy meal to bring us together to be what we eat. We are made to be the body of Christ, sent to live as that body in the world.

By the mercy of God, we gather, with the word of forgiveness and the thanksgiving for baptism drawing us into the triune presence of God. Then scripture and preaching lead to prayer, and thanksgiving and communion lead to sending. Or, in the largest outline: after our Gathering by the Spirit, Word and Meal lead to Sending. And next Sunday—and the Sunday after that—we will come again to these faith-making, mission-making gifts.

Sometimes, the scripture and the preaching lead not only to prayer but also to yet other important ways that faith is enacted in the assembly. The principal one of these is baptism. The note on page 226 of *Evangelical Lutheran Worship* (expanded slightly in LE, pp. 27–29) makes it clear that Holy Baptism, which best takes place in the gathered assembly, normally will follow the hymn of the day and precede the prayers of intercession. Then one might say that the pattern for worship is made up of five elements: Gathering, Word, Baptism, Meal, and Sending. Other rites of the church that echo and underscore our baptismal vocation—ordinations and installations, but also prayers for healing and for the blessing of a marriage—find their place in this same baptismal location. Or, as the notes again make clear, Holy Baptism may take place as part of the Gathering, before the greeting and the prayer of the day. Then the pattern might be said to be Gathering through Baptism, Word, Meal, Sending.

Still, this is not simply a list of five things but a *single* event, around a single gospel. The pattern is one of a flowing, communal action. Yet it is also a way of talking about the centrality of those things that God has given in order to bring us to faith and form us for love toward our neighbor.

The Pattern for Worship and Assembly Song

One way that has long been used to describe the flow of the classic Christian service involved the list of the common songs or chants that were sung at any festive celebration of the Western pattern of the Holy Communion: Kyrie, Gloria in excelsis, Credo, Sanctus, and Agnus Dei. These songs entered into the Roman rite for Sunday, beginning with the Sanctus in the fourth century and continuing with the Kyrie in the fifth century, the Gloria in the sixth, the Agnus Dei in the seventh, and the Credo more or less regularly only in the eleventh. They came to be the sung parts of the material that made up the "ordinary of the mass," and they seem to have been originally intended as communal song, though later the community was often replaced by the choir, increasingly using virtuosic musical settings that today are usually performed in concert settings.

However, the texts themselves, in this order, are not at home primarily in a concert hall but in the Christian assembly, helping to carry the flow of its pattern for worship. Called Kyrie, Canticle of praise, Creed, Holy, holy, holy, and Lamb of God in *Evangelical Lutheran Worship*, each of them have a place in the pattern for worship. Although four of these songs are not among the "weight-bearing walls," the songs themselves are nonetheless of lasting importance. They are a kind of well-distilled common song that has long expressed the acclamation of the assembly and the meaning of the shape of its worship. Still today, we may gather singing both Kyrie and Glory to God, crying out the need of the world and yet praising God with the angels at the incarnation of the Word. We may respond to the Word with the confession of the creed, perhaps singing it in the version of hymn 411. We almost always join the thanksgiving at table with the singing of the Holy, Holy, Holy. And we may bring to expression what is to happen in communion by singing the Lamb of God. These songs continue to unite us with God's people in many times and places. The ecumenical pattern for worship reflected also in *Evangelical Lutheran Worship* offers much flexibility in how this common body of song is used, especially within the Gathering. However, in Lutheran practice, these common songs (with the exception of the Creed, now rarely sung) continue to be a great treasure. While they may be seasonally varied, while they may be paraphrased and replaced with other songs functioning in similar ways, an assembly that leaves them out of its knowledge and ongoing life is likely to be impoverished. Lutherans have typically emphasized singing as a foundational and lively way of worship. Used rightly, the old "chants of the ordinary of the mass"—in musical settings both historic and contemporary—may continue to teach us that. They belong to the flow of the pattern for worship. They are not well understood except as they are seen to function within that flow. They are misused if they call attention to themselves, obscuring the flow and the pattern, or if they call attention to the musicians, obscuring the assembly.

And yet this common repertoire is but one example of how assembly song functions to carry forward the pattern for worship and to draw all of us into participating activity: through many ways of singing as we gather, through sung psalms and gospel acclamations, through the central hymn of proclamation, through singing as gifts are gathered, through singing around the table and as we are sent into the world.

Other Patterns?

One final comment: Some people, learning about the outline of Holy Communion, have wondered if the pattern might not be enacted in another order—Gathering, Meal, Word, Sending. There are two problems with this proposal. One is that it loses its connection to the widely practiced ecumenical shape and to the biblical and historical models, beginning with Nehemiah 8 and Luke 24. It seems like a local decision that chooses to disconnect from the more-than-local across both space and time.

But the more serious concern is that the Word–Meal pattern belongs to the deep, faith-making, mission-making logic of worship. If we eat first, before the proclamation of the gospel, we might easily forget what the meal is for, and we might also think that it is for us alone. Liturgy in our time has, after a long period of loss, again been gifted with the Sending. The promise of the gospel proclaimed leads us to prayer for the world. Then the gift of that promise in the form of food, as we now eat and drink the same word we have heard, leads us to care for and turn toward a hungry world, to "send portions . . . to those for whom nothing is prepared," as Nehemiah 8:10 says, and to be sent ourselves.

This pattern reflects the language of *The Use of the Means of Grace*, language that is helpful to recall:

> The two principal parts of the liturgy of Holy Communion, the proclamation of the Word of God and the celebration of the sacramental meal, are so intimately connected as to form one act of worship. . . . Our congregations are encouraged to hold these two parts together, avoiding either a celebration of the Supper without the preceding reading of the Scriptures, preaching, and intercessory prayers or a celebration of the Supper for a few people who remain after the dismissal of the congregation from a Service of the Word. . . . The simple order of our liturgy of Holy Communion, represented in the worship books of our church, is that which has been used by generations of Christians. We gather in song and prayer, confessing our need of God. We read the Scriptures and hear them preached. We profess our faith and pray for the world, sealing our prayers with a sign of peace. We gather an offering for the poor and for the mission of the church. We set our table with bread and wine, give thanks and praise to God, proclaiming Jesus Christ, and eat and drink. We hear the blessing of God and are sent out in mission to the world. [34, 34a, 34b]

Service Notes and Announcements

The Holy Communion pattern for worship in *Evangelical Lutheran Worship* can be considered an important form of "rubrics." That word was the name used to denote the directions and notes, written or printed in red ink (*rubrus* is the Latin adjective "red") on the edge of the actual liturgical texts in old manuscripts and books. As in the old books, the notes and directions for the services in *Evangelical Lutheran Worship* are still printed mostly in red, to distinguish them from the texts of the liturgy. "Service notes" or "notes on the service" are the terms used for this material.

But in *Evangelical Lutheran Worship* there are comparably fewer of these red-ink notes in the services. The ones that are there are intended mostly to make the structure or pattern of the liturgy clearer and to illuminate its many options, for example, pointing out leaders and postures as the assembly moves through the shape of the liturgy. In that sense, all these notes depend upon the Pattern for Worship as the most basic rubric of the book, even though that pattern is not printed in red. Beside the structural outline of Holy Communion that we have been considering, such a pattern is also found throughout the liturgical material of the book, just before the red tabs for each section: on pages 225–26 for Baptism, pages 248–50 for Lent and the Three Days, pages 273–75 for Life Passages, and pages 295–97 for Daily Prayer. All of those patterns are then further illuminated by yet another set of rubrics that are not printed in red: the important General Notes, on page 9 of both *Evangelical Lutheran Worship* and the Leaders Edition, and the extended Notes on the Services, on pages 9-52 of LE.

Someone who wishes to know the resources of *Evangelical Lutheran Worship* and to explore its possible uses should begin with studying these patterns, general notes, and notes within the services. Much of what follows in the second section of this book is commentary and reflection on these notes.

But it is important to say what these service notes are and what they are not. At least in Lutheran use, they are not ecclesial laws to be enforced. Neither are they trip wires set in place by ancient authorities and designed to trigger explosions if they are transgressed. Nor are they divinely-revealed rules. It is far better to understand them as a kind of concrete report of a long history of communal experience, written in a shorthand as a way to pass on that experience to a next generation of worshipers. It is as such a report of experience that we have been considering the Holy Communion pattern for worship. Wise leaders and wise assemblies do not simply walk past such a report of experience. But over time, rubrics are also living, changing things. Anyone who compares older liturgical books with newer ones will note both the similarities and the changes. One might say that the liturgy itself—especially in its central word and sacraments—is like a stream of fresh, life-giving water. Service notes are like the banks of the stream. They are not the water itself and cannot be. But they contain and channel the water, passing it on to those downstream and helping it not dissipate in an un-useful flood. Like river banks, these notes also change, gradually moving with the necessary moving and relocating of the river.

The service notes of *Evangelical Lutheran Worship* are written in a style influenced by that of the *Statement on Sacramental Practices* of the Evangelical Lutheran Church in Canada and *The Use of the Means of Grace* of the Evangelical Lutheran Church in America. They try to avoid sounding like laws and instead to give counsel and help. They intend to invite and teach, not compel. Much more often than in earlier rubrics, they talk about the reasons for an action or a text, about the why of the handed-down practice, doing so especially in the prose of the pattern for worship and in the extended LE notes. The purpose of the present volume—as well as the other volumes in this series—is in part to note those reasons and further expand upon them. But all of this is not to imply that the service notes of *Evangelical Lutheran Worship* are not important. On the contrary. They are important like the counsel of wise friends. They are important like the more-than-local. They are important like the banks of a stream are important and irreplaceable. But the gospel in word and sacrament is the living water.

One thorny and much-discussed matter is not addressed in the Holy Communion pattern for worship: Where shall we put the announcements? This matter is addressed in the red-ink notes interspersed in the service settings themselves, for example on page 114 of Setting One, as well as in Notes on the Services (LE, 17, 24). The counsel here, like that of a wise friend, is: Try to avoid interrupting the flow of the service with announcements. Either before the service begins or at the close of the Gathering section, just before the readings, let the presiding minister or some other leader announce what day it is, if that is useful, and make any brief comments that are needed for the assembly to know about the day's worship. That is all. Then, at the end of the service, just before the blessing or the dismissal, let brief announcements be made, especially those related to sending and mission — "those related to the assembly's participation in God's mission in the world," as the service note puts it. "Brief" is a key word. This may be a time for various people to let the assembly know of opportunities for service. It may be a time for the entire assembly to turn toward mission. It is not a time for further sermons or for lengthy lists of everything happening within the congregation. If the announcements drain the assembly of the impetus to go out in mission, it is time to rethink them. The counsel that divides announcements according to their function, places them at either end of the service, recommends simplicity and brevity, and welcomes many voices is wise counsel indeed. It may not be what you do. It may not, in this case, be local enough for your congregation. But it would be good to think about this proposal. It is one little part of the stream banks, intending to avoid a few people talking too much about programs, intending rather to accentuate the importance of our assembly work in worship and in mission, intending to let the water of word and sacrament — of Gathering, Word, Meal, and Sending — stay flowing clear at the center.

CHAPTER FOUR

Music and the Arts in the Assembly

The arts are an integral dimension of Christian worship. They play a critical role in grounding worship in a specific time, location, and context. Visual art and images, music of voices and instruments, poetry and drama, movement and gesture all serve to engage the assembly in multiple ways. The arts activate the human senses and connect us to one another and the larger communion of God's people as we participate in them together. In Lutheran worship, this critical nature is heightened still more.

A Lutheran understanding of the arts in worship sees them assisting in proclaiming the word in the assembly. This is much more than decoration or pleasant background. The various arts are among the human languages used to convey the means of grace as they proclaim the word and support the sacraments. Art forms that are more than verbal provide a balance to the spoken word, so that worship is not overwhelmed with words, but rather includes other forms of expression that are also gifts of God to engage the whole person.

The visual arts proclaim and support the means of grace within the physical environment for worship. Architecture can provide a welcoming home for the assembly in which the means of grace may be celebrated in their fullness and in which other arts may flourish. Paraments, banners, and other fabric art can focus the worship space, providing accent to the church's days and seasons, using color, shape, and texture to communicate. Stained glass, painting and other graphic arts, and sculpture can surround the assembly, highlighting witnesses in the communion of saints and opening up various aspects of God's work of salvation. Increasingly, churches are exploring the use of projected images, both still and moving, as effective means of visual proclamation and interpretation. Drama and dance can unlock new dimensions of meaning in the proclaimed word and the action of worship. All of the arts may be useful in developing an assembly's praise and proclamation.

Of all the arts, music has historically played an especially prominent role in Lutheran worship. Music invites the participation of the assembly, supporting and enlivening its voice. It is especially useful in the assembly's worship because it helps to form the community into one. Singing together helps make the gathered people into the assembly, connecting individual feeling to communal expression.

Music's importance to the Christian assembly centers on its ability to carry and enliven the words of worship. Martin Luther called the gospel the "sounded Word." A primary way in which the assembly enters into the sounding of God's word is through the assembly's song. In a particular context, at a particular time, the assembly takes up the proclamation and makes the word of God its own by using the language and art of music.

In *Worship and Culture in Dialogue*, studies prepared by the Lutheran World Federation, Mark Bangert writes about the unique way music bears this role of proclamation in the Christian assembly. "This is at the heart of being Lutheran: that is, Word is taken to be an oral thing, an enfleshed event, seeking a voice (vox), longing for fulfillment in song, hymn, or dance" (189).

Music provides connection in a community through its combination of word and organized sound. This combination serves to create meaning for those who join the song. As an assembly sings, so it may come more fully to believe and live. Music is a particularly effective means of holding several elements of worship or dimensions of meaning in creative contact with one another. Music in worship is continually juxtaposing text and tune, sound and silence, and it frequently accompanies and interprets the actions of worship. As it participates with a common voice in this combining of word, song, and action, the assembly often experiences an enrichment of meaning and experience that is greater than the sum of its parts.

Introducing a new song into an assembly's repertoire exhibits this confluence at work. For example, placing the Korean hymn of unity "Come Now, O Prince of Peace" (#247) next to the familiar apostolic greeting, "The grace of our Lord Jesus Christ, the love of God, and the communion of the Holy Spirit be with you all," gives both elements a new context. The contrast between the points of origin of these elements, combined with the complementary meaning of their words and a tune that evokes longing, has the potential to open up new avenues of meaning for the assembly.

So too we see new meanings possible even in the handing on of a previous generation's repertoire. "Children of the Heavenly Father" (#781) has made its way forward from at least three generations of previous Lutheran English-language worship books into *Evangelical Lutheran Worship*. Yet now it is surrounded by other songs and includes a stanza in its original Swedish language, and it becomes a hymn for another generation of worshipers. The generation of worshipers who will now sing this hymn will recreate it as they sing. It will no longer be the hymn it was; it will be a hymn carried forward to a new generation, who will find meaning from it in their own context.

As assembly song crosses from one time to another, or from one culture to another, we see its meaning and emphases shift. It becomes a vehicle that enables a transfer of praise and proclamation, lament and intercession from one assembly in one time and context to another. As this song travels from one assembly to another, it expresses a commonality among those assemblies, yet it often gains a distinctive place and fresh nuances in each new assembly. As people sing their songs, placing them next to prayers, scripture, and other worship elements, they activate the movement of the liturgy through time and place, their participation next to that of God's people of many times and places. No longer is a given assembly isolated, singing only its immediate expressions; now we open up the songs of sixteenth-century Germans or twentieth-century Argentines and discover that their words and music resonate deep within us.

Music's ability to hold together multiple layers of time expresses the *kairos* of sacred time. The great thanksgiving illustrates such multiple layers. At the conclusion of the preface, when the presiding minister prays, "with . . . the hosts of heaven, we praise your name and join their unending hymn," the assembly sings, "Holy, holy, holy Lord, God of power and might." These are the words of the seraphs, the heavenly hosts, which Isaiah heard in his vision. These ancient words found another layer of meaning when they were placed in the context of the church's thanksgiving for the gifts of life and salvation. And these words become new again when each newly-gathered assembly joins its voice to the song of thanksgiving each week. Music joins *this* assembly's voice to the church's song "of every time and in every place."

Through this deep connection to the great assembly of God's people that transcends time and space, through their immersion in such sacred time, worshipers may experience their connection and relationship to

God. Indeed, Christians have likened being "in Christ" to dwelling in the harmony of God, where there is ample room for dissonance and even single voices. This divine harmony is suggested and anticipated when we sing, but it is never fully realized in any of our holy songs.

The language of music also helps us understand that worship can open us to the reality that God's diversity is larger than even our most ambitious human imaginings. God's harmony is greater than ours, encompassing a wider breadth of expression than our music can ever achieve or even imagine. When we connect our songs to the actions and words and images of the liturgy, we see multiple layers of meaning emerge. When we set out the new together with the old, the traditional together with the contemporary, the unfamiliar together with the well-worn, we see God's revelation in ever-new ways. Diversity in our musical expressions helps us better to apprehend an image of God, of harmony in diversity.

Luther and the Church's Song

Martin Luther certainly believed that music had the ability to proclaim the word. He wrote that the gifts of language and sound were given to us by God so that we could praise God with cheerful hearts (*LW* 53:333). The ability to combine verbal and nonverbal dimensions into a unified, communal expression is a singular gift of the art of music, enabling music to carry God's word in the assembly. Luther believed that singing texts had the equivalent value of speaking them. In a letter to George Spalatin, Luther outlined his conviction about the value of music in teaching and proclamation: "Our plan is to follow the example of the prophets and the ancient fathers of the church, and to compose psalms for the people in the vernacular, that is, spiritual songs, so that the word of God may be among the people also in the form of music" (*LW* 49:68). Just as the word can be read in the assembly, it can also be sung. Just as one person can read the word, so also can the whole assembly sing the word. In fact, proclamation of the word by the assembly often happens most effectively when that word is sung.

Luther believed strongly in the distinctive ability of music to be a bearer of God's word, as a particular gift of God for human use. He declared that the prophets "held theology and music most tightly connected, and proclaimed the truth through psalms and songs" (*LW* 40:141). In his liturgical reforms, especially in adapting the mass to the German language, he was deeply concerned that music and the vernacular text could support one another.

Luther was unsatisfied with a chant setting that simply translated the Latin texts of the mass into German and left the chants intact. He felt this was a disruption to the sensibility of the mass and left a disjointed result. His solution for a mass with a German character *(Deutsche Messe)* was to use German chorales, folk-based tunes, and newly-composed tunes. These tunes were naturally suited to the German language. The liturgical texts of the mass were adapted and paraphrased in ways that would match the chorale tunes. In putting forward the German mass, Luther was offering an attempt at a form that took seriously the natural rhythm and character of the German language and its ability to be rendered in music. As he chose new tunes and adapted others, he consistently showed great concern for matching text and tune.

We can still see portions of Luther's German Mass in *Evangelical Lutheran Worship*, including several presented in sequence in the hymn section. "Kyrie! God Father" (#409) interposes the original Greek exclamation (*Kyrie eleison,* or "Lord, have mercy") with a vernacular text that adds a trinitarian interpretation. "All Glory Be to God on High" (#410) is a paraphrase of the Latin Gloria in excelsis. Luther's sung version of the Nicene Creed follows, "We All Believe in One True God" (#411). All of these hymns, among the most popular of the Reformation, continue to be strong entry points into vibrant assembly singing today. Luther saw these sung versions not as lesser alternatives to the liturgical songs they replaced but as worthy vehicles for those timeless songs of the church.

In addition to paraphrases of liturgical song, the early years of the Reformation saw new contributions to hymnody from Luther and others. In his preface to the Wittenberg hymnal of 1524, Luther notes that this new collection of German songs is offered so that "the gospel might be noised abroad." Luther was convinced that the reclamation of the gospel in the language of the people called for new songs to carry it. These new hymns were a further working out of Luther's commitment to use the gift of music to proclaim the word of God.

Music for the Sunday Assembly in *Evangelical Lutheran Worship*

Martin Luther's emphasis on communal assembly song is reflected also in the music of *Evangelical Lutheran Worship,* which includes liturgical song, psalms, and hymns in great variety, most of it useful within the service of Holy Communion. Some of the criteria Luther saw as important continue to have value today. Priority is given to song that is suited for bearing and proclaiming the word, that is accessible and invites assembly participation, and that can endure over extended time and use.

The use of vernacular language takes a different shape today than it did in Luther's day. Luther translated into German or sought out translations of Latin texts, which many people did not understand, so that people could sing in the language they understood. In our globally interconnected society today, the situation is quite different. Vernacular language in North America and the Caribbean includes a plurality of languages and cultures. English is not the only vernacular language used in our assemblies. There are members present and new worshipers arriving whose primary language is Spanish, or Mandarin, or Swahili. Recognizing this plurality of languages for worship, even in limited though symbolic ways, is an extension of the Lutheran priority that worship be in the language of the people. It also serves as a gentle corrective to the prevalent tendency to think of our own worship language and styles as universally normative.

Thus, *Evangelical Lutheran Worship* provides a setting of Holy Communion in which the sung portions are bilingual—English and Spanish (Setting Seven, p. 175). There are also hymns and liturgical songs with at least one stanza in Mandarin Chinese ("Midnight Stars Make Bright the Skies," #280), Zulu ("We Are Marching in the Light," #866), Swahili ("Gracious Spirit, Heed Our Pleading," #401), Muscogee Indian ("Hallelujah," #171), and Slovak ("Your Heart, O God, Is Grieved," #602), to name a few. Vernacular language in our time is not one language but many. Multilingual songs encourage our assemblies to discover the rich diversity around and among us and, in modest ways, to learn to express this diversity in singing together. Even assemblies that never sing in a language other than English will learn from the visible presence of other languages in this resource that the body of Christ has many members throughout the world. Also, those whose primary language is other than English who come into one of our assemblies may find a connection to their cultural identity when they encounter these multilingual materials. Although *Evangelical Lutheran Worship* is primarily an English-language resource, it includes a representative breadth of linguistic and cultural diversity.

Evangelical Lutheran Worship's organization emphasizes the centrality of the Sunday assembly. Ten musical settings of Holy Communion are provided, reflecting a wider and more varied musical palette than *Lutheran Book of Worship*. In addition to the musical settings of the liturgy, a service-music section provides further selections in a range of styles for use in the various services. Finally, the hymn collection has been designed primarily to support the Sunday meeting, with expanded sections for gathering song, communion song, and sending song, as well as an extensive collection of hymns for proclaiming the word in support of the seasons of the church year and the emphases of the appointed scripture readings.

In the years since the publication of *Lutheran Book of Worship* in 1978, musical languages for worship have expanded. The explosion of hymnody in the 1970s and 1980s brought folk and popular idioms into worship. Additional song from sources across the church and around the world have come into wide use. The musical settings for Holy Communion in *Evangelical Lutheran Worship* reflect some of this expansion. This variety is an indication of how the vernacular principle applies to music. Because no single musical genre can be said to be the musical language of the whole church, the service is presented in a number of musical genres, including some that are more easily adapted to a variety of performance styles and others that are more style-specific.

Holy Communion Settings One through Five use musical styles that will be familiar to most Lutherans. Setting One is a new compilation from the work of three Lutheran composers. It is in a genre that best lends itself to organ accompaniment. Setting Two also works well with organ, but can alternatively be effectively led with instruments such as piano, synthesizer, and guitars. Settings Three and Four are familiar from their use in *Lutheran Book of Worship*. And Setting Five is a chant-based setting that draws from a variety of sources, most of them dating back for centuries.

Holy Communion Setting Six is an African American gospel- and jazz-style setting. Setting Seven includes selections from Central and South America together with music by Latino composers from the United States. Setting Eight, with selections in various popular music styles, can be led by a keyboard or a larger praise ensemble. Setting Nine is another newly composed setting, commissioned for the Renewing

Worship process. Setting Ten is a hymn-tune setting along the lines of Luther's German Mass, pairing metric paraphrases of liturgical texts with familiar tunes. Though different instrumental accompaniments best suit one or another of these settings, all are designed to work with just a keyboard, whether a fine organ or a small piano. Singable and memorable melodies have been composed or selected, and most of them can be done quite simply, even without accompaniment. The settings may also be elaborated with choral and additional instrumental participation; festival settings of several of the settings have been or will be published.

While greatly diverse in their musical styles, most of these musical settings are united by the use of ecumenically-developed common texts, as a kind of musical testimony to unity in diversity. In every case, the music is designed to support the texts of the songs, prayers, and acclamations. Although ten settings may be more than most assemblies will be able to learn and know well, diving into one or more different musical settings is likely to open an assembly to new insights into its worship.

Taken together, these musical settings offer a breadth of possibilities, reflecting in a modest and representative way the plurality of musical languages sung throughout the church today. Some of them may come to serve as common settings, linking Lutheran worshiping communities across the geographic and cultural landscapes. Others may find greater use in specific contexts and settings. Still other musical settings are available, and more will no doubt be composed in coming years and added to the family of resources. Yet it is hoped that these core service-music materials in *Evangelical Lutheran Worship* will serve for many congregations as signs of unity and diversity, as the people of God in a particular local assembly find connections to other assemblies in the songs they sing around the word and the meal.

The Assembly's Core of Song

It is both a great privilege and a weighty responsibility to select, prepare, and lead music for the assembly. The Lutheran tradition offers a great deal from which to draw. To add to that, a wealth of new and valuable music awaits discovery by a local assembly. Balancing the contrasting and sometimes competing values can be daunting.

Thinking about an assembly's common core of music, those things which an assembly knows and sings with regularity over time, may be helpful in planning for its overall musical life. An assembly's common core would be the entire body of hymns and liturgical music that it knows well. When considering any given community's common core, at least four questions may be helpful:

- How many and which songs are currently well known by the assembly?
- What songs have the greatest value for the greater worship life of the congregation?
- What songs seem as though they will hold their value and appeal over years and decades?
- Approximately what number of songs would provide sufficient variety without overloading the congregation's capacity?

The assembly's current body of song.

If one took an inventory of the hymnody and liturgical song that the assembly knows well, what would be included? Taking such an inventory could be a helpful exercise for a worship and music committee and the congregation's pastoral and musical staff. How large is that group of songs? What are the familiar songs in this assembly? (Keep in mind that the perception of familiarity is often driven more by melody than text.) How will you answer these questions honestly for your assembly and not just its musical leaders? For some assemblies, the result might be 150 hymns and songs, and one or two settings of Holy Communion. For others it might be 300 hymns and songs, and five or six service settings. The current core will vary from assembly to assembly. Size of congregation, general openness to learning new material, musical resources and leadership, and the worship books or electronic resources that are available will all affect the outcome.

Assessing the value of the songs.

Hymns and songs become loved for many reasons: associations with a time or season, with a pastor, music leader, or family member, well-crafted words or melodies, and many more. Once the well-known hymns and other musical pieces have been identified, a second helpful step is to begin to determine the value of each one. This value may or may not be closely tied to the reason it became well known. For example, "Abide with Me" (#629) might have been a favorite closing hymn for midweek evening services, but it is at least as valuable for times like funerals when a poignant hymn of hopeful assurance is needed. Such an assessment will also helpfully lead to two more determinations: which of the current core of hymns might be moved into less-frequent use, and where are the "holes" where an additional hymn or song could be very useful?

The staying power of songs.

This factor is related to the previous one but applies both to currently known songs and those that an assembly might consider adding to the repertoire. Some new songs have immediate appeal to many worshipers, but for some reason such as simpler text or tune, they quickly wear thin for some people. It can be difficult to predict which hymns and songs will endure, and it will vary from one community to another. Also within a community, it is often worth pursuing a balance of sorts between lighter, more accessible songs and those that may be more challenging but also more nourishing. As the worship planners are working on a core, this is another evaluation to add to the mix.

The assembly's capacity for song.

This component is also difficult to determine, yet important to consider. Is the current inventory at or near the maximum that the assembly can be expected to know and sing well? Some assemblies have a larger capacity than their present core. Familiarity, too frequent repetition, and neglect of new materials may have kept this assembly core smaller than necessary. For others, the core may be too large. Once the number of pieces in the core grows beyond an assembly's ability to retain them in memory, pieces start to fall out of the core. Careful consideration of an assembly's abilities and limits is important.

The assembly's song ideally strikes a balance between the familiar core and the addition of new materials. For those assemblies whose core is already quite large and can't bear much expansion, introduction of new materials also means that some previous materials will need to fall out of the core. In most cases, this will be a gradual and organic change, as the assembly moves toward some resources and away from others. In places where the assembly's core and its abilities are different, however, care is needed in adding to or taking away from the core. Durable liturgical song grows stronger through repetition. In order for any new element to find a place in the core, carefully designed repetition over time is necessary. The assembly's core of song builds up from one generation to another across the decades. It is one of the treasures of the assembly, an organic treasure constantly and gradually being adapted to the assembly and the assembly's context.

Each assembly's core is different. While there are now few hymns that "everyone knows," there remain some that are familiar in most Lutheran settings today. Martin Luther's chorale, "A Mighty Fortress Is Our God" (#503–505), the American carol "It Came upon the Midnight Clear" (#282), Charles Wesley's "Love Divine, All Loves Excelling" (#631), and John Newton's "Amazing Grace, How Sweet the Sound" (#779) are examples of hymns that are part of the common core in most Lutheran congregations. Many other hymns and songs will be familiar in some assemblies but not others.

In planning worship, it is important to consider familiarity not only for the regular participant but also for the infrequent attendee and the guest. Regularly selecting at least some hymns that are shared widely with other Christians can be a great help in welcoming newcomers to an assembly. Many visitors coming into worship have little familiarity with Lutheran tradition. In the preceding examples, "It Came upon the Midnight Clear," "Love Divine, All Loves Excelling," and "Amazing Grace" are all from non-Lutheran origins. The first was written by an Anglican priest, the second by the founder of the Methodist movement, the third by a slave trader undergoing religious conversion. The judicious use of hymns from a common ecumenical core can be a welcoming and hospitable gesture.

Teaching and Learning Assembly Song

Teaching new song to the assembly requires skillful planning. When people learn something helpful or significant about the new song and are taught the music in an inviting way, they are likely to be more receptive. Some musical pieces require more introduction than others. Music similar to the assembly's core may need less introduction than musical styles outside the assembly's experience. Music that steps outside of comfortable boundaries will require strong leadership, patience, and care in its introduction—but may well be worth such an investment.

While different in each context, some of the ways to present new songs to the assembly include choir introduction, choir alternation, instrumental introduction, assembly rehearsal, and congregational communication tools.

Choir introduction

In many congregations, the primary or only role of the choir is to sing one or two anthems in the service. While such works can add beauty and depth to worship and be enjoyable for singers, limiting the choir to such a role is to sell them short. The primary role of the choir is to serve as a corporate assisting minister. If the assembly is to learn and "own" its song, there is no more effective way for that to happen than for them to hear a group of people singing their song—as a model, as a reinforcing and encouraging unit, and in alternation. As a hymn or song is being introduced, the choir can serve as a performing body so that the assembly can listen to what it will be eventually singing. Both adult and children's choirs are helpful here. There is timeless wisdom to John Wesley's recommendation that if one wants adults to learn a new song, let the children teach it to them. The wise choir conductor will spend a major part of rehearsal time in working on the next Sunday's assembly song with the choir so that they are able confidently to lead it. In fact, a piece that will soon be introduced to the assembly can serve well as a simple "anthem" a week or two prior.

Choir alternation

As a sort of next step, the choir (or, if necessary, a single cantor) might sing a stanza of the hymn, then the assembly sings a stanza. Or the assembly might sing a refrain, and the choir or cantor sings the verses. This kind of alternation can help the assembly from feeling overwhelmed in a new song, and gives continued opportunity to listen to what they will be singing.

Instrumental introduction

A keyboard instrument typically introduces a hymn before the assembly sings it. With new song, it is especially important to play the song all the way through as a teaching device, with the melody clearly audible. Further, on Sundays before the Sunday on which a hymn is introduced, the keyboardist might play the hymn as pre-service music, offering music, or as music during the communion, so that the assembly subliminally begins to learn the melody. Similarly, handbell choirs and other instruments may be used to introduce the music, as long as the new melody is clearly presented.

Assembly rehearsal

With care, a time of rehearsal just before the service begins is an effective way to learn new song. Such time is most effective when it is brief, focuses on the assembly music for that morning, and uses strong musical leadership. Unlike a choir rehearsal, it is not a time for repeating music for a thorough learning, but to introduce the assembly ahead of time to music they will hear again in worship. Whether this rehearsal is led by a cantor, choir director, or keyboard musician, visual contact with the assembly is particularly helpful, as is the assembly's ability to hear at least one confident voice modeling and leading the song.

Congregational communications

Communication is essential in the learning process. Consider ways to teach about new song through the congregation's publications—service folders, newsletters, and Web postings. This is an effective way to teach about the background of the hymn: where it came from, who wrote it, what kinds of assemblies have sung it, what theological meaning it holds, and its use in the church year—in other words, why this piece is worth learning.

Teaching a song orally

An important factor to remember about much assembly song is its origin in oral tradition. Historically, most corporate song has been transmitted orally, and that is still the way many people best learn a new song. At its simplest, this method involves call and response: a leader lines out part of a melody and the people respond.

"Come, Let Us Eat" (#491), familiar to many from *Lutheran Book of Worship*, is one of the simplest examples of such a method. The leader sings one line, the assembly repeats it, then the leader sings the other line and the assembly repeats that.

But there are many variations on call and response. "Listen, God Is Calling" (#513, Fig. 4.1), might be taught by the leader singing each two-measure phrase of the refrain one at a time, inviting the assembly to repeat each. Then double the length of the line to be repeated. Finally, the assembly flies on its own: the leader sings the two notes of "Listen," then the assembly sings the refrain. And the verses are easy because the assembly's melody is the same as the end of the refrain. In performance, the song models the life of the church in that the song

Listen, God Is Calling

Text: Tanzanian traditional; tr. Howard S. Olson, b. 1922. Translation © 1968 Lutheran Theological College, Makumira, Tanzania,
admin. Augsburg Fortress.
Tune: NENO LAKE MUNGU, Tanzanian tune, arr. Austin C. Lovelace. Arr. © 1968 Austin C. Lovelace, admin. Augsburg Fortress.

Fig. 4.1. Teaching song orally. *At its simplest, this method involves call and response: a leader lines out part of a melody and the people respond.*

is built around the interlocking structure of a dialogue between the leader and assembly. Neither part is sufficient on its own.

The interactive nature of song from a variety of oral traditions offers great benefit within a culture in which the entertainment paradigm encourages a tendency toward passivity on the part of gathered groups. Congregational song accents and calls upon the *interdependent* work of the assembly, and this is particularly true of songs from oral traditions. Such song requires the assembly's response in order for it to happen. The response is the gap that the community needs to fill. The song cannot happen unless the community enters into it.

Contextualizing the Song

Introducing less familiar types of song requires a deliberate and thorough approach to the assembly. Many forms of contemporary music, from pop and rock to various world musics, are new territory for most assemblies. Careful reading of the assembly's capabilities (quite possibly greater than they may first appear) and careful choices of music will help an assembly find musical expressions that it can grow into for its own praise and proclamation. Making such a process both gradual and thorough can yield well-grounded results that will endure in an assembly's core of song. That is, the songs will become contextualized—they will come to feel as though they fit within the assembly's unique context. Consider a process that uses some or all of the following steps in choosing new musical styles and songs to contextualize the assembly's musical repertoire.

Identifying the contextual location

The first step in contextualizing music for the assembly is recognizing the congregation's location—in several senses. First, literally: where is the congregation geographically located—rural area, city or suburban neighborhood, community, region? Chances are that a rural congregation in the upper Midwest will have experienced different influences from one in the center of San Juan, Puerto Rico. But beyond that, location also includes dimensions such as denomination, ecclesial tradition within a denomination, and congregational characteristics. The process of identifying location begins by noting the specific nature of each assembly, with its unique identity, while acknowledging ways it reflects larger unifying identities. Such a process also offers an opportune time to identify the common core of song and other liturgical repertoire for this assembly: what it owns for itself, and what it has in common with wider expressions of the church.

Each person in the worshiping community contributes to this process. While each person need not participate directly, it is important that the planning structure takes into account each person's gifts and abilities that relate to the assembly's worship. Are there any voices not heard? Such a question can be helpful in developing an inclusive planning process.

Naming a specific location is a process of claiming a worshiping community's identity. It is a way of saying both what it holds in common with other communities and what makes this assembly unique among others. No one assembly is normative for any other; each has its own identity, built from what it has inherited and what it continues to shape.

This process of naming helps a given worshiping community avoid thinking of itself as normative. That is, while a given assembly's traditions and preferences are valuable within itself, they won't be right for assemblies in other locations. Understanding that such differences exist can increase the possibility of mutual respect among communities. It also works against the idea that one community can simply be duplicated in another location. Each community has unique characteristics giving it an identity. Context adds the unique and particular elements distinguishing one assembly from others.

Identifying how meaning is articulated

The second step in creating or revising a body of music that fits within a given assembly is understanding how meaning is expressed. Worship expresses the deep values of its assembly. Because these values or meanings often go unnoticed or unrecognized in the assembly, this step in the process brings them into the conscious awareness of the assembly.

What does this community believe itself to be—under God and with God? The starting place is the Sunday assembly itself, the gathering around word and table. Aspects such as frequency of communion and richness of scriptural reading can reveal much. Then other dimensions may be helpfully evaluated—cultural expressions, styles of celebration, roles in worship leadership, for example. To discover what it communicates as important, an assembly can look, for example, at the ways it prays, the physical environment for worship, the vitality of its singing, and the ways visitors are welcomed.

Furthermore, the theological content of songs, hymns, and liturgical music in the assembly's common core are important to observe. How is God addressed and imaged? What images of God are present? Which are absent? What is the predominant relationship between God and creation? What kinds of ethical claims are made through the texts? Looking at sung texts in this light can reveal what the assembly has chosen to emphasize, either by design or default. What might be seen as omissions within a holistic view of worship? What is not being said that could be? What aspects of the divine–human relationship are not being addressed? How does the assembly's language reveal what it believes about itself and God?

The process of articulating meaning will help a community increase its own self-awareness. A worshiping community can assess not only what its history reveals about its values but what its vision is for the meaning it wishes to claim and express for the future.

Encountering expressions beyond the assembly.

This third step engages the assembly with musical resources from other communities, cultures, or traditions. As it does this, the assembly invites into itself expressions that contrast with its own identity. By this action, an assembly crosses outside its own local boundaries and encounters an expression that is new to it. And in this exchange, that expression takes on another dimension of newness, for now it is incorporated into a new context and thus also expresses new meaning.

It is here that issues of contact between and among communities arise. How much need one community know about another's resource before it engages it? Issues such as languages, cultural practices, and performance practices will need consideration. As one community learns about another, even if it is only through learning one of their songs, it enters an interdependent relationship with it. Relationships deepen and become more complex as a community engages more and diverse resources. This growing web of relationships becomes part of the assembly's identity.

Care in preparation is an important step in this process. Planners benefit by considering what would create an air of receptivity for new elements. If another culture is involved, how can the assembly learn about it? How could the assembly be introduced to the things that are highly valued in that culture? In relation to the songs in the *Evangelical Lutheran Worship* assembly edition, resources such as the Musicians Guide and the Hymnal Companion can be a useful start.

Introduction of the new element requires skillful teaching and learning. Are there a variety of presentations possible that would increase the assembly's contact with the music and enhance its learning? What gifts within the community might be tapped for presenting and leading this song? Repeated presentations over an extended period of time, employing variety, will give a broader learning experience and increase the possibility of the assembly's reception.

Developing meaning in the assembly.

The fourth step is meaning-making. The assembly that has encountered and engaged a new resource now asks itself: Does this resource carry meaning for this assembly? Is the word of God proclaimed for this people in this place through the use of this new song?

And when the resource moves beyond being introduced and is presented a variety of times in a variety of ways, the question of durability arises. Will the new expression be able to bear the repetition of this assembly over time? In the repetition of the song, does the assembly engage it? Is the assembly able to express itself through this new expression? Where are the connections between this expression and the community? Did the assembly develop a growing engagement with the expression over the course of its repetition?

Here the question of what is lacking in the assembly's repertoire may arise. Can the new expression fill a space within the local assembly? Does it say something new or fresh, providing a needed contrast to the rest of what the assembly sings? If the answer to most of the previous questions is yes, then this piece might find its way into the assembly's core.

Evaluation and assessment.

Finally, the assembly decides whether the new expression will have a regular place in its musical core. Often these decisions happen gradually and without conscious decision-making, as an assembly takes up a new thing and comes to own it. There is value, though, in assessing the expression's use and considering the ways it contributes to the assembly's worship. Connecting with other communities, enlarging the scope of one's own community, and proclaiming the word in fresh ways are among the values to consider. This is a deeper question than whether the community likes a particular song and is starting to take to it.

As assemblies engage new resources, they are widening their own horizons. They gradually embrace a more diverse and enriching whole, expanding their identity in ever-widening ways. Greater contrast offers potential for an assembly's expansion into greater wholeness.

An assembly that finds meaning in new and diverse musical expressions will be expanding its own identity and its own proclamation. In the contrast provided by these new expressions, an assembly begins to understand itself in new ways. Its own proclamation becomes more complex as it engages a growing richness of meaning.

A commitment to engaging an ongoing process of contextualization as described here holds promise for a community's maturity and growth, helping it retain its center and identity while at the same time expanding its horizons as it constructively learns to sing a new song.

CHAPTER FIVE

Leaders in the Sunday Assembly

"For just as the body is one and has many members, and all the members of the body, though many, are one body, so it is with Christ" (1 Cor. 12:12).

As it is with Christ, so is it also with the Christian assembly. Just as in the body of Christ there are many members, so in the Sunday assembly there are many ministers. The assembly is composed of individual members, just like the body of Christ, but each member has a different function. The individual members are present for the sake of the entire assembly in its worship. Together, these individuals form one body, the body of Christ, gathered at this specific time in this specific place.

In fact this *body*, all the individuals who gather for the Sunday assembly, itself becomes like a collective and essential minister in the assembly. The assembly itself is an active, participative voice engaged in the liturgy. Just like all other ministers, the assembly performs its function for the good of the whole. At times, the assembly proclaims scripture; at other times it raises its praises in song. Along with the other ministers, the assembly leads and follows; speaks and listens. Individual ministers lead along with, on behalf of, and in dialogue with this assembly minister.

Each kind of minister has particular functions that are needed for the whole. These leaders function effectively when their role is clear, both to themselves and the assembly. Presiding and assisting ministers, cantors and choirs, lectors, ushers, and altar guild members are all servants of the assembly. No leader leads with their own authority; rather each leader uses the skills they have for the good of the assembly. When leaders do their roles well and efficiently, worship becomes natural and may even appear effortless. When leaders get in the way through affected manner or overly-dramatic speaking, worship becomes awkward or stilted. When leadership is ill-prepared and becomes sloppy, the worship of the entire body suffers. When the various ministers go about their roles in the Sunday assembly, attentive and confident in their role, yet calling no undue attention to themselves, we get a little glimpse of the body at Christ in action; each one leading at the point of their gifts for the good of the whole.

Leaders in the Assembly

The various leadership roles serve the assembly. Remembering that the assembly is the body of Christ can be a helpful analogy in considering leadership roles. Just as in the body of Christ there are many members, each with its own function, so too the leaders in the assembly perform specific functions for the sake of the entire body. Keeping the roles clearly related to their function helps the assembly's worship.

The presiding minister is an ordained pastor who presides at the service of Holy Communion. The presiding minister leads at several points in the service, including confession and forgiveness, and often is also the preacher. When baptism is celebrated, the presiding minister presides at the font. At the communion table the presiding minister leads the assembly in the great thanksgiving, speaks or sings the words of institution, and becomes the principal server for the meal.

The assisting minister or ministers also serve the assembly in a variety of ways. An assisting minister leads the prayers of intercession, may read the scriptures, may speak an offering prayer, shares in serving communion, and announces the dismissal. While most often the presiding minister preaches, at times and under the supervision of the pastor or the bishop, an assisting minister may be the preacher. Assisting ministers arise from the assembly and are representatives for the entire assembly. The assisting minister is one with gifts for leading the assembly. There are varieties of assisting ministers; not only those who carry out the functions assigned in the rubrics to "the assisting minister," but also readers, altar guild members, musicians, ushers, acolytes, ministers of hospitality, and more. Understood together, these people come from the assembly's midst to help the assembly worship.

A Brief History of Assembly Leadership

Some sense of the history of leadership in the Christian assembly can help presiding and assisting ministers today as they think through their tasks. A thoroughgoing account of the many forms that such leadership has taken through the ages of the church, of roles and hierarchies, ordinations and appointments, is not within the scope of this volume. But some notes and fragments from that history call for our attention.

For example, it is useful to note that both the idea of many assisting ministries and the idea of the serving and focusing—but not all-dominating—ministry of a presiding minister are not new. We have already seen that Justin, when discussing the Sunday assembly of the church in mid-second-century Rome, speaks of a presiding minister who preaches, gives thanks at table, and enables the distribution of the collection for the poor, amid a liturgy that "we all" do. That same report tells us about "a reader" and several "deacons"—*diakonoi*, the Greek word for table-servers, is the name used for the latter. One might also suppose from the repeated "we" of Justin's report that there were people who helped the active assembly and its presiding minister with praying, setting the table, taking a collection, and distributing the collection to those in need. The assembly seems to have been assisted in its meeting by a variety of people reading, praying, serving, collecting, sending, and presiding.

With these diverse roles, Justin's community reflects something of the counsel that the apostle Paul gave about the gathering of the church. Paul knew that there were manifold gifts alive in the Christian assembly (1 Cor. 12:4-13, 27-30) and many contributions brought into that assembly by different people (1 Cor. 14:26-33). Still, he argued that what was done communally should speak the gospel intelligibly, build up the church, and be done in peaceful order (1 Cor. 14:26, 33, 40). The assembly imaged in Paul's writings is a participatory assembly with many ministries, but those ministries are called to account, being responsible for continually forming the church in the gospel of Christ. Similarly, the New Testament reflects many kinds of presiding leaders: elders (Acts 14:23), house-owners (Rom. 16:5; Col. 4:15), and prophets (1 Cor. 14:29; cf. Didache 10:7) seem to be three types of those who preside. For these leaders, too, authority alone is not enough. They must serve to build up the church in the mercy of God in Christ (1 Cor. 14; cf. Didache 11).

Women seem to be among these early presiding ministers. Women are named among the house-owners who were hosts to the church and thus most likely hosted the meeting and presided at the table. Women were probably also among the prophets; 1 Corinthians 14:34 demonstrates this practice by Paul's attempt to prohibit it at Corinth. Furthermore, the earliest Christian wall-paintings that we still possess—the catacomb paintings of second- and third-century Rome—include an image of a woman, in the ancient posture of prayer, giving thanks over a simple meal set out upon a tripod table. Only later in Christian history were the socially dominant ideas of patriarchy taken for granted in the leadership patterns of the Christian church. It has taken until the twentieth century for the churches to begin to rediscover something of their earlier, inclusive patterns. In any case, Paul's decent, building-up order was at least partly demonstrated by a presiding leader simply seated (cf. Luke 4:20; Matt. 5:1), peacefully and attentively presiding in the midst of an active assembly and thereby suggesting that the order of this meeting is profoundly and reliably centered in God. Such seemingly passive leadership, such focusing of the meeting by attending to the others gathered around the central matters, should be added to the list of active things Justin's presider did: preaching, giving thanks, seeing to it that there was a collection for the poor.

As pressures on the churches from both persecutions and internal disagreements continued, the patterns of leadership—so diverse at the outset—began to be regularized. Each orthodox local church took up the practice of turning to a bishop as its principal president. Beginning in the second century and strengthening in the third and fourth centuries, a single person from the local council of elders, called bishop—*episcopos*, or overseer,—was appointed as the primary leader. The "monarchical episcopate" emerged. These bishops began to be regarded as successors of the apostles. But even so, a variety of ministries did not disappear. The council of elders—presbyters, later "priests"—continued to assist the bishop in ruling the local church. Deacons—still both men and women—helped with baptisms, helped to serve the table in the church and also helped the bishop distribute support from the church to the poor. At least these offices, if not also others, were appointed with the laying on of hands and prayer. There also continued to be readers, and as time went on, there were doorkeepers or ushers, catechists, widows, cantors, subdeacons, acolytes, attendants, and more. The bishop was usually the principal presider in the church, but there were many other people who assisted the assembly in its work. Even then, the bishop could not preside everywhere. Early on in Rome, for example, it seems that portions of the bread from the eucharistic table of the bishop were sent to other places where the supper was being celebrated in order to be added to the cup in that place and thus signify local unity in Christ.

It was not long, however, until a single assembly in a single city, even by this bread-sharing method, was no longer possible, no longer big enough for all the Christians in the place. The presbyters or elders began to bear responsibility for local parish presiding. It is this late-antique, early-medieval development that has come down to us through all the ages since. Frequently a single presbyter—or priest or rector or pastor or minister, using the names that were diversely applied through history—was associated with a single parish and was then both its presider and its single minister. The diaconate increasingly became only a transitional way-station for a person on the way toward becoming a presbyter. Many of the other offices also fell into disuse. Not uncommonly, however, medieval- and Reformation-era parishes did continue to have a cantor, often the most learned person in the congregation, capable of being the parish historian as well as its music-maker.

In the late middle ages, preaching had often fallen out of the mass to become only an occasional thing. Made part of a special preaching service, held sometimes in the church building and sometimes in the open or in the streets, these occasional sermons often attempted some catechesis of the laity, strove to resist heresy, urged the use of penance, and in the late middle ages became the location for indulgence sales. A great many of these sorts of sermons were in the hands of the friars, new orders of traveling brothers and priests devoted to preaching. Nonetheless, while the practices and theories of the time tempted the local presider to become simply one who offered the "holy sacrifice of the mass," with the people as observers, there were repeated movements of renewal that called clergy toward the pastoral care of their congregations. Among the greatest of these movements was the Reformation itself, with its clear sense that pastors were to make the gospel of Jesus Christ available in the congregation through serving the word and the sacraments.

Since the Reformation there have continued to be diverse ways that ministry is organized in the churches. The late antique and early medieval idea of a single ordained parish leader was still found in most places. The episcopally organized churches regarded these ordained pastors and priests as locally presiding in communion with and at the appointment of the local bishop. Congregationally organized churches gave their ministers and preachers greater independence, though all of the various emerging polities sought some form of training and discipline for local pastors. Cantors and choirs continued to function in almost all the churches. In some places there were "lay readers" of scripture, sometimes trained and licensed by the local bishop. Some of the churches kept alive the liturgical ministry of deacons, though still largely as a transitional role of someone on the way to priesthood. Beginning in the nineteenth century, Lutherans in Europe and America experimented with a recovery of diaconal ministries—communities of deaconesses, for example, largely devoted to the care of the sick and the poor—though usually these deaconesses did not have a liturgical role. But mostly it was a lone ordained person, locally serving, that was meant when one spoke of a "minister." In the nineteenth and early twentieth centuries, many Lutherans simply had no idea there ever had been a time when the pastor—or perhaps the pastor and the choir—did not do everything there was to do in a liturgy, except sing the hymns.

It took until the late twentieth century for North American Lutherans to begin to recover in strength the old idea so clearly imaged in Justin's report and suggested by the New Testament: a presiding minister in the midst of an active assembly, with many other lay ministers assisting the assembly in its worship. It is this old idea that *Evangelical Lutheran Worship* continues to propose.

Now, with this venerable idea, a congregation may rightly look for, train, and support these ministries:

- leaders of prayer, including those who may serve as a principal assisting minister in the service, leading the intercessions (although the preparation and praying of these prayers could be an additional ministry role of an intercessor), praying the prayers at the offering and after the communion, and speaking the dismissal;
- readers;
- ministers of communion in the assembly, bearers of communion to the absent and sick, and visitors and caretakers of those in need;
- a cantor or cantors and a choir;
- ushers or greeters or doorkeepers;
- acolytes;
- altar guilds or sacristans; and
- among all the rest, a presiding minister.

It is a remarkable list, again inviting us to see the diverse gifts present in a congregation, again urging us to train all of these gifts so that they build up the assembly in the gospel.

In some places, a diaconal minister or seminary student may serve in one or another of these roles, though this important service should be undertaken only as the service of one among many, not supplanting gifted and trained local lay people. The congregation, in searching for assisting ministers, should look for people with gifts — to read, pray for others, sing, and graciously help people gather, among other such gifts — who are also willing to learn more about the liturgy and to have their gift further trained for communal use. These assisting ministers will be assisting the assembly in doing its work, side by side with the one who serves the assembly as its presiding minister. They are not so much assistants to the presiding minister in a hierarchical scheme as they are, together with the presider, assistants and servants of the assembly.

In looking for a cantor, an assisting minister who is so important to a Lutheran way of worship, the congregation should indeed seek out a gifted musician, but one who has a primary interest in the song of the assembly and is willing to continue to learn how to turn that musical gift toward support of the people as they sing around the gospel in word and sacrament.

In looking for a presider, the congregation engages in a call process, in company with the local synod and bishop, usually seeking someone whose gift for preaching and presiding in the sacraments and for communal care has been trained at a seminary and through further experience in the church. Lutherans teach that those who publicly preside in the word and the sacraments should have a public call and ordination (Augsburg Confession 14).

In calling and appointing people to all of these ministries, the congregation will be inviting them to one very particular way of living out the meaning of their baptismal vocation. When we are washed into the life of the triune God through baptism, we are united with the body of Christ and called to serve our neighbor. That service mostly takes place within the daily life of the world. But the mutual service we do to one another in the Christian assembly does continually form us in faith and mutual love, and it does give us one image of the kind of service to others that may fill our days in the world. We need some of the baptized, some of our number, as part of their baptismal vocation, to exercise the serving ministries that make the assembly possible.

The Presiding Minister

The stole typically worn by the presiding minister may be thought of as an image calling the whole assembly, together with the ordained minister, to mutual gratitude for the various ministries here, to respect, intelligent conversation, gracious critique, and prayer. "The Lord be with you," says the presiding minister at the outset of the great thanksgiving, singing or speaking out loud the truth of the presence of the risen Christ among us, praying for us that we may be enfolded in that presence, like the wrapping round of the stole. "And also with you," the assembly says back, singing or speaking the same truth, praying for the same enfolding for the presiding minister.

It is an important prayer. The task of the presider is a difficult task. She or he is to lead without dominating, serve without being servile, care about everyone in the room and yet not fill up the room with herself or himself. On most occasions it is the presider who is to preach a sermon that is responsible to the biblical readings of this meeting, attentive to real needs in the present time, marked by the genuine law of God, and full of the living and life-giving gospel of Christ. The presider is to do that Sunday after Sunday, in a lively way, and yet not let the sermon be centered on simply his or her own opinion. In addition, the presider is to pray at the table on behalf of the whole assembly, "as much as he can," as Justin says. When called for, the presider is to lead the assembly around the baptismal font as it receives a new Christian or as it recalls baptismal meaning. The presider is to see to it that a collection is made for the wider mission of the church, especially turning the attention of the assembly toward those who are hungry, imprisoned, and poor. The presider is to enable and encourage all the other assisting ministers, yielding place to them as they enable and encourage the entire assembly. Throughout, the presider is to peacefully anchor the whole meeting, turning the attention of the assembly away from herself or himself and toward God. It is a challenging task. It is also a wonderful task, a delight for those who are called to do it.

Presiding ministers need support for continually being renewed in this task. Indeed, education, shaping, and training in doing this presiding work should never be ended. Pastors are always learning, life-long catechumens also in this part of their baptismal vocation. One way that continual formation will take place is by the care and concern of the congregation. "And also with you" can be spoken metaphorically by the members of the congregation through the days of the week, as well as literally in the Sunday assembly, especially by genuine conversation about the assembly practice and its meaning, by intelligent support, and by ongoing personal or familial prayer for the pastor's well-being. Ongoing formation can also take place through the pastor's participation in continuing education events, some of which should be focused on worship, on the meaning of assembly around word and sacrament, and on the use of *Evangelical Lutheran Worship* and its unfolding family of resources. Congregations should encourage pastors—as well as assisting ministers and others from the parish—to take part in such events. Resources that will help in this formation, such as the examples listed in the bibliography, are another avenue for growth in the role and task of the presiding minister.

There may be a legitimate question about what to do when there is more than one pastor in a local congregation or assembly. The expectation of *Evangelical Lutheran Worship* is generally that there be a single presiding minister. In fact, when the assembly is served by a variety of lay assisting ministers, it is ordinarily true that one presiding minister is enough. It is a good thing for the person who takes the attentive leadership of the meeting also to preach and for this person who preaches also to preside at table. These tasks of the presiding minister mutually inform and interpret each other in meaning. Also, pastors who serve in congregations or educational institutions where multiple pastors make up the staff might take joy in simply being part of the assembly itself on those Sundays or festivals when they are not appointed to preside. The congregations that called them need to support them in this choice. Such pastors might certainly take turn at other ministries—reading or serving communion, for example—but then they might best do that task as baptized members of the people of God, as assisting ministers, wearing the alb but not the stole, for example. In any case, they ought not entirely supplant other gifted and trained lay people from the assembly in fulfilling these ministries. "Assisting minister" does not mean "associate pastor."

Still, for many pastors this proposal is a hard one. They wish to exercise those central tasks to which they said yes when they accepted call and ordination. They wish to see and be seen by the assembly that called them. They wish to say "The Lord be with you" and hear "And also with you." Rightly so. It is to be hoped that, in situations of multiple pastors, a fair roster of presiding leadership may be worked out. Perhaps, in these congregations, it may be wise, at least sometimes, to invite one pastor to read the gospel and preach and one pastor to preside by leading the confession and forgiveness or the thanksgiving for baptism, then greeting the congregation, praying the prayer of the day, bidding the peace, giving thanks at table, and speaking the blessing. It is not wise to have the pastors together do everything, eliminating lay assisting ministries. Nor is it helpful to parcel out the presiding task by the first half and the second half of the service, because it suggests a division between the "word service" led by one and the "sacrament service" led by another. The well-being of pastors doing their liturgical task must be balanced by the well-being of the assembly, rightly served by many gifted lay assisting ministers.

Further reflections upon the task of the presiding minister will be found in the detailed reflections on the pattern for worship in the chapters that follow.

Assisting Ministers and Their Training

As has been noted, assisting ministries arise from the assembly and are representatives for the entire assembly. Although one person in the service may carry out some or all of the functions assigned to "the assisting minister," typically there are also readers, altar guild members, musicians, ushers, acolytes, ministers of hospitality, and more. Understood together, these people come from the assembly's midst to help the assembly worship.

It is most useful for lay people to carry out these roles. While there are times when ordained persons take up roles designated for the assisting minister, these are vital opportunities for lay ministry in the assembly. The assembly's sense of its own calling and vocation is strengthened when people regularly witness or participate in these leadership roles.

Good leaders benefit from effective training. When every minister sees his or her role as an essential part of the fabric that contributes to worship, and understands how it fits in the entire service, that person's leadership becomes integrated with others. Each function is essential. None is more or less important. In fact, it could be that we should treat the weaker, less honorable member with greater respect and honor, as Paul reminds us (1 Cor. 12:22). Understanding not only their own roles but also how each ministry contributes to the whole can help leaders confidently and communally carry out their roles.

Each assisting minister has not merely a task but a ministry. A time of formation and training in that ministry—before beginning worship leadership—can convey both the practical and spiritual dimensions of the role. Whether reading scripture, serving on the altar guild, leading the prayers, or welcoming people to worship, each minister serves the assembly and its worship. In order for the assembly to worship well, each minister leads at a particular time or in a particular aspect of the work of the whole people of God.

Training assisting ministers is an ongoing process. Refreshing all ministers with training on a regular basis allows everyone to review their roles and serves to remind the varieties of ministers of their relationship to one another. It also demonstrates the importance of the individual assisting ministries, and proves an opportunity for various ministers to know one another and to be encouraged by one another's ministries. Consider bringing the various ministries together for initial discussion of assisting ministers' roles, then break into specific functions for further training. Encouraging all ministers to see their roles as integral to the assembly will help them to function cooperatively.

Cantors and Choirs

When a community gathers for worship, the primary voice is that of the assembly itself. This is the voice that welcomes and gives thanks for the gospel reading, sings the psalm, sings hymns and much more. The assembly's voice is central to the gathering, for it has its own role in proclaiming the gospel and celebrating the meal along with the other ministers. Here again we see that the assembly is itself like a minister. At times all in the assembly lead one another by proclaiming the word, singing praise, expressing lament. At other times the assembly responds with active engagement or listens to other ministers.

In assigning roles to other worship leaders, especially musical leaders, it is essential to keep the assembly's voice in mind. The assembly's voice may be reinforced and supported by the other ministers. When the ministers work together in this way, the assembly's voice remains central in dialogue with other voices.

Choirs and cantors add additional voices to the assembly. They encourage and assist the assembly. Cantors and choirs serve to strengthen and enliven the assembly's voice. Through training, preparation, and planning, these ministers augment the assembly's voice with their own. Sharing their gifts and talents with the assembly encourages and builds up the assembly's praise.

Cantors and choirs perform several different roles in assisting the assembly. These roles include reinforcement of assembly song, enhancement of assembly song, alternation with the assembly, and proclamation, singing independently on behalf of the assembly. Understanding the appropriate use of each role will serve to enliven the assembly's song.

Reinforcement

The choir or cantor's principal role is to provide a foundation for the assembly's voice with their own voices. In learning a new song, in supporting assembly song, in leading liturgical music, the choir sets an example for the assembly and encourages them to join the song. This role underscores the importance of congregational song, inviting all to participate. Reinforcement can also serve a teaching function, giving worshipers opportunity to hear rehearsed singers sing their part.

Enhancement

In this role, the choir may add certain musical dimensions to the assembly song. Descants and harmonizations are two examples. These additions allow the congregational song to become more complex as the choir adds their music around the song. When done with care, the assembly song is still primary, and isn't confused by the addition. The complexity adds beauty to the whole without detracting from the assembly's singing of text and melody.

Alternation

At times, the cantor or choir may alternate with the assembly. As discussed in the previous chapter, call and response hymns use this alternation method between a soloist or group of singers and the assembly. A long-standing tradition from northern Europe is for the choir to alternate with the assembly over the stanzas of a hymn, both to prevent fatigue and to provide the opportunity to consider a few selected stanzas while only listening.

Proclamation

At times the choir or cantor may sing independently, apart from the song of the assembly. But even here the choir, always serving on behalf of the assembly, gives voice to the assembly's praise in its song. The assembly participates through its engaged listening.

Choirs have the advantage of preparation time outside of the Sunday gathering. A choir that meets regularly for rehearsal and disciplined learning (which will include rehearsal of assembly song) can provide musical offerings that the assembly alone could not sing. When choirs understand that a part of their role (though not the primary one) is presenting music on the assembly's behalf, they see that their role is a ministry of the entire assembly.

It can be difficult both for choirs and assemblies to differentiate such proclamatory service from the entertainment encountered outside of church. One increasingly frequent result is the response of applause to a musical offering. Here again, it is helpful to take into account the local context. If it is a demonstrative assembly, generous with applause and vocal interjections during the sermon, their own song, and other liturgical moments, such a reaction to an anthem may be natural and good. But if the rest of the time they offer reserved silence, then for them at this one point to break into applause may communicate to the choir (whether adults or children) that they have failed at their attempt to integrate their gifts into the whole service and have rather become merely providers of an entertaining number. In that case, it may be good to look for other ways the assembly may show appreciation, or indeed to restructure the way music is used in the service so that it is more integral to the whole.

Understanding choral music as a ministry serving the entire assembly places special responsibility on the choir's musical choices for worship. Choir anthems, motets, and other offerings bring to the assembly the choir's best praises, and offer a vehicle for the assembly's praise as well. It is essential, then, that the assembly can enter into the music with the choir. Some of the ways music planners can assist this process include the following.

Ability to speak in context

Choices for choral literature, placement of anthems in a service, and placement of the choir are all choices for which the local context needs to be considered. When an anthem is chosen and performed well, it can enhance the entire worship. The ability of any musical piece to speak to an assembly is a complicated affair. It requires attention to both the choir's abilities and talents and to the assembly's abilities and limits. Careful judgment regarding the content and its relation to the proportion of the service is required. Choirs and assemblies can grow in their love and appreciation for new musical expressions. When assemblies are also brought into the process of understanding the choir's offering, there is a better chance they will be able to genuinely enter into their music, expressing their own praise with the choir.

Learning by the choir

The choir learns many technical elements about singing when preparing an anthem. Good breathing techniques, posture, and diction are all important considerations in preparing choral music well. Ignoring these will lead to ineffective choral presentation. There is more that a choir needs, however. In order to see and hear their own voices as a ministry, the connections between the music they sing and the worship in which they sing them is essential. As integral members of the assembly, their words function as praise and proclamation. The choir is bringing a proclaimed word to the assembly. Thus, when learning music, a choir that together also reflects on the text will develop a deeper understanding of the music's meaning and use in worship. This aspect of leading music is as important as learning the notes and other technical musical elements.

Intentional choral preparation is really a form of spiritual growth for its members. It allows choir members to connect their own faith to the musical expression. In times of spiritual dryness, the music and texts themselves can offer nourishment to a faithful choir member. In times of growth, spiritual and musical preparation become a weekly cycle of rehearsal, ministry, and reflection. As music from Sunday morning comes back in memory over the week, it continues to foster growth and spiritual development in the singer.

Learning by the assembly

What does the assembly need to know to enter into the choir's offering? This question may help music planners decide what kinds of information and teaching are appropriate for this assembly. The answer will be different with each local context, for each assembly has its own characteristics. For some, teaching about the background and composer of the choir's music is helpful. For others, a brief description of musical style and a listing of musicians will suffice. When introducing new musical expressions for the assembly, more extensive preparation will enable the assembly to receive the offering. It is also a contextual choice where and how to communicate this kind of teaching background. It may clutter a worship folder and can even distract from the worship itself. Perhaps a better choice is the church newsletter, where all can read at leisure. Or consider the use of a Web posting or blog of such material. Invite worshipers to reflect on the music's contribution to worship. Such communication tools could further enhance the choir's ministry.

Relationship to other worship elements

The choir's offering might offer a response to another element in the service, such as relating to the propers of the day or the season of the year. By providing continuity with the rest of the service, the assembly may more easily understand the choir's offering as part of an integrated whole.

Translation of texts

When the choir sings in a foreign language, it is helpful to provide a translation for the assembly.

Taking the assembly's role seriously in the choir's presentation serves to strengthen the relationship among all the ministers, keeping focus on the purpose and use of all music in worship. It can also lead to a deepening faith, both on the part of the choir member and of people in the assembly.

Placement of Musical Leaders

It can be challenging to determine optimal physical placement for cantors, choirs, instrumentalists, and other musical leaders. Every worship space has its own limits and possibilities. Here are some general considerations that can aid this reflection.

Priority of central signs

The places of the word, of baptism, and of the meal are the physical centers of the Sunday assembly and the visual foci of the worship space. Keeping these central signs in view allows the focus to remain clear. Blocking them visually with choirs, other musical leaders, and equipment can lead to distraction and confusion. Although some occasions and some architectural layouts may make such a situation unavoidable, keeping the central signs visually central will ultimately aid the assembly.

When musicians are in the assembly's view

Some music works best when the musicians are visible to the entire assembly. Call and response music, noted earlier, is aided by a leader the assembly can see. In such cases, the cantor's welcoming gesture can be effective in inviting the congregation to lend their response. It requires care not to call undue attention to oneself, as if the cantor is a performer, but rather to be present in an assured way that encourages the assembly's response. An advantage to having musicians visible to the assembly is that the visual aspect of leading the assembly's song may add another important dimension to the communication between leaders and the assembly. Often, this placement also makes it easier to have the choir closer to the assembly and thus be understood as one group rather than separate forces.

When musicians are not in the assembly's view

Sometimes being seen by the assembly is not critical to effective musical leadership. For example, in basilican architecture, organs have often been placed in rear galleries. In this case, it is the sound itself that leads the congregation, providing its cues and musical support, the sound coming in the same direction as the assembly's voices rather than coming at them. Choirs too are often placed in the gallery for proximity to the organ. An advantage to having musicians not in view of the assembly, when it is not critical to the music being led, is that it may help to avoid having strong personalities dominate the musical leadership and attract the assembly's attention to themselves.

In determining the best placement for musicians, consideration of the space itself in combination with the music and its own requirements for effective presentation will yield an effective solution. Awareness that different kinds of music may require different placement is a helpful concept in working with the worship space over time. Principles of visual and musical clarity, when taken together, will aid in finding the best solution in each space.

Clothing for the Liturgy

The baptismal vocation of all of the assembly's ministers comes to symbolic expression in the basic clothing of liturgical leadership.

It is not uncommon for all of us to put on some kind of festive clothing when we gather with the Christian assembly. In some communities, the "Sunday best" is worn, celebrating how God's grace has made us to be whole and healed as human beings. We then come before God and one another showing the respect of our very best. This practice especially marks more traditional congregations and communities that have known a great deal of poverty, the splendid clothes being a kind of festival protest against that poverty. In other communities, casual clothing may be worn to church, perhaps out of an unspoken idea that God's grace has brought us to rest and to a cessation of the kind of competition that can be present between us in displays of fine clothing. This practice may mark communities of working people who keep festival by getting out of work clothes, or it may be found in communities of class-conscious people who celebrate by neglecting obvious displays of class. Both traditions may be present in your congregation. Both practices can be seen as festive practices. It may be helpful to have a mature conversation in the congregation about these practices—about the meaning of the clothing we wear to church—especially if that conversation can be turned toward mutual understanding, toward education about the meaning of the liturgical assembly, and away from legalisms of any kind.

But the most ancient festive garment Christians have worn to church is the garment of our baptism. Already in the first centuries, when people were baptized, each one—fresh out of the water—was clothed in a new or newly clean and bleached white robe: the *tunica alba* (alba means white) or the alb. This garment was, in fact, the basic garment of men and women of all classes in the ancient Mediterranean world, covering the whole body graciously, and ready with a hood to be used also outside. Washed and bleached clean, this garment became one of the basic symbols of baptism. It expressed the idea that to be baptized was to "put on Christ" and to join that multitude of people who had "washed their robes and made them white in the blood of the Lamb" (Rev. 7:14). To walk in the baptismal way was to walk in the freedom and grace of such a robe. Even when the styles changed in the ancient world, this garment continued to be used in baptism. It was this garment, especially, that leaders of the assembly wore. They may have worn other garments or insignia over it, but the root garment for someone who was serving the assembly was the assembly's garment, the baptismal garment, the alb.

Fragments of this idea continued down through the ages. Even when the white garment for adult baptisms had largely disappeared—because there were so few adult baptisms—a "christening gown" for infants, a tiny alb, continued to be one of the most cherished traditions of many Christian families. Even when the alb for community leaders had largely been lost, it still sometimes appeared as a large, white over-garment—a "surplice"—pulled on over the dark monastic habit or academic gown or court apparel which came to mark later generations of Christian leaders.

The old idea of the alb has been rediscovered in the last generation. Leaders of the assembly are invited to put on the assembly's garment. Many North American Lutheran pastors—like many other presiders in other churches and places throughout the world—have taken the alb as their basic liturgical garment (Fig. 5.1). When at least some of the lay worship leaders on a Sunday morning join the presiding minister in wearing the alb, it reinforces the message that this festive clothing is a sign of the baptismal identity we all share. The garment does not signify ordained ministry. It signifies baptism, and it belongs thereby to us all. Leaders of the assembly wear it on behalf of us all, showing another way of festive clothing than either "Sunday best" or casual clothes. Indeed, our leaders can thereby step out of the ways in which our current clothing so inevitably communicates gender, sexual attraction, class, and wealth, inviting us to another way of considering the human being.

Here are some proposals: Consider purchasing or making a whole set of albs for the congregation, of diverse sizes, so that anyone who serves as an assisting minister may be able to find an alb to fit. Make sure you have enough that are fully cut so that they can truly fit amply and can extend to just above the shoes on anyone who will use them. Use the same style for both men and women, remembering the baptismal assertion of Paul: "As many of you as were baptized into Christ have clothed yourselves with Christ. There is no longer Jew or Greek, there is no longer slave or free, there is no longer male and female; for all of you are one in Christ Jesus" (Gal. 3:27-28). Keep the garment simple.

A band of lace, for example, draws the eye to the lace and away from the alb itself, and in current Western culture lace is gendered in meaning. Think carefully about the use of the cincture, which is usually a braided rope that has sometimes come to be used as a belt along with the alb. Cinctures are not needed; they do not belong to the root-symbolism of the baptismal garment, and they may make the alb difficult for many people to feel natural in wearing.

Consider using these same albs at adult baptisms in your congregation and whenever members of the assembly are affirming their baptisms, to

Fig. 5.1. The alb. *Its name means white, and it is the ancient festive garment that represents our baptism. The alb has been rediscovered in many North American Lutheran congregations for use by both pastors and lay worship leaders.*

help unfold the meaning of baptism itself and to lead the assembly to see the baptismal connections of the garment its leaders are wearing. Think about which assisting ministers in your assembly will then wear an alb: perhaps someone who acts as the principal assisting minister; perhaps the communion ministers; perhaps the acolytes; perhaps especially the choir. While many choirs have adopted garments that have their origin in academic apparel or the performance wear of touring choirs, it may be wise, if an opportunity arises to change or renew the vestments of the choir, to consider its baptismal calling and identity.

When people put on albs, invite them to consider all else that they wear as well. Shoes, watches, and other visible adornments frequently function in our society to indicate wealth, status, physical appeal, and personal self-expression. There is nothing inherently wrong with this. Clothing and body decoration choices have long been part of human cultures. But when the minister puts on the alb for us, the minister puts on a simpler and more direct way of being a human being in Christ, one that transcends our cultural moment. The minister puts on the baptismal vocation of the whole assembly. Think about what clothing or adornments will be in the assembly's view. Will they call attention to themselves—and might they best be put aside for the time of the service? Some worship leaders have found, for example, that putting a wrist watch in a pocket or purse helps to free them—and the assembly—from a constant visible reminder of our current society's obsession with time. At least these things can be thought about and gently discussed. Baptismal clothing is communal clothing in the mercy of Christ, not the transitory clothing of individual choice.

If you do decide to use a cincture, Figure 5.2 shows a simple way it may be tied. The cincture can help some people avoid tripping on an overly long alb, but it does not have to be interpreted symbolically. The most important Christian symbolic garment is the alb itself. From its origin, a cincture is simply a help to the alb. It would ordinarily be in the color of the alb, not in the various church year colors, which only serve to call more attention to it.

In this model of clothing for the liturgy, the presiding minister also wears an alb. The presiding minister comes to the task of presiding also out of his or her baptismal vocation, putting on Christ, walking in freedom and love, wearing the garment that belongs to the whole assembly, joining those who assist the assembly in its liturgy.

Fig. 5.2. Simply-cinctured alb. *Tying the alb on the side can help worship leaders avoid tripping on a long alb, but the cincture does not need to be interpreted symbolically.*

Then, over the alb, the presiding minister may also put on one or more further symbols of the particular calling to be one who presides in this assembly and to be an ordained minister of word and sacrament. The most common of these symbolic garments is the stole (Fig. 5.3). Among Lutherans, it is a common practice that a pastor puts on a stole, over an alb, if she or he is going to preside or preach at a service of Holy Communion or if he or she is going to otherwise exercise the role of an ordained minister: announcing the forgiveness of sins, preaching at any service, and presiding at a baptism or at one of the Christian passage rites. At its root, the stole is simply a badge of colored cloth used to mark our principal leader in an assembly. Its origin seems to be in similar cloth markers that were given to local leaders in the ancient Roman empire. Among Christians, however, it quickly came to have some secondary connotations. Sometimes it was regarded as like the ancient prayer-shawl of the Jews. Called an *orarion* in Greek, it marked a leader of prayer. Or sometimes it was taken to be like the towel of service that a servant puts on (cf. John 13:4) or the yoke of Christ for the learner, the yoke that is, paradoxically, easy and light (Matt. 11:29-30). In any case, if several persons are wearing the baptismal garment for us all, showing forth their service to the assembly, then one of them wears this long cloth as a sign of presiding among us. In this understanding, the colorful stole itself is the symbol, and it does not need to carry further embroidered words or symbols—symbols upon symbols.

One other important garment comes from ancient Christian times and continues to be worn in some Lutheran communities: the chasuble (Fig. 5.4). It too is put on by the presiding minister over the alb and stole, for a service of holy communion, and is usually worn throughout the whole service, signaling the unity of word and sacraments. If the alb was originally the basic garment of the Mediterranean world, the chasuble was the traveling garment, the poncho or coat, of the same world. Called *casula,* it was the "little house" one carried along on a journey, sometimes simply rolled up on one's shoulders until it was needed. Christians seem to have admired and used it because of its

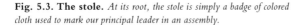

Fig. 5.3. The stole. *At its root, the stole is simply a badge of colored cloth used to mark our principal leader in an assembly.*

great fullness and beauty. It could be taken to stand for love which covers all (1 Peter 4:8) or for the robe with which the waiting father clothed the prodigal son. Worn by the presider with this sense, it could seem to be embracing and covering everyone, put on the whole assembly. Some scholars have supposed that it always carried with it the idea of traveling. The presider comes among us to preach and lead and pray, with the authority of the old sent and traveling apostles, with the apostolic gospel. The presider calls us together to be as a journeying people, to get on our gospel coats, traveling in mission to the world and in a new Exodus. In any case, once again the garment itself, cut fully of beautiful cloth, is the symbol. It can be quite simple, not needing applied symbols.

Fig. 5.4. The chasuble. *Its name comes from the casula (little house), a poncho or coat that was a basic traveling garment in the ancient Mediterranean world. It may be worn by the presiding minister for a service of Holy Communion.*

Another garment used in some places is the cope. The cope, a great coat-like cape, similar to a full-cut chasuble yet with only a simple fastening in front instead of a full seam, may be worn over an alb by anyone leading a festive form of evening prayer or morning prayer. It is sometimes worn on other occasions, such as a festive procession.

None of these things is required. There is no rule or law about clothing for worship in North American Lutheran practice. Indeed, there are many variations among us on the use of alb, stole, and chasuble, let alone other garments and personal adornments. Some communities clothe one or two assisting ministers in the traditional dalmatic or tunicle over the alb; these are simpler forms often related visually to the chasuble. Some pastors add a large cross to their vestments, wearing it on their chest, hung from their neck, even though the oldest tradition is that such a pectoral cross has been worn in liturgies primarily by bishops. Some pastors wear a cincture, and when they are presiding at the Holy Communion they cross their stole over their breast to make an X or chi, the first letter of the word Christ in Greek, holding the stole in place by tucking it into the cincture. Some pastors make use of an academic gown, sometimes marked with a colored stole, sometimes with an academic hood, sometimes further decorated with a ruff-collar or with "preaching tabs." The academic robe, of course, points toward the university origin of the preachers of the Reformation as well as to the academic formation of this particular pastor. The elaborate collars usually had their origin in court clothing, the ministers in a land where the prince ruled the church often taking their clothing clues from what people wore at court. Some pastors wear the old monastic cassock, a black robe with its origin in monastery practice and peasant clothing, covered with the alb cut large to form a surplice, to which then a stole is added. And some pastors opt for the "Sunday best" suit or a type of casual clothing inspired by their particular context.

None of these things is right or wrong. To some extent, such choices are dictated by local custom, by ecclesiastical fashion changes, and by personal piety. But the major point here is that thoughtful leaders in local congregations will consider the meanings of what they wear. Vestments only for the pastor, vesture that is too complicated to understand clearly, clothing that refers primarily to academic rank, adornment that calls attention to wealth or sexual attraction or individual flair—these are probably not good ideas for Christian communal worship.

But the baptismal proposal of the alb is a brilliant proposal, worthy of our attention in the present time. It underlines the baptismal vocation of the entire assembly, clothing at least several of the ministers of the assembly with a symbol of that vocation. "As many of you as were baptized into Christ have clothed yourselves with Christ" (Gal. 3:27). Then the presider's stole—or stole and chasuble—can call the presiding minister to serve among these other servants in the assembly, doing so in the specific ways of ordained ministry: gathering us around the font, preaching, praying at table, and calling us to turn toward the needy world.

PART TWO

Liturgy for Sunday:
Reflections in Detail

CHAPTER SIX

Gathering

God initiates our worship, gathering us by the call of the Holy Spirit. God calls us to observe Sabbath and keep the day holy for God (Ex. 20:8). As Christians we come together on the "Sun-day," the day of Christ's resurrection. This pattern of gathering on Sunday begins on the first Easter morning, when the women go to find that Jesus has risen. From that time, Christians have gathered on the day after the Sabbath day, the first day of the week. This first day of the week is more than Sabbath; it is also the day of resurrection, the completion of creation, the eighth day of creation. We gather on Sunday, the great first day of the week and the eighth day of creation.

God initiates our gathering; we respond with our presence in a local assembly. Week after week God calls us to come together; to hear God's word and receive Christ's meal; to be sent out again. This cycle contains God's continuing invitation to participate again and again in this life-giving, faith-developing event. God is the giver; we are the receivers. We praise and thank God for this invitation, gathering each week to receive again the word of life and the meal of life. This is the nourishment for our lives, the sustenance for our life in the world.

What the Gathering Is — and Isn't

When Christians gather for worship, they are forming community. This community is fluid, different each time it gathers, called together by the Holy Spirit. The Gathering is important, essential even, so that we acknowledge ourselves to be in God's and one another's presence. This kind of gathering reminds us that worship is not just about a relationship between God and me. It is also not just a human gathering. This gathering is the threshold, preparing us for the word and meal that await us. In our individualized culture, such a gathering reminds us that our meeting is unlike others we may have attended during the week; now the Holy Spirit has gathered us as a community. We are being formed as church; the church on this day, in this place.

This gathering is not simply a gathering of friends, although friendships may develop in an assembly. This gathering is not a gathering of like-minded folks, though the community shares deep meaning and values. This gathering is not a civic occasion. All of these things are perhaps good in themselves, but do not reveal the essential nature of the assembly. This gathering welcomes all into its midst, expecting to meet Christ in each one who enters.

Christian gathering takes Christ's command seriously: "I was a stranger and you welcomed me" (Matt. 25:35b). This is the great equalizer in Christian community. Christ is found in the stranger, in each member and guest in any assembly on any day. Christian gatherings assert that they are forming the body of Christ, and no one is excluded. There are no prerequisites here, no credential required, and no admission fee. Rather, this gathering includes and invites all to the word and meal, all to come to the gathering of Christ's body. This is the radical, countercultural nature of the Gathering in Christian worship.

Gathering begins as soon as worshipers enter the church doors. In fact, gathering sometimes occurs before one ever enters the church. In some times and places in the church, worshipers have gathered outside the church building for confession and forgiveness, then proceeded into the building for the word and the meal. In gatherings today, it may be only on occasions like the Easter Vigil and the Sunday of the Passion that worshipers gather outside for opening singing and greeting before moving into the church. In some cultures the procession into the church itself is a regular part of the assembly's gathering.

In any case, gathering begins as soon as people are present. The way we welcome and greet others in the assembly is both a sign of hospitality and an initial liturgical action. Gathering is hospitality, welcoming sisters and brothers in Christ, welcoming the stranger, establishing the bond among all who are present. Generous hospitality brings the newcomer into the assembly as a welcome addition, acknowledges all present as equally members of the assembly. Gathering acknowledges our oneness in Jesus Christ, who calls us to gather.

That said, the Gathering can contain as many variations and permutations as fit any assembly. The description of the Gathering section is expanded in *Evangelical Lutheran Worship* (AE, 92) to encourage variety and flexibility in length and content. For example, in addition to an order for confession and forgiveness, there is also a rite of thanksgiving for baptism. Depending on the day's theme or season, one or the other may best suit the gathering. The thanksgiving for baptism includes prayer at the font and can also contain song and a tangible sign of baptism such as sprinkling of the assembly. The Gathering section can be as simple as an invocation and prayer or as elaborate as an extended baptismal thanksgiving with gathering at the font, singing, praying, sprinkling, and procession.

The thanksgiving for baptism is a new opportunity for congregations to live into their daily baptismal identity in Christ. Using this option at the Gathering, we acknowledge our identity in Christ as the foundation for our assembly. Reminding ourselves that our primary identity is found and formed in baptism, we can live into the daily dying and rising of our lives of faith in Christ.

What else do Lutherans do in their gathering together? They sing, of course! Singing during the Gathering forms the community by joining all voices in song. Each one present adds her or his voice—trained or timid, reluctant or expectant—to the fabric of song, weaving the community together. Beyond that, this time is flexible. Over the centuries Christians have sung some form of the Kyrie and/or the canticle of praise (historically, the "Glory to God"). Gathering may include an extended time of singing, including hymns, songs, canticles, praise choruses, chants, and refrains. This is a time for the congregation to put its best resources forward in gathering all the people in song, inviting everyone to take part.

What place does an organ or other instrumental prelude have in the Gathering? Many assemblies begin with an organ or instrumental prelude as people gather. In this case, the musicians are offering a musical gift for the assembly. Worshipers receive that gift by listening, perhaps using that time for personal reflection and preparation for worship. At first glance, such a quiet time may appear to contradict the welcoming nature of a gathering. A prelude prepares the community by giving time and space for centering, praying, and reflecting together. This kind of gathering is forming the community from its inner core, connecting with the community's spiritual center and prayer life. It can be an important time for forming community, sitting together in silence, listening, and reflection.

The church's building will affect where and how the gathering happens. When there is a prelude in the woship space, consider what other place is available for meeting and greeting people as they arrive. Greeters and ushers can assist this process, offering welcome and conversation as people enter, and guiding them in the assembly's custom of listening to a prelude.

In other assemblies, a series of gathering songs welcome people in the worship space. In this case, it may be appropriate to meet and greet one another during the singing, and to join into the singing as well. This more informal style of gathering accommodates several things going on at once: meeting, greeting, and singing. Here, the welcoming may look more like a family gathering for a celebration. People gather, the singing continues, friendly conversation and greeting develop as the assembly continues to arrive.

Still another possibility is to use song, but of a more reflective and centering character, as typified by many of the pieces from the ecumenical community in Taizé. Repeating such pieces many times can help bring a community into readiness for corporate worship.

The way a community gathers speaks to member and visitor alike about the assembly's values. Greeting, conversation, meditation, singing, and prayer can all have a place in forming the community. How the assembly orders these and which elements to choose on any particular day influence everyone. Not all types of gathering can happen in one service, and some elements work best to the exclusion of others. Consider carefully the function of the Gathering, the assembly space, and the nature of the service to follow in deciding how the Gathering will take place.

The Gathering is the first contact a visitor likely has with a worshiping assembly. Imagining the Gathering through the visitor's eyes is a helpful exercise for those who know the routines and habits of the assembly well. Asking how the visitor would see the Gathering can assist in remaining welcoming and open to all. Consider questions that a visitor would likely have, and plan a gathering that avoids unnecessary barriers.

- Is the entrance to the church clearly marked from the street? Does it appear welcoming or forbidding?
- Does a visitor know where to enter the church building for worship?
- Where will a visitor be greeted or welcomed?
- Will a visitor know where to go once inside the building?

- Is signage clear and consistent in the building? Are restrooms, coatrooms, and child-care locations clearly marked?
- How does a visitor receive a service folder or any other items needed for worship?
- Is it clear what a visitor is to do during pre-service and gathering music?
- Can a visitor find the information needed to identify worship books, order for worship, communion practice, and the like?
- Can a visitor remain anonymous if so desired? Is there a method for noting visitors?

There is no substitute for personal welcome and greeting. Clear signage and accessible worship folders assist the visitor and member alike, but in no way take the place of the human greeting. A human greeting begins a clear declaration that a community is forming, person by person. It also begins forming the body of Christ gathered on that day in that place.

Attention to the importance of the Gathering also keeps the assembly mindful of its role in welcoming and greeting new members and visitors to the assembly. This is not a time to visit with friends, do business with one another, or simply be mindful of oneself. Rather, it is a time to welcome one another in Christ's name, seek out the stranger, greet one another into the assembly, and join together in praise.

In our day of various forms of electronic communication, the human greeting already changes the nature of our culture's communication pattern. The countercultural nature of worship appears already at this initial contact. We are people forming relationship, not merely exchanging information. The impersonal nature of much contemporary communication pales in contrast to the welcome at the Gathering, beginning with the first human greeting. Those who have worshiped before know that this greeting foreshadows the sharing of the peace to come, in which we will declare to one another Christ's peace in and among each one gathered. A simple greeting begins to draw each one away from an individual and solitary life into the community of the body of Christ.

Gathering is God's action, and ours as well. God gathers us; we gather in Christ's name. God extends welcome to us; we extend welcome to one another. In this very human event, we already acknowledge God among us, leading our gathering, bidding us welcome, and inviting us to the feast to come.

Changing the Gathering with Seasons and Circumstances

The Gathering can take on the character of the church's season with great variety. It can be shortened or lengthened as the needs of the assembly vary from Sunday to Sunday, but it may be best to aim for some consistency within a season. During a penitential season, a simple Gathering could be:

Greeting

Prayer of the Day

Yes, a Gathering can be accomplished without any singing, without any music at all, and in a community that is used to singing at that point, it will be all the more striking for that. More extensively, the Gathering in that penitential season could be:

Prelude

Gathering Songs

Penitential Psalm

Confession and Forgiveness

Opening Hymn

Greeting

Kyrie

Prayer of the Day

Here the Gathering time is extensive, quite a ways from the stark simplicity of the first model, yet it still can highlight the somber nature of the season.

In both cases, the Gathering places the community in its specific physical and liturgical locations. Gathering reminds the community who it is—the body of Christ—gathered on this day in this place to enter God's saving actions for all. Varying the elements in the Gathering keeps the assembly attentive to its purpose and deters automatic or thoughtless participation.

On festive Sundays, the Gathering can also be simple or elaborate. A simple form could be:

Thanksgiving for Baptism

Greeting

Prayer of the Day

Or, more elaborately, it could be:

Prelude

Songs and Psalms of Praise

Thanksgiving for Baptism

Gathering Song—"This Is the Feast," with sprinkling
Greeting
Prayer of the Day

These are examples of the many possible combinations of gathering elements. When planned with skill and care, the Gathering gives the community time to form for that day and prepares the assembly to hear God's word. The Gathering welcomes the guest, rejoices in the day, joins its voice in praise, and focuses on the God who called the assembly to gather.

Gathering: Confession and Forgiveness

One of the possible components of the Gathering is the act of confession and forgiveness. If this part of the Gathering is used, it will usually constitute the first liturgical interaction between the presiding minister and the assembly and the first spoken communal texts of the meeting. It will be seen as a preparatory act of the community as, drawn by the mercy of God, we begin to assemble around word and sacrament.

Sometimes, however, when there is a particular need to help the assembly understand a thing that is to happen in the day's liturgy or rehearse a song they are to sing, brief announcements may be made first by someone—the cantor, perhaps, or another assisting minister, or the presiding minister. Congregations that have the practice of "announcing the day," of having someone speak two or three sentences about this particular Sunday or festival in the church year and about the readings of the day, might also use this place—or the time after the prayer of the day and before the readings begin—to do this task. But such announcements should be very simple and helpful, not extensive and complex. It may also be that confession and forgiveness will be preceded by a musical prelude. Such a prelude may help us move into the reflective character of the confession to follow, or it may draw us into music we are later to sing, perhaps the hymn of the day. Some congregations may use yet other musical ways for us to assemble, including choral music or singing by the assembly itself, as has been described above.

In some congregations one of the most beloved and traditional ways to mark the beginning of the service is to ring the church bell immediately before the first liturgical interaction, in this case confession and forgiveness. If the congregation has a bell, one way for it to be rung to mark the beginning of the Sunday service is seven times with double notes followed by three spaced single notes. The three notes thus stand out as an invocation of the holy Trinity, in whose presence the assembly gathers and begins. If one seeks further interpretation, the seven notes might be thought about as the seven gifts of the Holy Spirit, poured out upon the baptized (AE p. 231; cf. Isa. 11:2-3a), that very Spirit who gathers us into the assembly around Christ.

The order for confession and forgiveness itself may be seen as the Christian assembly's return to the gift of baptism. In the Large Catechism, Luther wrote of this "approach and return" with characteristic vigor and graphic language:

> Therefore baptism remains forever. Even though someone falls from it and sins, we always have access to it so that we may again subdue the old creature. But we need not have the water poured over us again. Even if we were immersed in water a hundred times, it would nevertheless not be more than one baptism, and the effect and significance would continue and remain. Repentance, therefore, is nothing else than a return and approach to baptism, to resume and practice what has earlier been begun but abandoned. [Large Catechism 4:77-79]

Many Christians through the ages have regarded an assembly of Christians coming together on Sunday as having something baptismal about it. Justin, already in the second century, proposed that the weekly meeting was one way that Christians reminded one another that they were baptized. Pools of water have sometimes marked the entrance ways of Christian churches throughout the world, intentionally recalling the water of baptism. In the last century or so, many Lutherans have enacted such a return to baptism by a brief order for confession and forgiveness at the outset of the service, coming into worship by way of the font of living water.

At its origin among Lutherans, however, this act of confession and forgiveness was not held on Sunday morning at all. Rather, in order to prepare for the Sunday communion, several different practices were urged in Lutheran parishes: private confession and absolution with the pastor sometime during the week, or an individual meeting with the pastor for instruction and spiritual conversation, or a communal gathering in the parish for a service of public confession and forgiveness, often on Saturday. All these things still exist in Lutheran practice, though none is required before communion and none is widespread in use. Lutherans have long taught that there are many worthy ways to prepare for holy communion, but that the truest preparation is simply to trust the words of Christ: "given for you" and "shed for you for the forgiveness of sin" (see the Small Catechism, AE p. 1166). The forgiveness of sins is surely and reliably proclaimed in an act of absolution. But so is it in the communion itself, as also in faithful preaching, as also in "the mutual conversation and consolation of brothers and sisters" (Smalcald Articles 3:4). Still, slowly throughout the Lutheran world, and especially in North American practice, that separate service for confession and forgiveness was drawn to Sunday morning, coming to be for many the regular way a congregation began its Sunday service. It is not a requirement, not a law that must be followed. It is rather one more way among the many extravagant ways given us that the promise of God's forgiveness is proclaimed and showered upon us. As the Notes on the Services say:

> The service may begin with confession and forgiveness or with thanksgiving for baptism. Neither of these forms is an essential beginning to the service nor a prerequisite for participation in holy communion. However, many Christians express the desire to acknowledge sin on a fairly regular basis and to receive the assurance of God's forgiving word, or to be reminded again of the gift of baptism: forgiveness and new life. Thus this preparatory act may be pastorally advisable in many contexts. [LE, 17]

It is important for a congregation to continually learn again how this act has baptismal resonance. The mercy of God in baptism made us one people in Christ, an assembly gathered to proclaim God's saving deeds and to turn to our neighbors in witnessing service and love. The forgiveness of sins restores us to this vocation, reconciles us to the purposes of the baptized assembly. There is certainly a need for individual confession and forgiveness—the "particular preaching of the gospel," Luther called it—to be available for the Christian (see AE pp. 243–44). But this Sunday act is communal. Together we confess our sins. Together by the mercy of God we are restored to being the baptized assembly, first to gather around word and sacrament here and then to be the body of Christ for the sake of the world.

It may be that people who are not baptized will be part of the assembly on many or most Sundays. It is to be hoped that they will find the act of confession and forgiveness moving, even amazing, as it grounds the identity of this assembly in the overflowing grace of God. Members of the assembly can be prepared to help such people understand that because of Christ this grace is also for them, that the word of forgiveness is a word for them this day, and that the way of baptism is also open to them. The baptismal resonance of confession and forgiveness, the continual presence of a baptismal grounding to Lutheran assemblies for worship, can be one way that interest in baptism and the Christian life can be awakened.

One important possibility for helping to make this baptismal meaning clear is that confession and forgiveness be led from the font. Especially if the baptismal font of the congregation is at a visible place in the room — at the entrance, indicating the entrance into the assembly, or at a central location in the midst of the assembly, indicating that baptism is a foundational matter of the assembly's life — the presiding minister should take a place at the font, facing the majority of the assembly across the water of the font. The principal assisting minister and other leaders of the service can also be nearby. In certain circumstances — especially when there is ample room around the font or when the entire assembly will participate in the entrance procession — the whole assembly may gather at the font. Figures 6.1–3 show several possible configurations for the act of confession and forgiveness.

In such a practice, the font should be kept filled with clean water. The notes rightly say:

"Keeping the font open and filled with water at worship services is a strong symbol of the importance of this sacrament" [LE, 18].

The water and the word, the word next to the water, the water flowing with the authority of the word — these things all resound in this "return and approach to baptism."

Other possibilities for leadership in this act include having the presiding minister lead from the entrance of the assembly room, whether

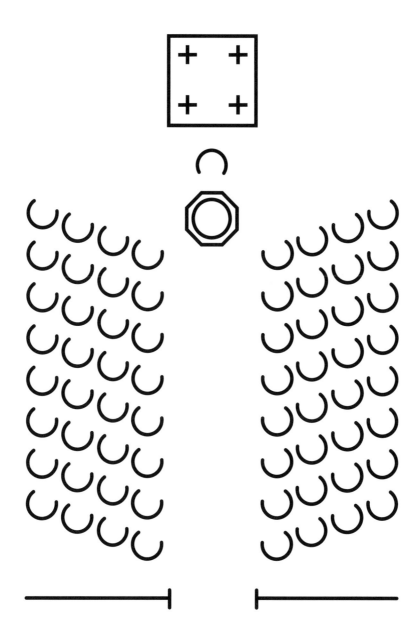

Fig. 6.1. Possible configurations for confession and forgiveness. *Leading confession and forgiveness from the font—if it is located in a central or visible place in the worship space—will help link it to its baptismal meaning.*

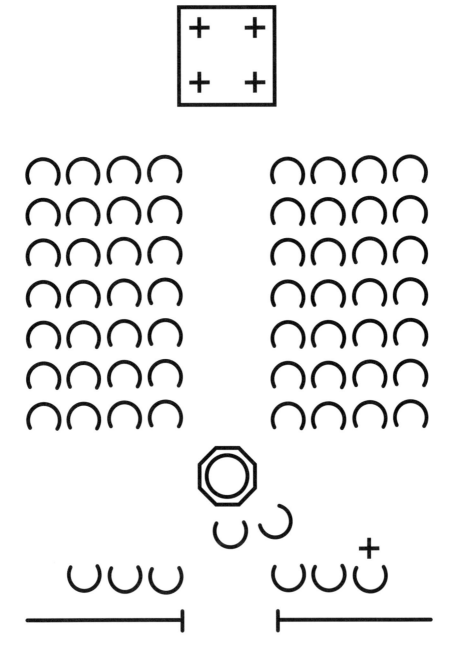

Fig. 6.2. Configurations for confession and forgiveness. *Leading confession and forgiveness from the font—if it is located in a central or visible place in the worship space—will help link it to its baptismal meaning.*

Fig. 6.3. Configurations for confession and forgiveness. *Leading confession and forgiveness from the font—if it is located in a central or visible place in the worship space—will help link it to its baptismal meaning.*

or not the font is there, as an indication of the preparatory character of this order, or having the presiding minister lead from the midst of the assembly, perhaps at the head of a central aisle.

As the prelude concludes or as the church bell rings out its last three notes—or at another signal known in the assembly, perhaps simply a handbell or the rising of a few leaders in the front—everyone who is able to do so stands and faces the font, if the order is to be led from there, or otherwise faces the presiding minister.

Consider whether such communal standing really needs to be announced or signaled by the presider's gesture. In fact, consider whether such announcements and gestures can be minimized or eliminated altogether. They tend to communicate that the assembly does not need to be particularly active or knowledgeable, that the pastor is a controlling figure who manages movement and posture, and that posture is more important than it really is. Once people are trusted to move together, they will. Visitors will usually sense the communal movement and join it. Perhaps, if a congregation has long had a habit of depending upon the pastor to make hand gestures indicating posture, a simple and gracious announcement, made at the beginning of the service for a few Sundays and indicating the communal signal, will help the assembly discover the freedom of doing without such directions. Of course, if this assembly is not regularly together—if we are discussing a one-time gathering—some announcements, made graciously and briefly, may be necessary, such as: "Will the assembly please stand." The use of such indications of posture or participation, whether orally or in print, should be sensitive to what the notes say:

> Recognizing that some individuals may not participate in these actions or postures, these notes describe the action of the assembly as a whole. So, for example, "the assembly sings" or "the assembly stands" are notes affirming what the whole body is doing on behalf of all who are gathered—even though the action may not be possible for some of us. [AE p. 9]

Then the presiding minister begins to speak. The first words are either the baptismal words from Matthew 28 or an acclamation of the triune God, using passages from Psalms 103 and 136 or another such acclamation. These other possibilities include: texts from *Sundays and*

Seasons or from the *Evangelical Lutheran Worship* family of resources as they come to be published, or similar texts from ecumenical sources, especially from those church bodies with which the Lutheran churches enjoy a full-communion relationship. The point of this text is that we begin in the presence of God, remembering the promise of baptism. The first words speak of God or to God, with the sense that the triune God is powerfully present. The assembly assents with a spoken amen.

As these words are being spoken, anyone who wishes to do so may make the sign of the cross on his or her own body, as indicated by the small red cross shown among the printed words. If using this sign is a practice in the congregation, it will be important that repeated and simple teaching, in many venues, continues to make the meaning of the symbolic act available. The act recalls that in baptism we were immersed into the death of Christ (Rom. 6:4) and marked with the cross forever. Christians believe that the cross is our only hope and the sign of our identity in Christ. Using it may recall the whole of baptismal practice and meaning for us. Luther teaches us to use this sign morning and evening (AE pp. 1166–67). It has come to be one good way that Christians together make a nonverbal sign of faith. One manner for making the sign is to use an open hand, touching first your forehead, then your lower chest, then your left shoulder, then the right, bringing your hand finally to your heart. Eastern Orthodox Christians frequently form the hand into a sign of the Trinity and of the two natures of Christ (two fingers and the thumb held together, with which to touch the body, and the two other fingers folded down on the palm) and reverse the touching of the shoulders. Another way to make the sign is simply to use your hand or thumb to trace a cross on your forehead. Still, it is important to note that there is no prescribed way to make the sign and that its use is not required.

If the sign is being made in the congregation, the presiding minister too may make it. She or he is also baptized, also claimed by the cross, also in need of this baptismal return and proclamation. If the presiding minister does make the sign, she or he also makes it on her or his own body (Fig. 6.4), not in the air toward the assembly, as in a symbol of absolution or blessing.

Then the presiding minister may pray one of the prayers of preparation. Once again, God's action here in the assembly is acknowledged. Only by God's gift and help may we truly confess our sins and come to newness

Fig. 6.4. Sign of the cross. *If the sign of the cross is made in the assembly at the start of worship, the presiding minister also may do so, tracing the cross on the body using an open hand and starting by touching the forehead.*

of life, and we confidently ask for that help. Again the assembly speaks the amen. During this prayer—as during all prayers—the presiding minister may take the posture of standing prayer, the *orans* posture, with hands upraised. For suggestions regarding that posture, see the comments related to prayer of the day.

The presiding minister then invites the community into the confession of sins. It will be important for the presiding minister next to observe a space of silence of significant length to allow time for people genuinely to examine themselves and, at the same time, to communally indicate the weight and importance of the action in which they are engaged. No best length of time can be specified; the presiding minister must sense what is right and enough before beginning the communal prayer of confession with its opening words.

In some congregations, the assembly will kneel for the silence and remain kneeling both for the prayer of confession and for the announcement of forgiveness. In many places, this kneeling is treasured as a sign of humility. However, if the assembly is facing a font at the entrance to the church and if the kneelers would then have the assembly turn their backs to the font, it would be wiser to have the assembly continue to stand. The font with its concrete connection to baptism should not be lost as the central focus of this rite. On the other hand, if the congregation is facing in a direction that makes kneeling quite possible without turning, then the presiding minister should join the assembly in kneeling. For example, if the presiding minister is leading the assembly from a central aisle, she or he might simply kneel in place. Or if the presiding minister is facing the assembly across the font, then she or he might come in front of the font and join the assembly's kneeling there. Nonetheless, kneeling is not required. Indeed, the ancient Christian posture for the Sunday assembly is standing—standing with the Risen One, standing around the Risen One.

Two optional prayers of confession are provided. Others may be chosen, as the rubric and the Notes on the Services (LE, 17) indicate, although the words of this alternate will need to be supplied to the assembly.

The presiding minister then declares the forgiveness of God. Again, two optional patterns are provided, and other forms may be used as well. If the presiding minister initially began this rite facing the assembly across the font, then she or he makes this proclamation from the same place, returning there if she or he moved away for the prayer of confession. If the presiding minister knelt, she or he stands. In any case, the presiding minister faces the assembly. In both of the provided declarations, the grounds for the authority to forgive sins are made clear: the act of God in Christ; the name of Jesus Christ; the power of the keys given by Jesus (John 20:22-23); the action of the triune God. One of the texts is a traditional formulation, long in use among North American Lutherans. The other is a compilation of biblical texts (Eph. 2:4-5; Acts 3:6, 10:43; Eph. 3:16-17). Both directly proclaim God's forgiveness.

During these words, the presiding minister may hold one or both hands open and toward the assembly, as if testifying to the reliable truth of this proclamation or as if putting this forgiveness upon the people. With or without this hand gesture, the presiding minister may also make the sign of the cross during these words, as indicated by the small red cross among the printed words. In this case, the sign of the cross is made with a large gesture in the air, toward the assembly. One hand of the presiding minister in such a gesture is usually held open and flat, with the fingers together (Fig. 6.5), and the other hand may rest against the torso.

Anyone in the assembly may also respond to these words by making the sign of the cross again on his or her own body, as if to take this

Fig. 6.5. Sign of the cross while proclaiming God's forgiveness. *While declaring God's forgiveness, the presiding minister may turn toward the assembly and also may—as shown here—make the sign of the cross.*

word of forgiveness, this return of the baptismal gift, into one's own bodily existence, one's own life.

Then the service continues with gathering song, the assembly standing if it had been kneeling. If a time of gathering song has already preceded the confession and forgiveness, it might be possible in some situations to continue with the greeting and the prayer of the day. However, at least one sung element in this place (hymn, psalm, Kyrie, canticle of praise) will help to set off the confession and forgiveness as the preparatory order that it is.

Gathering: Thanksgiving for Baptism

Another way to begin, proposed by *Evangelical Lutheran Worship*, makes the baptismal character of our coming together even more explicit. A thanksgiving for baptism may be the preparatory act in which we engage as we gather for this service of word and sacrament. Here the assembly recalls how God has joined us to Christ through baptism and so clothed us with mercy and forgiveness. We are being clothed anew in this garment as the Holy Spirit draws us together. The thanksgiving praises God for all of God's actions to save through water and the word, praying that this present assembly will be renewed by the Spirit in forgiveness, grace, and love. The assembly is being spoken of as a whole, as a subject of the "one baptism" (Eph. 4:5) given to the world in Christ. The very saving word of God spoken of here—and the very sustenance and renewal of life God promises—are also freely available to people in the assembly who are not baptized. The importance and beauty of this thanksgiving might be one of the things that could awaken their own calling to come into Christ through this water.

This thanksgiving for baptism is an alternative to the order for confession and forgiveness. Another option, of course, as discussed above, is that neither of these options will be used and the service will begin immediately with gathering song or simply with the greeting and prayer of the day. If the thanksgiving for baptism is used, however, it may be wisest to use it for a season, for several Sundays in a row. The eight Sundays of Easter (including Pentecost) or the varying number of Sundays in the Time after Epiphany present two such seasons when this thanksgiving might be especially apt to the content of the readings and to the congregation's practice of baptism itself.

This act may be preceded by music, by announcements, and/or by the ringing of the bell. See above, in the section on confession and forgiveness, for notes on these practices.

It would clearly be best if the thanksgiving for baptism were led from the water-filled font. Again, see above for notes and diagrams.

The first words of the service, in this case, are either again the baptismal words of Matthew 28 or an acclamation of the triune God, composed of rich biblical images for the God who acts in baptism, drawn from Jeremiah 17:13, Deuteronomy 32:18, and Psalm 27:1. The presiding minister speaks these words, across the font, facing the assembly, and the assembly assents with its amen. The sign of the cross may be made by the assembly and by the presiding minister, each person tracing the sign on his or her own body. For this sign, see the preceding section.

The presiding minister then invites all to give thanks and proceeds to pray the thanksgiving prayer. The assembly speaks the amen. It may be a good practice for the presiding minister to extend her or his arms in the *orans* posture during the prayer, from "We give you thanks, O God . . ." through "in the unity of the Holy Spirit, now and forever." See the comments at the prayer of the day, pages 140–141, for a discussion of this posture. But other visible or audible signs may also accompany the prayer. An assisting minister might pour water into the font after the invitation to give thanks and before the prayer begins or during the prayer itself. A large pitcher full of water may be standing at the side of the font or nearby for this purpose. Or the presiding minister may dip a hand into the font during the prayer, raising and releasing water again as thanks is given for the water.

Two further possible tangible signs that might be used are clearly described in the notes (LE, 18):

After the prayer of thanksgiving, the service continues with gathering song, during which assembly song related to baptism is especially appropriate. A sign recalling the gift of baptism may be used during the singing. For example, the presiding minister, accompanied by an assisting minister carrying a bowl of water, may move through the assembly sprinkling the water upon the people as a reminder of the gift of baptism, using an evergreen bough or another convenient means of dispersing the water. Or, the assembly gathered around the font may approach and touch the water, making the sign of the cross upon themselves.

If the bowl of water is used, it may have been dipped out of the font. While the assembly is singing, the presiding minister and assisting minister may then find a graceful way of moving through the assembly, back to the font again (where the bowl and branch are left), and then to their places for the prayer of the day. If the assembly is large, however, more groups of assisting ministers may move through the congregation with additional bowls and branches. Alternatively, if the assembly is gathered around the font and is invited to touch the water, people may make the sign of the cross with water upon their own foreheads or, with respectful care, upon the foreheads of their neighbor in the assembly.

Even without one or the other of these additional signs, the service may continue with the time of gathering song.

Gathering Song

"Gathering song" is the phrase used by *Evangelical Lutheran Worship* to describe the singing that takes place in most situations when an assembly gathers. "Song" is a purposely ambivalent word that can describe a single musical piece or the singing of multiple musical pieces. As noted above, varying the singing during the Gathering can heighten the liturgical season, particular day of the church year, or highlight a reading or theme to follow. This can also be a time to introduce new hymnody to the assembly, especially if there is extended time for singing in the Gathering.

The character of the gathering, the season of the church year, and the practices of the local context are among the factors that will help determine choices for gathering song, for its leadership, and for what takes place during the singing. Ministers, or ministers and choir, or ministers, choir, and the whole congregation might enter singing an opening hymn. Or, especially after the thanksgiving for baptism, they may be singing a responsive song or psalm on a baptismal theme. Or, at some festivals and in some contexts, they may come dancing, or dancing and singing, accompanied by percussion instruments. See the notes in the next section for more discussion about the entrance.

Many North American Lutheran assemblies have a familiar pattern of singing a gathering or entrance hymn at the beginning, often after a preparatory act such as confession and forgiveness. Such a hymn may be selected from the Gathering section of hymns and songs (#520–533), but many other hymns are equally useful. A hymn invoking the Holy Spirit is appropriate at this point.

Singing one or more psalms at the time of gathering is an ancient practice well worth considering. The introit that was in common use through the middle of the twentieth century was a remnant of this entrance psalm. Creative use of psalm settings in various forms could help revive the custom and add richness to the service.

Some of the church's long-treasured liturgical songs and biblical canticles are especially useful as gathering song. The Kyrie and canticle of praise are set to music in each of the ten settings within *Evangelical*

Lutheran Worship, and additional settings are in the service music section (#151–167). Kyrie eleison, most often sung today as "Lord, have mercy," is an early Greek Christian hymn to Christ. Known already in the third century AD, this is a plea and a prayer for the gathered assembly and for the whole world. Various forms exist, including three-, six-, or ninefold repetitions of the plea itself (see, for instance, service music #151–156 and 158), and the litany version placed within the ten settings and at #157. Its cry for mercy, peace, and salvation may be especially fitting in Advent and Lent. Other options related to the Kyrie include "Holy God" (#159–161), an Orthodox form of this plea for mercy; the Great Litany (#238), particularly fitting in Lent and at times of great need; and hymn paraphrases such as "Your Heart, O God, Is Grieved" (#602) and "Kyrie! God Father" (#409). The Kyrie may also be used alongside a canticle of praise for the great church festivals.

The canticles of praise express the joyful and celebrative nature of the Gathering. "Glory to God" has as part of its text the Lukan account of the angels' response to Christ's birth. It has been used in the church since at least the sixth century with the Latin text, "Gloria in excelsis Deo." However, this hymn, in its Greek form, was likely used in liturgies of daily prayer already in the fourth and fifth centuries. "Glory to God" is useful during much of the year, and especially during the Christmas season, on the Baptism of Our Lord and the Transfiguration of Our Lord, and on The Holy Trinity. "This is the feast" is another, more recent, canticle of praise, introduced in *Lutheran Book of Worship*. The text, drawn from Isaiah 25 and the book of Revelation, is a summation of Jesus' triumph over sin and death. Its use is especially fitting during the Fifty Days of Easter and on some of the lesser festivals, such as Holy Cross Day and All Saints Day.

Although the options mentioned above have a long history of use in the Christian church and in Lutheran practice, other possibilities for selecting and arranging the time of gathering song are available. Some congregations use a sequence or medley of songs, led by a praise team or song leader, that are often selected to convey a progression of thought or sensibility. Some congregations sing a hymn or a song set as the assembly is first gathering, before any other service elements, while others will place the song after the initial greeting. See the *Musicians Guide to Evangelical Lutheran Worship* for a fuller description of the possibilities. One thing to keep in mind is this: although listed as one of the four sections of the service, Gathering is secondary in importance to Word and Meal.

There are times when an expansive Gathering section is appropriate, but in many cases an over-extended gathering section, especially one that always employs every option for song, is likely to detract from the central things the assembly has gathered to do around word and table.

When the assembly is invited to join in singing at the Gathering, it may be helpful to have a cantor lead the people. The term *cantor* is used in this discussion to denote the function of a song leader. Thus, a cantor may be an individual, a choir, an organist, or a praise team. Any of these groups serve to lead the people in song and are therefore functioning in the role of cantor. The cantor may announce the songs (musically or verbally), invite people to join (simply and graciously), and continue welcoming as people gather. When the cantor is placed in clear view of the assembly, visible gestures can encourage the assembly in joining the song. An open gesture, with an uplifted arm, welcomes people into the song and lets them know when to sing. The cantor may also lead with the singing voice as encouragement to the singing. At times, she or he may sing in alternation with the assembly, in a call-and-response dialogue. The congregation may repeat back a refrain from the cantor, or may sing their own part in response to the cantor. For example, in "We've Come This Far by Faith" (#633; Fig. 6.6), the assembly is invited to sing the refrain, and the cantor sings the verses.

Careful consideration is needed to determine whether cantors will use amplification. The priority of congregational song remains central to the decision. Will amplification encourage the assembly in its singing? The assembly needs to hear its own voice as a part of the entire musical fabric. Amplification that fills the room with the cantor's voice may not leave room for the assembly's voice. Capable song-leading leaves room for the assembly as an essential element in the song. The assembly is not an afterthought or an unnecessary addition but the integral part of assembly song. When determining the use of amplification, consider:

- Size and shape of the room. Can people hear the cantor from all places in the room?
- Natural projection. Do the instrumental and vocal leaders have the ability to project clearly to the entire assembly?
- Primacy of the assembly's voice. Is amplification needed for the music to lead the assembly? If so, what needs amplification, and how can the assembly's voice remain primary?

Refrain – All

We've come this far by faith, lean-ing on the Lord;

trust-ing in his ho-ly word, he's nev-er failed us yet.

Leader
1 Just remember
  the good things God has done...

Leader
2 Don't be discouraged
  with trouble in your life...

Text and music: Albert A. Goodson, 1933–2003. Copyright © 1965, ren. 1993 Manna Music, Inc

Fig. 6.6. Cantor-led gathering song. *The cantor can lead the assembly in a number of ways, including by singing the verses of a song and inviting the assembly to sing the refrain.*

- Leadership. Are the leaders prepared to lead so that the entire assembly can hear their directions and respond?

In some cases the gathering song choices themselves can teach the assembly about the nature of the Gathering. "What Is This Place" (#524; Fig. 6.7) connects the physical gathering, its people, and the worship environment with the formation into the body of Christ in that place. The hymn reminds the assembly what its purpose is in the Gathering and in the Word and Meal to follow. By singing this hymn, the assembly already announces the connection between its gathering and the proclaimed word and shared meal it will join. The lively musical character of the hymn supports the text well, adding a musical vigor to the text's strength.

"God Is Here!" (#526; Fig. 6.8) is another hymn that teaches about gathering as the assembly sings it. In it the assembly declares "may we find in fuller measure what it is in Christ we share." The hymn continues in connecting the table, font, pulpit, and cross as the central signs in the assembly. Placing such a hymn in the gathering song can

1 What is this place
where we are meeting?
Only a house, the earth its floor.
Walls and a roof
sheltering people,
windows for light, an open door.
Yet it becomes a body that lives
when we are gathered here,
and know our God is near.

3 And we accept
bread at this table,
broken and shared, a living sign.
Here in this world,
dying and living,
we are each other's bread and wine.
This is the place where we can receive
what we need to increase:
our justice and God's peace.

Text: Huub Oosterhuis, b. 1933; tr. David Smith, b. 1933. Copyright © 1967 Gooi en Sticht BV, Baam, The Netherlands. Exclusive agent for English-language countries: OCP Publications.

Fig. 6.7. Gathering songs that teach. *The words and melody of "What Is This Place" together emphasize the connections of gathering, word, meal, and sending.*

1 God is here! As we your people
meet to offer praise and prayer,
may we find in fuller measure
what it is in Christ we share.
Here, as in the world around us,
all our varied skills and arts
wait the coming of the Spirit
into open minds and hearts.

2 Here are symbols to remind us
of our lifelong need of grace;
here are table, font, and pulpit;
here the cross has central place.
Here in honesty of preaching,
here in silence, as in speech,
here, in newness and renewal,
God the Spirit comes to each.

Text: Fred Pratt Green, 1903–2000. Copyright © 1979 Hope Publishing Company.

Fig. 6.8. Gathering songs that teach. *"God Is Here!" and other gathering songs can help the assembly understand what it is doing as it gathers, and give it focus and direction for the elements that follow.*

help the assembly understand what it is doing as it gathers, and give it focus and direction for the elements that follow.

Gathering: Entrance and Apostolic Greeting

In some congregations, the Gathering is symbolized by the choir and at least some of the ministers of the service entering to take their places for the Word section of the service, while some of the gathering song is being sung. In other places, it is not uncommon for the entire congregation to enter together, singing. In yet other places, it may be only the presiding minister or the presiding minister and a principal assisting minister who so enter. In still other places everyone is in place from the beginning. In some congregations, these entrances vary by season or festival. Such variations are local and cultural. No one way is right. It is only important to note that if some of us come in formally, they do so in the name of us all, symbolizing our gathering. They do not come in as if they were the performers of a play and we were the audience. Having a sense of coming in *for* the assembly—serving the assembly in this way—may be clear even by the manner in which people walk. But that astonishing gift and privilege of service will certainly be an important matter for choir and ministers to think about as they enter the room, in whatever formal or informal way they come.

An entrance procession can be organized in any number of ways. One classical way would have the choir come first, to help the assembly's singing as soon as possible, followed by the assisting ministers and the presiding minister. In some places the choir would be preceded by someone carrying a processional cross, sometimes immediately flanked by two persons carrying burning candles, reflecting the importance and the light of the cross. If the Bible or the lectionary book that will be used during the service is also to be carried into the meeting, it can be carried by someone who immediately follows the cross and the candles, or it can be carried later in the procession, perhaps also flanked by two additional burning candles, reflecting the light of the word of God. The person who carries the Bible or lectionary book might hold it high, so that we may see it as it is brought to the center of the meeting to be at the very heart of the liturgy of the Word. If incense is to be used in the procession—or later in the service—it can be carried first, in a bowl or in a thurible, before the cross, as if to signal the "fragrance that comes from knowing [God]" and the "aroma of Christ" (2 Cor. 2:14-15) spreading in procession throughout the world. All of this can be done straightforwardly, joyfully, without fuss. None of it is required. Unnatural hand positions for those carrying the cross and torches, such as with the fingers forward, can easily communicate pomposity. This is an entrance of servants of the assembly, not a parade of nobility. The presiding minister comes last, not as the monarch but as the principal servant of this gathering.

When the choir and the ministers enter, they should be able to go, simply and directly, to the places from which they will rise to lead during the meeting. It is especially important for the presiding minister to have a place—a chair and a place to stand in front of that chair—where she or he may be seen. Much of this minister's presiding is found in a peaceful presence in this chair, as the presider pays attention to the assembly and to the readers. The opening greeting of the service and the prayer of the day, as well as the conclusion of the prayers of intercession, the invitation to the peace, any necessary announcements, and the blessing can all be led from this place, if it is clearly visible.

In some congregations, the ministers or the choir make a simple bow before the altar table in the assembly's space or before the cross—or both—on their way toward their chairs. This also is not required, though it is treasured as a gesture in some places. For example, the altar, on which the holy supper is set out as Christ's gift, is taken as a strong symbol of Christ in our midst and the bow is taken as an acknowledgment of the gift of holy communion. People in congregations where this gesture is treasured might also consider another gesture: a bow made by at least some of the ministers toward the assembly. The principal sign of the body of Christ in the room is this people who have been baptized into Christ and assembled in his name. That truth may be honored. Of course, since the American Revolution, Americans rarely bow to anyone, perhaps rightly wanting instead to guard their equality. But perhaps Western Hemisphere Christians, in the assembly, could learn from Asian Christians about the deep significance and courtesy of a bow. Honoring the others in this way can be a sign of Christian mutuality. Again, such a gesture is not required and greatly depends upon local receptivity and local practice.

At an appropriate time during the Gathering, the presiding minister greets the whole assembly with the words used by the apostle Paul (2 Cor. 13:13) to greet the churches. Then the assembly greets the presiding minister in return. In the letter to the Corinthians, these words accompanied Paul's greetings from all the other churches and his encouragement for the Christians in Corinth to greet each other in peace and love. Now, here, these are words that mean to do what they say. In God's mercy, the words convey the very grace, love, and communion of which they speak. In this mutual greeting, with apostolic authority, the presider and the assembly are established and held in the triune life of God. This assembly is to be the communion of the Holy Spirit around the grace of Jesus Christ and the love of God, spoken and given in word and sacrament. Furthermore, the assembly, by its response, acknowledges and prays for the triune God to be with the one who is presiding for them. With this prayer, the presiding minister is acknowledged and welcomed again as one who presides here. It is as if the call of the pastor is renewed. This moment of mutuality in the living word of God constitutes one of the seminal moments in all Christian liturgy. With it the Gathering comes to clear expression and the service clearly begins.

The appropriate time of this greeting may vary. In a simple service, it can be the very first thing that occurs. In a service involving extended gathering song, it can take place after some initial gathering song—once the ministers are in their places—after which the gathering song may continue. Or, the greeting may be exchanged after the time of gathering song is concluded, just before the prayer of the day.

But two things might be considered. First, since it so strongly begins the service itself, it probably best takes place when the presiding minister has reached the chair or the place from which she or he will preside during the Word part of the service. Its effectiveness in establishing the assembly for this service will be less clear if it is spoken in another place.

Second, it does not need to be repeated or echoed. Many pastors who have used *Lutheran Book of Worship* will remember a practice that involved the apostolic greeting before the Kyrie and hymn of praise, and another greeting or salutation, with a "may" rubric, just before the prayer of the day. That duplication has been eliminated in *Evangelical Lutheran Worship*, even if the greeting is separated from the prayer of the day by some further song. The greeting establishes this pastor as the one we ask to pray for us in this Gathering, just before the Word begins, and that sense of mutuality and appointment may only be weakened by repetition. The exchange "The Lord be with you. And also with you." will take place as part of the ancient dialogue at the very beginning of the Meal part of the service. But then it is clear that a powerful dialogue of greeting has two locations in the service, in slightly different words, both coming before the most important prayers prayed by the presiding minister: the prayer of the day and the great thanksgiving or prayer at the table. In both locations, the assembly is greeted and the presiding minister is again appointed to do these major tasks. In both locations, the greeting is intended to signify love, trust, mutual service, and the hope in God, who makes such service possible.

When the presiding minister leads this greeting, the presiding minister will be facing the assembly and standing in a place the assembly can see. The presiding minister may extend both arms toward the assembly, in a posture of welcome and greeting (Fig. 6.9).

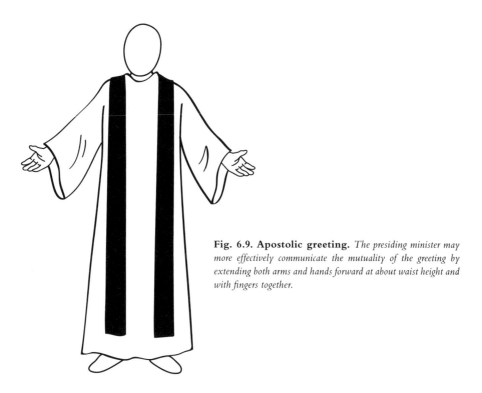

Fig. 6.9. Apostolic greeting. *The presiding minister may more effectively communicate the mutuality of the greeting by extending both arms and hands forward at about waist height and with fingers together.*

Such a gesture may better communicate the mutuality of this moment than one in which the hands are raised as if in blessing. To make this gesture, it will be important for the presiding minister to have empty hands. A book or ceremonial binder can be put down, because the minister knows the text of 2 Corinthians 13:13 by heart, or it may be held by an assisting minister standing beside the presiding minister. The book is an important resource for our gathering, but the liturgy is a living thing, and it will be better for this greeting gesture, if used at all, to be unimpeded by the book.

Some presiding ministers respond to the assembly's "And also with you" with a deep or partial bow. The use of a bow at this place is intended to indicate honor and respect for the assembly as the body of Christ and a willingness to serve this assembly. Still, the spirit of service, the use of appropriate and loving authority in Christ but a refusal to "lord it over" this people, is important for any presiding minister, whether or not there is a bow.

Gathering: Prayer of the Day

As a summary of the entire Gathering section, the presiding minister prays the prayer of the day. This prayer—in earlier generations called "the collect"—rightly collects us together in prayer before God and turns us toward the scripture readings we are about to hear. It is the principal presidential prayer of the first part of the liturgy and, in the pattern for worship, it is the seam between Gathering and Word.

Evangelical Lutheran Worship provides the church with a renewed set of prayers of the day, appointing one such prayer for each set of lectionary readings. Thus, for most Sundays and festivals there are three prayers of the day, to be used according to the current lectionary year. This collection of prayers of the day (AE pp. 18–63; LE pp. 60–137) includes refreshed translations of almost all of the traditional collects, long used in Lutheran churches, together with a number of prayers drawn from ecumenical sources, some from ancient writings of the saints, and some newly composed for *Evangelical Lutheran Worship*. For further information about the prayers themselves as well as about their use, see *Keeping Time: The Church's Years,* another volume in the leader guide series for *Evangelical Lutheran Worship.*

A classic prayer in the "collect form" follows a simple outline. First, God is addressed, sometimes with great simplicity and brevity—"O God" or "Almighty God"—and sometimes with an image— "O God our shepherd," for example, or "O God our rock." Then a sentence is proclaimed in acknowledgment and thanksgiving for what God has done, especially what God has done in Christ and God's acts to which the scriptures of the day will testify. These prayers depend upon the faith of the church that ours is a God who acts and that the scriptures bear witness to this action. Then the prayers make a direct request, a petition, frequently again drawing on imagery and promises found in the day's readings. Then the prayer concludes. The terminations of the prayer generally follow two patterns, one fully trinitarian ("through Jesus Christ, our Savior and Lord, who lives and reigns with you and the Holy Spirit, one God, now and forever"), the other simpler ("through Jesus Christ, our Savior and Lord"). The notes, however, make two important points in this regard:

> Either form of termination may be used with any of the prayers. Whatever termination is used, careful inflection and pacing on the part of the leader will help the assembly confidently respond Amen. [LE, 14]

Knowledge of this structure can significantly help the presiding minister pray the prayer with meaning. It can also help the assembly hear it. Furthermore, knowledge of this structure is necessary in those places where the prayer of the day is chanted or intoned by the presiding minister. The inflections in the chant are a kind of punctuation, based upon the collect structure and the meaning of the prayer itself, as the example on page 705 (LE) makes clear.

The prayer of the day is prayed by the presiding minister. This prayer is one of the important services the presider does for the assembly, standing with us before the triune God and, in prayer, turning us toward some of the scriptural themes of the day. It is not wise for the presiding minister to pass off this task to someone else. Nor is it helpful to ask the entire assembly to read the prayer. Unlike the creeds or the Lord's Prayer, this text will not be known by heart by the assembly and will not easily be read by a large group of people. Furthermore, the effect could be as if people are being forced to pay attention to the prayer, rather than receiving the ministry of the prayer—its enunciation in the mouth of one whom we have asked to do it in our name—as a gift.

Though the presiding minister should be visible when speaking the prayer of the day, it is not generally necessary for him or her to move to a certain place such as ambo, lectern, or altar. It will communicate more clearly that we are still in the Gathering if the prayer is led standing at or near the presider's chair.

As one of the two most important prayers articulated by the presiding minister, this may be one moment when the minister will choose to adopt the ancient posture of Christian prayer, the *orans* or "praying" posture (Fig. 6.10).

Fig. 6.10. Orans or praying posture. *This ancient posture of Christian prayer requires empty hands. If the prayer hasn't been memorized, an assisting minister can hold the book.*

If the presiding minister uses this posture, it will be best if her or his hands are empty. A book in the hands will blunt the image of openness and vulnerability originally intended by this gesture. Again, if the prayer of the day has not been learned by heart by the pastor, an assisting minister might hold the necessary book for the presiding minister, the image of mutual help being a wonderful image for us to see.

Most widely known in our day as a communal posture used in Pentecostalist churches, the gesture of open arms—formed like an empty chalice or like a cross, open to the sky but also open to the community—is widely found in images from ancient Christianity. The Roman catacombs show many Christians from the second and third centuries praying in this way. The second century Odes of Solomon, a collection of Christian hymns, has one poem (number 37 in Syriac) that reads, in part: "I extended my hands out toward the Lord, and to the Most High I lifted up my voice." Medieval and Reformation images show that priests and pastors continued for generations to pray this way at important moments in the liturgy. The posture is certainly not required, but it is available to us. Furthermore, it is available to us all. It is possible for everyone in the assembly, if they wish, to raise their hands in prayer during this prayer of the day. Then the assembly says "Amen" (or sings it, if the prayer has been intoned) and is seated.

We have been gathered. Now we begin to hear the word, the first reason for our gathering.

CHAPTER SEVEN

Word

Lutheran Christians stand in the church's long tradition by passing on to contemporary assemblies the words of scripture. We do this through the readings, prayers, and responses we speak to one another and through the songs and hymns and liturgical music we sing together. In our musical choices we honor the church's great tradition, while at the same time we add new songs and expressions of current practice.

As Lutherans, we understand that the word of God is proclaimed in scripture reading. We value the public reading of scripture, often including an Old Testament reading, psalm, and New Testament reading in our Sunday assembly. We read the gospel of the day, the assembly standing to show the prominence in our midst of this testimony to the living Word, Jesus Christ. We hear and participate in God's word as an active and living proclamation through preaching, as God's own voice speaking to us today to arouse faith, to confront sin and brokenness, and to strengthen us with the good news of our salvation.

We also hear proclamation in the singing of scriptural texts and in the prayers and responses of the entire assembly. Music is a vehicle for the proclamation of the word of God in and by the assembly: this understanding is a strong emphasis in Lutheran worship and a continuing witness we can offer to the whole church. The singing of the psalms is a practice that has been rediscovered in many places. We welcome the risen Christ by singing Alleluia at the gospel reading. Hymns can be proclamation too. For example, "A Mighty Fortress Is Our God" (#503–505) proclaims God's fierce strength in time of trouble, bearing the words of Psalm 46 through the interpretive framework of Luther's experience during the Reformation and into our mouths and hearts. "Neither Death nor Life" (#622) uses a strong gospel pulse to drive home the assurance of God's unassailable love voiced in Romans 8. "O Day Full of Grace" (#627) weaves together biblical images from the whole salvation story and joins our voices in the "endless praise" of heaven and earth. These and many other powerful expressions of God's word are carried to the assembly by the assembly, carried through our own voices.

The Word Proclaimed in the Scriptures

At the heart of the Word section of the service of Holy Communion stands the reading of scripture. Together, these readings are one of the primary centers of the service. As *The Use of the Means of Grace* says: "The public reading of the Holy Scriptures is an indispensable part of worship, constituting the basis for the public proclamation of the Gospel" (7). The pattern for worship in *Evangelical Lutheran Worship* celebrates that indispensability, regarding all three of the readings, plus the sung responses to those readings, the sermon based upon those readings, and the intercessions that flow from the whole Word-event to be part of the structural walls of the edifice of Sunday worship, to be part of the "central elements of the liturgy." Each of these elements is listed in the pattern (AE p. 92; see also p. 45–46 of this volume) with bold type.

The ordering schedule whereby the churches publicly read the Bible in assembly is called "the lectionary." That word can also indicate a book containing these readings in order. We here are using the word in both senses: the list of readings and the book containing them printed out in full. *Evangelical Lutheran Worship* itself includes simply the list (AE pp. 18–63; LE, 60–137). Since at least the eighth century and until the mid-twentieth century, the standard list in the Western churches had involved a one-year cycle, appointing usually two passages of scripture for any celebration. That list almost always indicated, for any Sunday, the proclamation of a section from one of the New Testament letters (epistles) and of a section from one of the four gospels. The practices of the Christian liturgical year together with generations of Christian piety were established around these readings. However, even before that list of scripture readings was fully organized, ancient Christians also had the practice of reading from the Old Testament. Already in the second century, Justin's report indicates that the Sunday assembly he knew in Rome read from both the New Testament and from the Old. Other churches throughout the early Christian world did the same. For a variety of reasons during the middle ages, those readings from the "law and the prophets" were much diminished or eliminated—at least on Sunday—and that diminishment and disappearance carried over into the centuries following the Reformation. The twentieth-century biblical and liturgical movements have brought about the recovery of the more ancient Christian practice. The Hebrew scriptures are being read again in fullness, side by side with the traditional practice of an "epistle" and a "gospel." Furthermore, the great diversity and richness of both Testaments have led many Christians in the present time to favor a three-year rather than a one-year cycle. The result has been a three-year lectionary that presents three readings for any Sunday or festival service: a core reading from the gospels, preceded and supported by a reading from the Old Testament or from Acts and a second reading from the New Testament letters or from the Revelation to John.

In providing for those three readings, *Evangelical Lutheran Worship* makes available and recommends the Revised Common Lectionary, the three-year calendar of scripture reading that has the widest ecumenical acceptance. This lectionary is printed in the Propers section of *Evangelical Lutheran Worship*. It is for this lectionary that all the other propers in the book, together with many other helps for hymn selection and for preaching, have been prepared. Some Lutherans in North America certainly do read from other lectionaries—the old one-year lectionary listed in earlier North American Lutheran hymnals, for example. Some Lutherans use no lectionary at all, depending upon the pastor to pick the reading or readings they will use in a Sunday liturgy. But the recommendation of the Evangelical Lutheran Church in America and the Evangelical Lutheran Church in Canada, a recommendation embodied in *Evangelical Lutheran Worship* itself, is that Lutheran congregations in North America make use of the Revised Common Lectionary. This is a wise recommendation. *The Use of the Means of Grace* indicates why:

> The use of ELCA-approved lectionaries serves the unity of the Church, the hearing of the breadth of the Scriptures, and the evangelical meaning of the church year. [7a]

Those three reasons bear further reflection. The Revised Common Lectionary (RCL) is the fruit of a long ecumenical discussion that has now produced this list of readings being used by many different Christians throughout the world. In the very neighborhood of your own congregation, there are other churches of other denominations listening to these same readings on the same Sundays. Local clergy gatherings may share preparatory text study as one important sign of Christian unity. Publications of many different church bodies help an ecumenical church reflect on and use these readings we have in common. Perhaps even more important, the people of your congregation may know ahead of time what passages of the Bible will be read in the Sunday assembly. They too may join in text study, alone or in congregational events. They may come prepared to Sunday church. If they miss the assembly, they may know what was read. In addition, Sunday school teachers, choral music planners, and those who choose the hymns or care for the worship space all have, in the lectionary, a central resource for their work, so that parish education relates to worship and the Sunday assembly is truly gathered around a shared set of scriptures. These scriptures are given to the church—all together—and not simply to a single planner, say to the pastor, alone. The use of this common lectionary serves the *unity of the church,* locally and more-than-locally.

Furthermore, the very point of this three-year lectionary has been to make *a greater range of scripture* available to be read in church. The lectionary invites us to read large amounts of all four gospels and a great deal of the New Testament letters, together with a larger proportion of the Old Testament than has ever been regularly scheduled for Christian public reading. Pastors or congregations that are tempted to abandon lectionary reading should consider how their own selection of texts may thus significantly narrow the range of scripture read in their assemblies and known by their people. For example, the pattern of reading Matthew, Mark, and Luke through three subsequent years and of reading John at festival times in all of the years has already brought many congregations to a new awareness of the gospel books and their contents.

Additionally, the feasts and seasons of the year, as they have developed among us today, come to their clearest meaning when they are unfolded by the texts that the lectionary appoints to be read at those times. This three-year lectionary is so organized that the readings invite us to encounter the living Word, Jesus Christ, present in the midst of the scripture on every Sunday and festival, pouring out the Spirit and drawing us into faith. The church year may best be understood as a way we *read the Bible through time,* a way we have been given to set the proclamation of the scriptures next to our experience of the year. Indeed, the very use of a lectionary may help to symbolize this *evangelical meaning of the church year.* If we use the common lectionary, we do not locally choose or control the readings. They come to us as a gift. As such, they may help us remember that all of the scriptures and all of the good news to which they bear witness come to us as a gift. God's mercy in Jesus Christ, proclaimed in the scriptures, saves us in our times. According to the story in Luke (4:14-30), Jesus himself was given the scroll of the prophet Isaiah when he came to read in the synagogue. Even he did not choose the reading. But he did proclaim its fulfillment. Christian faith trusts that the Jesus of that story is also in the midst of the assembly today, proclaiming the fulfillment of God's promises and the coming of release and good news. "The year of the Lord's favor" (Luke 4:19) is encountered in the church's year.

At the very heart of an evangelical and Lutheran understanding of worship stands this rich practice of reading from the scriptures. Far from being a burden, these three readings offer the exciting and real contents of the Bible, its rich images and stories, unfolded Sunday after Sunday. The very hearing of images and stories read aloud can help us in a time of decreased literacy, a time when many people are more used to seeing images on television than they are to reading texts by themselves. The biblical texts, read in community, can call to our imaginations. Indeed, the complex and layered character of three readings—rather than simply one reading or even simply a few biblical verses, as practiced in some churches—helps us to see that, for us, the scriptures are not primarily a source of religious ideas nor the basis for a single, ideological, and legalistic message. They are not merely a source for moral advice. They are rather a place for meeting the God who knows us and has heard the cries of need from the earth (Exod. 3:7). Our many real stories, stories of sin and loss and death, are echoed here. Our hope and faith can be genuinely awakened. One text balances and responds to the other text, and yet a third widens the circle still further. The various texts tell the story of God and of the world in differing, balancing ways, with room for us in the telling. We are held by these scriptures, as if they were witnesses, as if they were the elders and the four living creatures, singing around the throne of God (Rev. 3:4-8) and drawing us into the song. In the assembly, it is as if we see the Lamb open the seals of the book (Rev. 5:1-10). In the preaching, we hear Christ interpreting what is read of his death and resurrection, and our hearts burn within us as he opens the scriptures (Luke 24:32). In the liturgy, we praise the God who is present in the reading (Neh. 8:5-6). In the whole liturgy of the Word, we encounter the Spirit who makes the letter of the book to be life-giving (2 Cor. 3:6).

Lutheran assemblies, then, gladly use the full range of the lectionary—all three readings and the psalm and acclamation that respond to and welcome them. On rare occasions, a simple service may call for only two readings, most likely then omitting the second, as the Notes on the Services recommend (LE, 15, 19). Perhaps, for a weekday service, only the gospel will be read (p. 19). Still, as the notes say further, "on Sundays and festivals, the assembly's participation in the word of God is best supported when all three readings are used" (p. 19).

Of course, such a practice will be experienced as a gift and a strength especially if the readers do so with confidence and skill. It is important for congregational leaders to look for persons who are gifted to read in the assembly, persons who love the Bible and who have the aptitude and the will to serve in this way. Then, it will be important for those same persons to spend some time together—perhaps with an experienced reader, perhaps with the pastor—in training to do this ministry. Readers need to read the passage of scripture beforehand, understand its sentence and paragraph structure and its meanings, and know something of its literary genre, whether poetry or prose. The Study Edition of the lectionary (one volume each for years A, B, and C), prepared as part of the *Evangelical Lutheran Worship* family, provides helps for pronouncing difficult words as well as other hints for the reader. Further, in preparation, readers should practice projecting their voices, without straining. It will be good for them to practice using their ordinary voices, speaking honestly, and not adopting some supposed churchly style. They need to avoid over-dramatization while also avoiding under-expression. As they are able, they should stand upright at the place of the word, with a clear and direct presence. Then, when it comes time to read, they will proclaim the scripture as if they themselves are listening to the text, not over-mastering it, and, yet, as if they themselves find it an honor and a delight to be able to serve this assembly with the word of God, reading so that each one in the room may hear.

For further reflections on the Revised Common Lectionary, on its origin and structure, on its uses in worship and on the ministry of readers, see *Keeping Time: The Church's Years* (Using *Evangelical Lutheran Worship*, vol. 3).

The Scriptures: Place, Version, Responses

Three further things need to be said. The first has to do with the arrangement of space for the meeting of the assembly. The counsel of the Notes on the Services is:

> The unity of the proclamation of God's word is reinforced when all the readings and the preaching are led from a single place of the word. [LE, 19]

For some congregations this will be a new idea. A single place of the word, whether it is called ambo, pulpit, lectern, or reading desk, can be used for all of the reading and preaching. The old chancel arrangement still present in many of our churches, with lectern on one side and pulpit on the other, seems to have arisen from a time when the ceremonies directed that the gospel book be carried toward the north. This practice is now long lost. In some places, a subsequent meaning may have taken its place: the pulpit is a place where only a pastor may stand. That clericalization of space probably ought to yield, in our current practice, to the greater importance of the idea of a "place of the word." Other congregations may have yet other practices: people rise from their places in the room to read or the scriptures are read from the altar. Arguments can be made for all of these practices. Still, a single place of reading and preaching, a single, beautiful, and focused ambo (pulpit), perhaps with burning candles on either side marking the importance of God's word, can matter. It can set the Bible at the heart of our meeting, help us see the unity of the scriptures, and emphasize the relationship of preaching to all the readings, not only the gospel. It may take some time to establish this practice in some assemblies, requiring a new decision about the best place for reading and preaching and the best way to introduce this change and make any necessary alterations to the assembly's space.

It is important to note, however, that this idea is not meant to counter another practice used by some assemblies: the gospel procession. In some congregations the Bible or lectionary is carried into the midst of the assembly while the gospel acclamation is sung, with the whole assembly turning to face the place where the gospel is then read. This movement, meant to indicate the community's trust that the risen Christ is among us, is a welcome practice, though it is certainly not required. But it can also be done by congregations that have a single place of the word, with the Bible or lectionary being carried from and returned to that place where the other readings have been proclaimed and where the preaching will occur. Some congregations save the gospel procession for great festivals. Others practice it every Sunday. Yet others have never used it. Such diversity is welcome. "We do both and require neither," as Luther said of such ceremonies and of their absence.

A second concern involves the choice of the biblical translation for these readings. A great diversity of Bible translations is currently available, sometimes leading to considerable confusion. This choice of translation, of course, is entirely a local matter. Still, *Evangelical Lutheran Worship* has used the versification of the New Revised Standard Version (NRSV) of the Bible in presenting its lectionary list, and people using other versions will need to compare verse numbers to make sure about the scope of any reading. *Evangelical Lutheran Worship* has also referred to the NRSV in its many quotes from the Bible, with the exception that its version of the psalms for singing is a modern, Lutheran revision of the Coverdale Psalter of 1535, the psalter long used in the Book of Common Prayer. On the whole, for most congregations, the NRSV probably remains the best version currently available for public proclamation, combining fidelity of translation and clear, up-to-date American English with the literary strengths drawn from the old tradition of the King James Version and the Revised Standard Version. Augsburg Fortress makes available a series of resources using the NRSV text, including lectionary books that can be used in worship. Among these books, both *Lectionary for Worship* and *Readings for the Assembly* present the lectionary texts in order, drawn from the NRSV, but the latter also modestly emends the NRSV text to attend to a number of language matters.

There is a great variety of practice in North American congregations in regard to whether or not the biblical text of the readings is in the hands of the entire assembly. Some congregations have pew Bibles, hoping that members of the assembly will find the texts during the service. Some congregations print the lessons for every Sunday or purchase bulletin inserts, distributing these to worshipers. Some congregations print the readings but, on any given Sunday, pass out the readings for the following Sunday, to assist in preparation and study at home. Some congregations do none of these things, reflecting their sense that the reading is a communal oral/aural event rather than an occasion for individual reading, and that extensive use of paper and disposable Bible texts is to be avoided. Whatever practice is followed in your congregation, it is important that the readers read well enough that people will be able to look up and listen, together, and it may be helpful to encourage the assembly to attend to the readings (and the readers) in this way even if the texts are in printed form and available for reference at other times in the service.

The third matter concerns the responses to and acclamations around the readings. In the three-year lectionary and in the *Evangelical Lutheran Worship* pattern for worship, the psalm is not a fourth reading. What it is instead is a response to the first reading. With the psalm appointed for the day, listed along with the readings of the day, we are given a text from the word of God to sing or to speak together, full of themes that have been present in the first reading. Having heard the Bible, we are gathered into biblical words, held together in a response to what we have heard. The verse of the psalm that is suggested as a refrain or antiphon, indicated in the propers of *Evangelical Lutheran Worship* (AE) with a small, red number in parentheses and written out in full in the Leaders Edition, can especially show us the way that the appointed psalm or other biblical song reflects on the text we have just heard. This response then leads us to be ready to hear the further readings.

The gospel acclamation intends to be exactly what its name says. In *Evangelical Lutheran Worship*, the gospel acclamation is not a song or a choral piece by itself, one in a series of unrelated liturgical events. It is also not, in the first place, a response to the second reading. Rather, it involves the assembly in standing and welcoming the reading of the gospel as if they were welcoming the very presence of the risen Jesus Christ. Alleluia means "praise to the Lord," and Christians have taken the "Lord," in this case, to be the risen Christ, known to us in the scriptures. The verse interspersed among repeated alleluias may be the proper one chosen to coordinate with the gospel to follow (these are listed in the Leaders Edition along with the readings) or the common one printed in the musical setting. Whether it is sung by the choir or a cantor or the congregation, the verse is usually addressed to Christ, who meets us here. The passage from John 6:68, included in most settings of Holy Communion, is paradigmatic: "Lord," we say to Jesus along with Peter, "to whom shall we go? You have the words of eternal life." Indeed, those words of life are about to be read to us; that Life-giving One is here with us in the reading. The proper verses of the various appointed gospel acclamations also function like this. So Luther, in his "Brief Instruction on What to Look For and Expect in the Gospels," said:

> When you open the book containing the gospels and read or hear how Christ comes here or there, or how someone is brought to him, you should therein perceive . . . the gospel through which he is coming to you, or you are being brought to him. [LW 35:121]

Generally, the use of the psalm and the gospel acclamation in the liturgy gives a clear indication of the way scripture is being read in this assembly, a clear indication of the meaning of the lectionary. God meets us here. God puts true and gracious words in our mouths, the word of God gathering us into the word of God. Then, in the readings, by the power of the Spirit, God brings us face-to-face with the risen Christ. The other, fixed acclamations of the service say the same thing: "Thanks be to God," we say after each of the first two readings. "Glory to you, O Lord," "Praise to you, O Christ," we say around the gospel reading, addressing the Risen One who meets us there.

Word: First Reading

The assembly has been gathered, in ways discussed above, simple or complex. The assembly is then seated. As they are sitting down, the reader rises from wherever his or her place is in the assembly and walks or moves peacefully and directly to the place of the word. Some congregations have the custom that the reader will pause briefly before the altar/table on the way, perhaps with a bow to this sign of Christ's gift. Others do not. Whatever is done should be done simply, without fuss. At this point, the important center is the place of the word, the place of reading. That place is now the symbol of God's self-giving. Indeed, congregations that practice "reverencing the altar" might here consider instead a certain "reverencing of the ambo and the book." However, none of this is required. What is needed is the direct and peaceful approach of the reader, with a heart ready to give this reading into the hearing of the assembly.

It will be important that the reader has already checked before the service to see that the Bible or lectionary is ready, so that she or he will be able quickly to locate the right reading. It will also be important that the reader has stood at the ambo, checked its height and its light and, if necessary, its sound equipment. Then the reader can approach the reading task in peace. Some readers may need to stand beside the lectern or sit there in their wheelchair, with the Bible or lectionary book in their hands, in order to see the reading and to be seen as they read. Similarly, some readers will need to make sure that the right braille pages are open at the place of reading. In any case, it may be wise that the reader come with nothing in hand, so that there need be no struggling with where to put things down at the lectern. Reading from the bulletin or another loose piece of discardable paper, however, sends a particularly unhelpful signal at this moment in the service. At the heart of the assembly gathered around Christ the living Word there is nonetheless a *book*, and we need to help people think of these words as being something other than temporary. Such a simple habit has a greater subliminal effect than we may usually recognize.

The reading that is to be read will be the first one listed in the lectionary list for the day. On most Sundays and festivals, this will be a passage from the Old Testament. On the Sundays of Easter, it will be a passage from the book of Acts—the "book of the acts of the risen Christ in the church," as some people have called it. In about half of the year—the Sundays in the Time after Pentecost that are indicated in the propers with lectionary numbers—the reader will need to know which of the two series of Old Testament readings his or her community is following. The first reading listed is part of a series that has been chosen to complement the gospel reading of the day. In congregations of the Evangelical Lutheran Church in America this pattern is generally followed. The second possible Old Testament reading, listed with its answering psalm at the end of the list of readings for the day, is part of a semicontinuous series in which parts of the Hebrew scriptures are read in a relatively sequential way. Congregations of the Evangelical Lutheran Church in Canada generally follow this pattern. It is about these two possibilities that the Notes on the Services say:

> The goals of the lectionary are best realized when one series or the other is used consistently throughout the Time after Pentecost. Church bodies may recommend one or the other of these approaches for normative use. [LE, 15]

The church bodies have indeed made the respective recommendations indicated above.

The reader then begins. First the reading may be announced. Looking at the assembly, the reader says simply, "A reading from _____," naming the biblical book. Neither the chapter nor the verse numbers of the passage need to be announced. Such citations may be noted in printed materials. The announcement is an invitation to listen to the communal event of the public reading. After a brief pause, the reader begins the passage. The notes again helpfully observe:

> When the speaker is not identified in the beginning verse of a reading, or if a pronoun is used without a clear referent, the reader may substitute a proper name or add a clarifying phrase. A lectionary book designed for use in worship will provide helpful guidance in this regard. [LE, 15]

The lectionary books provided for use with *Evangelical Lutheran Worship* provide those sort of clear beginnings to the readings.

Then, with dignity and beauty and clarity, the scripture is read into the life of the assembly. Throughout the reading the reader may focus on the printed text; making eye contact is not necessary, for it is the written word that is speaking to us now. The notes observe:

> Upon completing the reading, the reader may pause briefly before addressing the assembly with "The word of the Lord" or "Word of God, word of life" and waiting for the assembly's response, "Thanks be to God," before moving from the place of the reading. [LE, 19]

God is praised by the assembly at this point because of the deep trust of the assembly—and of the tradition of *Evangelical Lutheran Worship*—that God is the giver of this word and that God is active in these readings to give faith, forgiveness of sins, and new life (see *The Use of the Means of Grace,* 5).

Word: Psalm

Lutheran Book of Worship restored psalm-singing's important place in Lutheran assemblies. Providing psalm texts for those psalms that appear in the lectionary along with single and double psalm tones gave assemblies easy access to chant-based psalm singing. Many assemblies took up the practice while using *Lutheran Book of Worship* and continue singing the psalms today.

The psalter is filled with psalms of praise, thanksgiving, petition, penitence, and lament. The biblical book of Psalms is the hymnal of ancient Israel. Many of the psalms were written for use in worship in the temple. Others were written for pilgrims to sing as they journeyed to Jerusalem. They range from songs of trust to songs of thanksgiving; royal psalms to wisdom psalms; personal expression to corporate praises. Their intrinsic beauty and spiritual depth give them a timeless value for communal worship. The psalms have continued in use from their inception until today. Thus, when we sing the psalms we are joining our assembly with the praises of God's people from ancient Israel, continued with Jesus and his disciples, and handed down to us today. As the best biblical source of communal singing, we do well to sing them in our assemblies today.

Now, with the publication of *Evangelical Lutheran Worship* there are many new and expanded possibilities for singing the psalms. The pew edition includes a textual version of all 150 psalms that has been specifically prepared and laid out for singing, allowing assemblies the full expressive range of the psalter. Many of the psalms are appointed for use in the Sunday and festival lectionary; others can be used in services of daily prayer, on other occasions, and in personal devotion.

Sixteen psalm tones are also included (AE pp. 337–338). As in *Lutheran Book of Worship*, the psalm texts are pointed—using short vertical bars to indicate the first change of pitch in each of the two halves of each verse—for ease in singing. Singing the psalms should resemble the pace and accents of natural speaking. The introduction to the Psalms (AE pp. 335-336) clarifies this process of turning speech into psalm singing.

In addition to psalm tones, there are many other ways to sing the psalms. Metrical psalms are stanza-based hymns that paraphrase the words of the psalm. "All People That on Earth Do Dwell" (#883) is a metrical setting of Psalm 100 from the Genevan Psalter. This Reformation-era collection is the earliest form of a metrical psalter. It was developed in the Calvinist Reformation as a way of teaching psalms to those Reformed congregations in Switzerland. Other metrical psalms include "My Shepherd, You Supply

My Need" (#782) and "The Lord's My Shepherd" (#778), both based on Psalm 23, and "On Eagle's Wings" (#787), based on Psalm 91.

Refrain-based psalms have a repeating portion of the psalm that is alternated with verses carrying the rest of the text. "Shepherd Me, O God" (#780), a setting of Psalm 23, is an example of a refrain-based psalm. In this type of psalm the assembly may sing the refrain, in alternation with the cantor, or may sing the entire psalm.

Psalm Settings for the Church Year and *Psalter for Worship* are among the many resources available to assist congregations in singing the psalms in a variety of ways. Adding instrumentalists, handbells, descants, and choirs will also help enliven psalm singing in the assembly.

Singing the psalms engages the assembly in actively proclaiming the word together. As a response to the Old Testament reading, the assembly gathers its voice in words from the Old Testament's song book. Reviving and strengthening this ancient practice in our current assemblies connects us to this Old Testament practice, to Christians' ongoing use of the psalms, and expands into new ways of singing the psalms today. The psalms contain the highest joys and the deepest laments of the human soul, laid out before the God of all. Giving the assembly the ability to sing these together each Sunday can nourish the congregation's praise. Over time, these psalms may become treasures of the assembly, rich words given to us from another time and place for use in our own places.

Exploring the various ways of singing the psalms is a trajectory begun in *Lutheran Book of Worship* and continued in *Evangelical Lutheran Worship.* For those assemblies who have not regularly sung the psalms, simple treatments with skilled leadership may be the best way to begin. For those who have been chanting the psalms from *Lutheran Book of Woship,* there are now many new and varied ways to sing the psalms. Exploring these can help to keep psalm-singing fresh and energizing in the assembly, and can enable an assembly to grow in its love and use of the psalms.

Strong leadership and clear directions will assist the assembly in joining the singing. When there is alternation with the cantor or choir, this leadership should model for the assembly the style in which the assembly responds. The text remains primary; the music serves to bring the text clearly into the assembly. The possibilities for psalm singing have expanded in *Evangelical Lutheran Worship* and its companion resources to become almost endless. Careful choices for singing the psalms can lead an assembly to make this portion of the service a place of praise and thanksgiving, petition and lament. It is an important time for strengthening the assembly's voice as it participates in this piece of the day's proclamation.

Word: Second Reading

(On ways for the reader to prepare this reading, approach and stand at the place of reading, and begin and conclude the reading, see the discussion above related to the first reading.) It may be that the reader for the second reading is the same assisting minister as the reader for the first reading. In that case, the reader might consider remaining near the lectern during the singing of the psalm, instead of returning to her or his place in the assembly. If that practice is followed, it would be good for a copy of *Evangelical Lutheran Worship* to be on a chair nearby, with the psalm of the day marked, so that the reader might be seated and easily join in the psalm-singing.

Toward the end of the singing of the psalm, the reader rises and approaches the reading desk so as to be at peace and ready to read when the psalm concludes.

It will be useful for the reader to understand something of the role of this reading in the lectionary. Lutherans, of course, have found the witness of Paul to be of extraordinary importance for the life of the church. This second reading will frequently contain that witness, proclaiming justification by grace through faith, the theology of the cross, or the doctrine of vocation, to name only three of the central Pauline themes important to Lutheran identity. But whether or not the reading on a particular Sunday is from one of the central Pauline epistles, the second reading will connect this assembly to the life of the earliest churches by bringing to us a letter that was sent among those churches, meant to be read aloud in them when they met as we do today.

In the three-year lectionary most of the passages listed for this second reading during the Christmas and Epiphany cycle and during Lent have been chosen to complement the gospel reading of the day. But on the Sundays of Easter we read passages from 1 Peter in year A, 1 John in year B, and Revelation in year C. These texts are taken as ancient celebrations of the resurrection. Similarly, on the "green" Sundays that occur between Pentecost and Advent, the assembly listens to semi-sequential readings through several epistles. In year A, these epistle selections are from 1 Corinthians, then from Romans, Philippians, and

1 Thessalonians. In year B, they continue from 1 Corinthians, then come from 2 Corinthians, Ephesians, James, and Hebrews. In year C, 1 Corinthians is finished, then we read from Galatians, Colossians, Hebrews again, Philemon, 1 and 2 Timothy, and 2 Thessalonians. It will be good for the reader to know this sequence, enabling her or him to follow the structure of the text and make sense of it as it is proclaimed in the assembly.

Again, at the conclusion of the reading, a dialogue of acclamation between the reader and the assembly may be used. God is praised as the giver of this word, alive in the churches.

Word: Gospel Acclamation

The gospel acclamation is a high point of celebration in the assembly. It is the assembly's opportunity to welcome the reading of the gospel in its midst, to rejoice for the great gift of God's word, and to gather around the reading. It is an anticipation of the gospel reading to come and a response to the word it has already heard. The choir may have a role in leading the acclamation, providing a descant or singing the proper verse. However, on most days it is not advisable for the choir to sing the entire acclamation in the assembly's place (the days of Lent and Holy Week may be an exception, when the proper acclamations are less easily sung by an assembly). This is the assembly's response, and at least the alleluia needs the entire assembly's voice.

Usually the gospel acclamation contains an alleluia, our most basic word of praise. In the Lenten season, we sing a less festive text without an alleluia, "Let your steadfast love come to us, O Lord. Save us as you promised; we will trust your word," or another suitable text. In all other seasons, we may simply sing the alleluia or we may pair that singing with a proper verse for the day. For each Sunday there is an appointed text for the gospel acclamation (LE, 60–137; also in the Liturgies Accompaniment Edition).

Some of the musical settings offer options for singing the alleluia with or without the proper verse. Setting Nine (Fig. 7.1) is one of these. The alleluia can be sung first, followed by a proper verse set to a tone, then returning to the alleluia. Or, just the alleluia may be sung, without the proper verse.

Likewise, the service music section contains acclamations that have an alleluia and a tone for singing the proper verse (#168–170), acclamations

Fig. 7.1. Gospel acclamation. *Some of the settings for holy communion, including Setting Nine, provide options for singing the alleluias with or without the proper verse.*

that are simply alleluias (#171–175), and Lenten acclamations (#176–177). Using a variety of acclamations will help keep them fresh and vital for the assembly's singing. Changing them with the seasons is another way to highlight their importance in the assembly.

On occasion, a hymn—especially one with alleluias that is closely related to the gospel or the season—may be substituted as a gospel acclamation. "We Know That Christ Is Raised" (#449), for example, might be suitable for a Sunday during Easter.

Word: Gospel

The reader of the gospel is usually the minister who is preaching at this service. The point of this practice, suggested in the notes (LE, 19), is not that the gospel text is the only text that the preacher will use. Rather, the clear continuity between proclaiming the gospel text and preaching the sermon is meant to indicate the interpretive principle that an evangelical Lutheran assembly uses: Jesus Christ, his cross and resurrection, and the faith that is through him, are at the heart of the scriptures. The preacher is to use that principle in preaching at this service from some or all of the readings. The gospel text stands for Jesus Christ in our midst.

Similarly, the gospel text may not be the text of the day most filled with good news. Indeed, Jesus can sometimes appear as a harsh preacher of the law. But, as Luther has said, he is himself the life-giving gospel.

On any given Sunday, that good news of God's grace might be found in greatest clarity in the first reading or in the second reading. We stand and sing acclamations around the gospel not because it is the "best" or even the most important reading, but because it is the story of Jesus Christ, the living heart of our readings.

As noted in chapter 5, it may be wise for the presiding minister of the day also to be the preacher of the day. There may be reasons why this is not the case, however. Nonetheless, the pastor of the congregation bears responsibility for the whole service, and the preaching takes place under the care of this pastor, whether or not she or he is the presiding minister on a given day. *The Use of the Means of Grace* provides:

> While other persons may sometimes preach, the called pastor of a congregation has responsibility for this preaching, ordinarily preparing and delivering the sermon and overseeing all public ministry of the Word in the congregation. In congregations without a called pastor, the synodical bishop assumes this responsibility, often by providing an interim pastor. [9b]

When the gospel acclamation begins, the assembly stands. Whoever is the reader of the gospel also rises at this time and moves to the place of the word. Again, see the notes related to the first reading on ways for this reader to have prepared this reading, and on ways to approach and stand at the reading place and to begin and conclude the reading. In this case, however, there are acclamations both before and after the reading. On reaching the place of reading, the presiding minister—or the preacher or other reader—finds the text and then stands, waiting while the gospel acclamation continues to be sung, meanwhile keeping his or her eyes on the text. The book and the text are at the center of this acclamation by the assembly—or by the assembly and the choir. The gospel-reader will only redirect and diffuse this attention if she or he, for example, turns toward the choir as if this were an independent choral piece, or if she or he otherwise loses focus. The gospel acclamation finished, the gospel-reader announces the reading: "The holy gospel according to Mark," for example. Again, chapter and verse are not needed. This is the announcement of an oral event. Other words are, of course, possible: "The gospel according to St. Mark" or the "The holy gospel of our Savior Jesus Christ, according to Mark" or "Hear the holy gospel according to Mark" are not wrong. It is simply that directness and consistency are a virtue here, and the basic text suggested by *Evangelical Lutheran Worship* is all that is needed.

Some Christians have the custom, during this announcement, of using their thumb to inscribe a small cross on their forehead, lips, and breast in turn, a way of praying, "May this gospel be in my head, on my lips, and in my heart." This practice, which was originally used in medieval times by the person who was publicly reading the gospel of the day, may be recommended or not as is felt helpful.

After this announcement, the assembly says or shouts, "Glory to you, O Lord." *Evangelical Lutheran Worship* no longer provides music for this response, nor for the one that immediately follows the reading. These responses could, of course, be sung, but most likely only if the gospel itself is to be sung, perhaps on the old gospel-tone used by Martin Luther (see *LW* 53:56–57, 76–78, 86–89). In any case, it will be good for a congregation to be taught how important these words are, addressed to Christ who comes to us here in words, so that they learn to make this response easily and freely. Then, after a brief pause, the reading itself commences. At the conclusion, again after a brief pause, the reader announces: "The gospel of the Lord." And the assembly says or shouts, "Praise to you, O Christ." Usually, then, the assembly is seated and the preacher begins to preach.

The actual reading comes from one of the four gospel books of the New Testament. The Gospel of John is read in all three years, on Christmas Day, the Second Sunday after Epiphany, during much of Lent, on Maundy Thursday and Good Friday, on most of the Sundays of Easter, and in the summertime of year B. On the other Sundays, Matthew is largely read in year A, Mark in year B, and Luke in year C. Thus, in any given year the synoptic gospels and the Fourth Gospel are in a dialogue of witness to Jesus Christ. It will be good for the congregation to be assisted to understand this simple pattern and thus begin to distinguish between and appreciate the emphases of the four books.

In those places where a gospel procession is practiced, the procedure is slightly different from that described above. There are several ways for such a procession to be enacted. Usually, an assisting minister approaches the ambo and picks up the Bible or lectionary. Then, holding up the book to be seen, she or he begins to walk toward the center of the church, while the gospel acclamation is being sung. The presiding minister—or the preacher of the day or another appointed reader—then follows the assisting minister who is carrying the book. While they move, the assembly turns to face them. When they have reached the place of reading, the assisting minister turns toward the reader, holding up the book and resting its top against his or her chest, while the reader finds the place. When they are ready and when the gospel acclamation has finished, the reader announces the reading and the assembly speaks or shouts the first gospel response, as above. During the procession, the person carrying the book may be accompanied by two other persons carrying burning candles, perhaps the very two candles that stood on either side of the book during the first two readings. The resulting configuration, when this group reaches the center of the church, is shown in Fig. 7.2.

The cross may be added to this grouping to lead the procession; however, it is not needed, because in this moment the book itself is the chief sign. Furthermore, in some Lutheran communities that know this practice and perhaps especially at festivals, this whole movement may be accompanied by incense. If incense is used, then the person who carries the bowl or thurible will go first. At the place where the gospel is read, after the announcement of the reading and before the reader begins the reading itself, this person will make the incense available to the reader who will use it to sign the book. After the announcement, the response, the reading, and the final acclamation, those who carried the book here will return to their places. If the cross was in the procession, everyone will step to the side to let it go first, also in the return movement. The book could be carried back to the ambo by the assisting minister who brought it forward in the first place. Or it could be carried by the preacher, who now takes the responsibility to proclaim what has been read. During this return movement, the alleluias of the gospel acclamation could be sung once again, or instrumental music may be played.

Yet other variations of this practice may be practiced locally. Perhaps the presiding minister will simply carry the book alone into the midst of the congregation to read. Perhaps she or he will be joined by the children of the congregation gathering around this reading. Perhaps some of the older children may carry candles. If there is a children's sermon, perhaps it will follow, right there in the aisle, after the reading is concluded, everyone sitting down in that place. Perhaps the assisting minister who carries the book will be a dancer, gracefully moving it

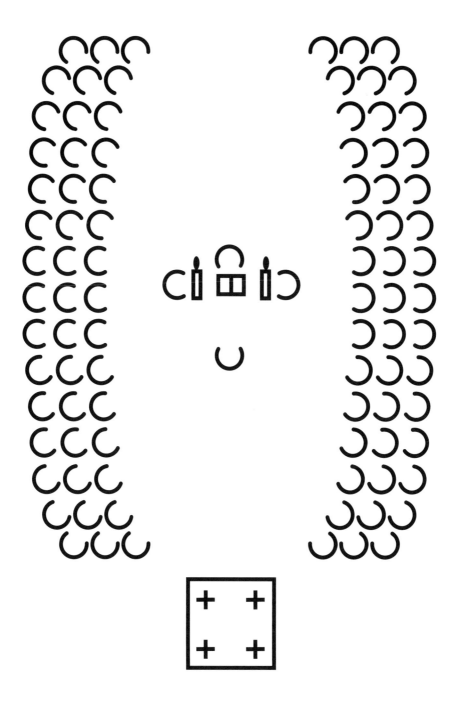

Fig. 7.2. Gospel procession. *The presiding minister, an assisting minister carrying the book, and sometimes two candle bearers process to the center of the assembly, whose members turn to face them.*

among the assembly before and after the reading. Perhaps a full gospel procession will be celebrated and will be joined by banners.

Read in simplicity or with fuller ceremony, the gospel forms the heart of the readings, themselves one of the centers of the service. As the pattern for worship says, "We acclaim the living Word, Jesus Christ, present in the gospel reading."

Word: Sermon

Then preaching follows. The pattern for worship says simply: "Preaching brings God's word of law and gospel into our time and place to awaken and nourish faith." *The Use of the Means of Grace* elaborates:

> The preaching of the Gospel of the crucified and risen Christ is rooted in the readings of the Scriptures in the assemblies for worship. . . . Preaching is the living and contemporary voice of one who interprets in all the Scriptures the things concerning Jesus Christ [Luke 24:27]. In fidelity to the readings appointed for the day, the preacher proclaims our need of God's grace and freely offers that grace, equipping the community for mission and service in daily life. "Only under extraordinary circumstances would the sermon be omitted" from the Sunday and festival service of Holy Communion. [9 and 9a]

So, among us, preaching is not omitted. It belongs to an assembly gathered for worship in word and sacrament. It is one of the most important centers of the service. It is a communal event, the assembly praying for the preacher and the preacher caring for the assembly. Furthermore, it responds to and deals with the texts that have been read. A faithful preacher may particularly focus on the interpretation of one or another of those texts as the core of his or her sermon, but he or she will not ignore the texts or announce still another text. The assembly needs these very texts—the ones that have been read side by side in this service—to be interpreted and proclaimed. And, among us, this proclamation has a clear purpose: in the power of the Spirit, to speak of Jesus Christ in these texts so that we may again come to trust in God with our lives—come to faith—turning then in faith toward our neighbors with service, witness, and love.

In doing this task, the preacher speaks of "our need of God's grace." Using the texts of the day, the preacher preaches the law—that is, the preacher speaks the truth about our sin, loss, failure, and death. Preaching is a time for truth-telling about the human condition. But the preacher also gives the very grace we need. The preacher does not simply speak *about* God and forgiveness and life. Rather, growing out of the texts and because of the presence of Jesus Christ and of his outpoured Spirit, the preacher forgives sins and gives the possibility of hope and life. From the starting point of the day's readings, the preacher leads us into the presence of the life-giving God.

Of course, this event can occur in many ways. There are many different styles and patterns of preaching, and there are many different preachers, all bringing their own experience to the task. Preaching may indeed sometimes occur in "dialogue, drama, cantata, and visual forms," as the notes (LE, 20) suggest. Furthermore, in some congregations, preaching has been divided into two parts—first a "children's sermon," then the sermon proper, largely intended for more mature listeners. Each of these forms needs to be used carefully so as to bring "God's word of law and gospel into our time and place to awaken and nourish faith" (AE p. 92; LE, 164).

The preacher, then, approaches the place of the word—the place where the readings have taken place—and begins to preach. Some preachers use alternative places: they go to a pulpit that has otherwise been unused, they walk about, or they use the table. Again, arguments can be made for each of these places. But preachers might well consider the importance of the symbolic continuity between the readings and the sermon and avoid anything that calls too much attention to themselves and their own idiosyncrasies. God's mercy is the focus here. Furthermore, preaching is a communal ritual event with ritual expectations, and the preacher ought not violate the communal expectations by acting like a "loose cannon." The word of God may be challenging and disturbing. The preacher's posture ought not be so. For example, walking about in the manner of television talk-show hosts may seem friendly and informal. In fact, it involves a large exercise of power and can be experienced by assemblies as far from friendly. The preacher needs to be deeply respectful of the assembly, not "in your face."

Many congregations have locally diverse practices around the sermon. Some congregations stay standing until the preacher has greeted them, perhaps with a biblical greeting, drawn from the New Testament letters, like "Grace to you and peace from God our Father and from the Lord Jesus Christ," or a baptismal invocation, like "In the name of the Father, and of the Son, and of the Holy Spirit" or "In the name of Jesus." In those congregations, the assembly then says "Amen" and sits down. Some congregations and preachers are used to beginning here with a prayer or a quotation from the psalms. There are similar traditional patterns around the conclusion of the sermon, the most common being that the last words of the sermon will evoke from the assembly a strong, assenting "Amen." All of these diversities are welcome. None are required. After the gospel, the preacher may simply begin. At the conclusion of the sermon, the preacher may simply end. It is the sermon itself that is to lead us into the encounter with the grace of the triune God.

Assemblies and preachers that make use of a children's sermon may need to exercise a special care. Thought will need to be given to the placement of this moment so that the flow of the pattern for worship is not disjointed. Even more, thought will need to be given to avoiding common dangers here: The children also need to hear a word of gospel-grace, not simply a religious or moral object lesson. Most importantly, the children should not be put on display for the amusement or entertainment of others. One wise idea is for the preacher to speak simply to the children—not over their heads to the rest of the assembly—while everyone else simply waits. Following that idea, if the preacher has a portable microphone, then to avoid the sense of display it is best that the microphone be turned off. In any case, a children's sermon is not required. If it is used, it should speak the gospel to the children, from the day's texts, or it should use the occasion for some simple worship-related instruction, about, for example, the water in the font or one of the symbols in the room.

But amid all these diverse patterns of preaching, it is very useful for the congregation itself to know what we expect preaching to be. The words "preaching" and "sermon" have sometimes borne negative connotations in our society, implying a kind of judgmental scolding. On the contrary, the evangelical Lutheran expectation is that preaching mercifully speaks out loud the truth of our awful need and, at the same time, gives away God's free grace in Christ, making it possible for us to believe in God again and to turn in service to our neighbor. *Evangelical Lutheran Worship* beckons assemblies and preachers to renewed delight in this gift and task of preaching. Assemblies need to pray for and encourage their preacher or preachers. The preacher needs to see the clarity of the task again and take courage from the promises of God.

After the sermon, *Evangelical Lutheran Worship* continues the past practice of encouraging a time of silence for reflection. A lot of words have been directed at the assembly through the readings and the sermon. Silence here provides the opportunity for the hearers to process that message, and to let the Spirit move them. Because silence can be very uncomfortable in today's busy world, occasional pastoral direction may be helpful. The assembly can be reassured that there is no particular expectation for this time. It is only an open space so that "reverberation" from the spoken word can take place. On the other hand, it is not a time for filling out a communion card or (as most often) for finding the next hymn. There will be time for that, but this, now, is the gift of some moments to just be, before the aural activity of the service continues.

Word: Hymn of the Day

The hymn of the day is one of the few central elements that is distinctive to the Holy Communion pattern for worship as practiced by Lutherans. Its importance for contemporary Lutheran assemblies can hardly be overstated. Essentially, it is a central way in which the assembly takes its part in proclaiming God's word for the Sunday or festival. Thus, although some call this a sermon hymn, the hymn of the day is something more. The hymn of the day is the principal hymn of the service and a key component of the day's proclamation. It is intended that this hymn be related to more than one text or to the sermon. Rather, the hymn of the day gathers up relationships among the day's readings and the season within the church's year. It may respond to the scripture readings and may certainly reinforce preaching that is based on the appointed readings. First and foremost, however, the hymn of the day gives the assembly the responsibility and opportunity to proclaim and respond to the word. The assembly has heard God's word read and preached and now joins its voice to that proclamation.

Because of this demanding role in giving voice to the proclaimed word, this hymn needs to be substantial enough to be up to the task. Prime candidates are texts that are well grounded in scripture and that offer mature devotional or theological reflection on the word in the context of Christian faith and life. Other texts may be considered for their ability to bear the word on this day and season of the church year. The tune also needs to be durable, singable by all, and an effective complement to the text. Although the hymn of the day may employ the expression of many different poetic and musical genres, texts that are theologically shallow or tunes that are too repetitive or difficult can hinder the assembly's proclamation. Skillful hymn of the day choice involves considering a particular assembly's resources and selecting the strongest texts and tunes this assembly is able to use—or learn to use—with assurance.

The hymn of the day is a historic feature of Lutheran liturgical tradition. Martin Luther made use of it, assigning chorales to seasons and times of the liturgical year. In this way, assemblies in Luther's day built up a core of scriptural and liturgical hymnody in the vernacular language. The *de tempore* hymn tradition precedes Luther, however. Before the Reformation, there were particular chants and songs assigned to saints' days and other festivals. Luther and other reformers built upon this tradition, reinforcing the importance of the assembly's voice—not only the choir's—taking its part in singing the word of God. Still today, teaching assemblies about the hymn of the day and its purpose helps them understand their role with regard to the word in worship. Claiming this practice as a particular Lutheran treasure, our assemblies can build a treasury of song that will nourish the faith and life of all who worship from one generation to another.

Choosing a hymn of the day involves attending carefully to the church's day and season, the scripture readings and psalm, and the assembly's abilities. Here are two examples of hymns for the Advent season that may help illuminate the principles involved in choosing the hymn of the day. "Savior of the Nations, Come" (#263; Fig. 7.3) is one of Luther's hymn of the day choices for the Advent season. Luther translated into German the Latin text attributed to Ambrose; Johann Walter set the tune for congregational singing. This chorale was published in the earliest hymnal of the German Reformation, the 1524 *Geistliche Gesangbüchlein*. Its text incorporates several Advent themes: human yearning for redemption, God's Son coming among us, the story of salvation. Singing it as the hymn of the day on the first or one of the other Sundays of Advent is a tradition, begun by Luther, that may well be continued today.

Savior of the Nations, Come

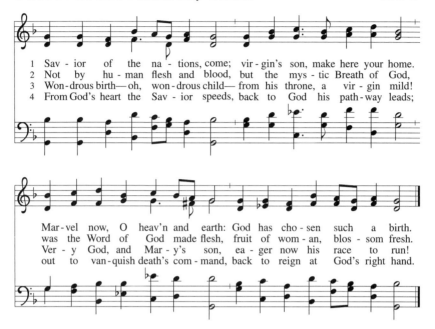

1 Sav - ior of the na - tions, come; vir - gin's son, make here your home.
2 Not by hu - man flesh and blood, but the mys - tic Breath of God,
3 Won - drous birth— oh, won - drous child— from his throne, a vir - gin mild!
4 From God's heart the Sav - ior speeds, back to God his path - way leads;

Mar - vel now, O heav'n and earth: God has cho - sen such a birth.
was the Word of God made flesh, fruit of wom - an, blos - som fresh.
Ver - y God, and Mar - y's son, ea - ger now his race to run!
out to van - quish death's com - mand, back to reign at God's right hand.

5 Now your manger, shining bright,
  hallows night with newborn light.
  Night cannot this light subdue;
  let our faith shine ever new.

6 Praise we sing to Christ the Lord,
  virgin's son, incarnate Word!
  To the holy Trinity
  praise we sing eternally!

Text: attr. Ambrose of Milan, 340–397; Martin Luther, 1483–1546; tr. hymnal version
Music: J. Walter, *Geistliche Gesangbüchlein*, 1524
Text © 2006 Augsburg Fortress

NUN KOMM, DER HEIDEN HEILAND
7 7 7 7

Fig. 7.3. Hymn of the day. *Choosing a hymn of the day involves attending carefully to the church's day and season, the scripture readings and psalm, and the assembly's abilities. This hymn was one of Martin Luther's choices for Advent.*

"Come Now, O Prince of Peace / *Ososŏ, ososŏ,*" (#247; Fig. 7.4) is a new possibility for a hymn of the day during the Advent season. This hymn was written in the late twentieth century as an expression of hoped-for reconciliation between North and South Korea. In the larger context of worship by Christian assemblies in many other places, it speaks of the Advent longing for Christ's reconciliation of all the

Come Now, O Prince of Peace 247

Ososŏ, ososŏ

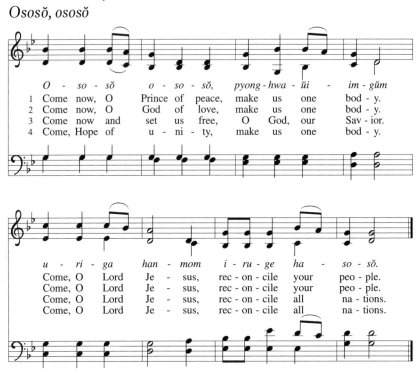

Text: Geonyong Lee, b. 1947; tr. Marion Pope
Music: Geonyong Lee, b. 1947
Text and music © Geonyong Lee

OSOSŎ
6 5 5 6

Fig. 7.4. A newer hymn of the day. *"Come Now, O Prince of Peace / Ososŏ, ososŏ" was written late in the twentieth century to express hope for reconciliation between North and South Korea, but more broadly it speaks of Advent longing for worldwide reconciliation.*

world. With its haunting Korean tune, this hymn offers a new musical style for the hymn of the day. It expresses the longing of the Advent season, and it captures in word and music the world's longing for peace and reconciliation.

A table of hymn of the day suggestions is found in Appendix B in this volume. Additional hymn of the day suggestions, along with suggestions for other hymns that relate to the readings and the various roles hymns play in the service, may be found in *Indexes to Evangelical Lutheran Worship*—one of the other volumes in this series of leader guides—and in the annual publication *Sundays and Seasons.*

Word: Creed

When the hymn of the day concludes, the assembly, still standing, may sometimes confess the creed. In current Lutheran practice, the Apostles' Creed, the creed associated with baptism, is usually chosen for Lent, as the season of baptismal renewal and preparation, and for all of the Sundays in the Time after Epiphany and the Time after Pentecost. The Nicene Creed is usually chosen for festival days and during the seasons of Advent, Christmas, and Easter. On the other hand, the creed might be omitted altogether, the service moving on to the prayers of intercession immediately after the hymn of the day.

If the creed is used, it may be enough for the presiding minister to simply begin confidently, "I believe in God, the Father almighty . . ." or "We believe in one God . . .," expecting the assembly to join in on the next phrase. This is especially true if the presiding minister allows enough time after the hymn for people to locate the creed. Adding the brief invitation provided in the Leaders Edition may give the assembly more confidence: "With the whole church, let us confess our faith." Or, when visitors or regular participants are learning to use the book, it may be gracious to announce the page number of the creed. For example, "The Nicene Creed, on page 104," could be a sufficient announcement, followed either by the Leaders Edition invitation or the creed itself.

Those who have used *Lutheran Book of Worship* have become familiar with the practice that the creed may or may not be used in the service. This choice is rooted in the fact that the creeds were originally teaching documents, at home in baptismal catechesis, learned by heart by baptismal candidates and then used in the celebration of baptism itself, not in the regular Sunday liturgy. In the West, the Nicene Creed came to be used regularly in the Sunday eucharistic service only in the eleventh century. The Apostles' Creed began to be used in the Holy Communion service by North American Lutherans only in the twentieth century. The deep sense of leaders of the liturgy in the Western churches has often been that the reciting of the acts of God and the confession of triune faith takes place in the Sunday liturgy most strongly through preaching, communal singing, and the great thanksgiving at the Lord's table. In all of these, biblical language, rather than doctrinal and creedal language, are more appropriate. The Christian liturgy is mostly made up of scripture and biblically inspired hymns and prayers. The creeds do rightly belong more clearly in baptismal practice. Used on Sunday morning, outside of the context of teaching and conversation, they can seem to some people like shibboleths, like words to test loyalty and ward off strangers. Still, baptismal faith does come to expression when the assembly gathers. The sermon does have some teaching character, illuminating the meaning of the triune God for us. And the creeds can be one way that the assembly responds to the preaching of the word of God. Preaching is intended to lead to faith, and the assembly responds by singing that faith in the hymn of the day. It can also respond with the confession "We believe" or "I believe." The trinitarian character of these confessions corresponds to the trinitarian character of the whole Sunday event: the Spirit gathers us here into the word and presence of Jesus Christ, bringing us thereby to stand in faith before the One who sent Jesus, the One called "the Father." In that sense, every Sunday is Trinity Sunday, and the confession of trinitarian faith belongs to the celebration.

In most Lutheran congregations in North America, the Nicene Creed and Apostles' Creed will continue to have a regular and important place in the Sunday service. As these creeds are used, however, it will be important for parish education to help people see the reasons for the slight changes in language present in the versions used in *Evangelical Lutheran Worship* and the reasons for the footnotes below those versions. The Notes on the Services (LE, 20) are helpful in this regard and should be consulted. The very ecumenical character of these creeds comes to expression by our using the best current ecumenical translation, the 1988 version prepared by the English Language Liturgical Consultation that was printed in *With One Voice* and is used here. In fact, besides being better translations of the original Greek and Latin, both the "became truly human" of the Nicene Creed and the "descended to the dead" of the Apostles' Creed also more adequately represent classic Lutheran theology than did the old translations. In the incarnation, God is saving all humanity. In the death of Jesus, God is proclaiming forgiveness and life wherever there is death, even in the very place of the dead. Furthermore, in modern American English a masculine pronoun necessarily indicates a person of male sex. God as God is not a male and therefore the words *he* and *his* in the old translations had become misleading when used of the Father and the Spirit. We indeed confess that Jesus Christ was and is fully a human male, but the new creed-translations express the hope that we can articulate the trust in the other two persons of the Trinity with better, more faithful, and more accurate language.

The third ecumenical creed, the Athanasian Creed or *Quicunque vult,* with its length and complexity, is now rarely used in corporate worship and is thus not included in these core worship resources.

Whether or not the creed is used in response to the reading and preaching of the word, the assembly continues to stand for the prayers that follow.

Word: Prayers of Intercession

If the readings followed by the preaching are together meant to bring us again to trust in God, to bring us again to faith, then one of the first ways we are invited to exercise that faith is by praying for the needs of all the world. "Grounded in the word and promise of God, the church prays, in the power of the Spirit and in the name of Jesus Christ, for all the great needs of the world" (LE, 21). Said another way, the word of God calls us again to our baptismal vocation as a priestly people of God. That priesthood is now undertaken as we together pray for people besides ourselves and for the needs of all of the creation. We stand before God on behalf of others. Here then are those prayers of which 1 Timothy 2:1 speaks: "First of all, then, I urge that supplications, prayers, intercessions, and thanksgivings be made for everyone."

The counsel of *Evangelical Lutheran Worship* is that these prayers should be locally prepared, be truly prayers of intercession, and be led by an assisting minister, a lay person who is chosen and trained for this ministry. No text is provided in *Evangelical Lutheran Worship* for these prayers beyond a suggested invitation to pray at the beginning, three possible responses throughout the prayers and one possible conclusion that the presiding minister might make. *Evangelical Lutheran Worship* does, however, provide a fine list of matters to consider, reflecting "the wideness of God's mercy for the whole world" (AE pp. 105, 127, 218; and in all ten settings and Service of the Word in LE).

One sound practice is that these intercessions are prepared by the person who then leads them. In other congregations, people are identified for this ministry of preparing intercessory prayers, and while some of these people also publicly lead the prayers, others who may be less comfortable in such a public role hand on the prayers they have written to another person to lead.

In such preparation, the person or group assigned to this task may take the list of concerns in *Evangelical Lutheran Worship* and then begin to think: For whom specifically in the church universal shall we pray today? Where is there a church in need, in persecution, in turmoil? What missionaries or ministries are we supporting? Who in ministry is frequently not remembered at all? For what other non-Lutheran local churches shall we pray, asking God to empower their witness and bring us all to unity? And what is the name of the national or presiding bishop of our church body and bishop of the local synod so that we may be sure to pray for them as well? Then, how shall we pray for the creation today? What are the local, regional, and worldwide ecological needs? Can we name local rivers and streams, local forests and fields, and pray to God for their restoration and health? Can we pray for endangered species, for the well being of the animals? Can we pray for those who care for the land? Then, where are the situations today where peace and justice is threatened? For whom in the nations and among those in authority, specifically, shall we pray today?

And this is only the beginning. On and on the questions may go, using the remarkable list in *Evangelical Lutheran Worship*. The person who prepares the prayers of intercession may also take the readings of the day and the kinds of needs in the world that they suggest, the day's newspaper and the urgent events that will be on everybody's minds, and his or her own caring experience of local and more-than-local realities. The result will be a long list of real situations and people for whom we need to pray.

To pray: it is important that we genuinely pray. A person who is beginning in this ministry might begin with prayers that simply list the people and needs for which we pray. "For the churches in the Lutheran World Federation; Lord, in your mercy . . . For Christians in Palestine; Lord, in your mercy . . . For our neighbors, the First Presbyterian Church; Lord, in your mercy . . . For our bishop _name_ and our bishop _name_; Lord, in your mercy . . . For the rain forests, for the polar bears; Lord, in your mercy . . . For the farmers in our county; Lord, in your mercy . . . For children in foster care; Lord, in your mercy . . . For the homeless people in our city; Lord, in your mercy. . . ." Such intercessions can be very moving and very real. They can invite us all into the ministry of intercession for others. Such a pattern is never too simple.

As the leader of prayer gains confidence in the task, she or he may add a few more words—a biblical image from the readings of the day, a purpose for the prayer: "For our neighbors, the First Presbyterian church, that they may be renewed in the gospel; hear us, O God . . . For children in foster care, that they may grow up into safety and hope; hear us, O God. . . ." Models of intercessory prayer that can be found in various published resources can also help a leader of prayer move toward richer language.

But an important thing is to avoid so building up the words that they become more like little sermons or announcements about what we should do, than genuine, beseeching prayer, trusting in God. We do need to talk together about what we will do about needs in the world, but at this point what we are doing is speaking the prayer of faith, genuinely naming urgent needs before God, believing that there is a God and that God answers prayer. A turn of speech that often indicates that the prayer is turning into a message to ourselves is "Lord, help us to remember that . . ." or "For those who are poor, that we may do more. . . ." For all of the good intention of these seeming petitions, they wind up being prayer to or, at least, *for* ourselves. Here, except for one or two bids toward the end of the prayers, we are invited genuinely to pray for others.

A further tendency to beware of is disguising parish announcements as intercessions. A gross parody of this would be something like: "For the ladies of the Dorcas Guild who are meeting at Helen Johnson's house on Tuesday at seven. . . ." It is fine to pray for the Dorcas Guild, but save the details for a more appropriate time. Similarly, prayers for the sick or those who have died best simply name the person, omitting details about illness, hospitalization, or funeral arrangements. Remember that we are speaking to God. It is worth considering whether any names beyond baptismal (first) names need be used in prayer: "For Kristine, Morrie, and Olaf. . . ." The Notes on the Services rightly counsel us about these local prayers: Prayers prepared for use in the assembly are those that the assembly can assent to and make their own [LE, 21].

The prayers should not be an imposition upon these gathered people, a political or social position–taking, but a gracious invitation into prayer for public needs. The notes continue: "The assembly voices [its] assent by responding after each brief portion of the prayers with one of the suggested responses or with similar words." Thus, each of these bids or a group of these bids together may be concluded with a line that invites the assembly to join the prayer. Three of these lines and their responses are provided in *Evangelical Lutheran Worship*. Other forms of this dialogue are also possible. One way to introduce an alternate form is by using the opening invitation to prayer to indicate also the response, adding it to the end of the invitation: "With the whole people of God in Christ Jesus, let us pray for the church, those in need, and all of God's creation. At the bid *God of mercy,* we respond *hear our cry.*" Whatever the response, it should be kept consistent throughout the prayers of intercession of a single service, and should be brief enough to be held easily in memory.

The assembly may also be invited to join directly in these prayers. One way this may be done is by the leader of prayer leaving a space of silence during which names or needs may be spoken aloud or silently by the assembly: "For the sick, for Ralph Larson, for Mary Smith, and especially for these people whom we name aloud or in our hearts *(silence);* Lord, in your mercy. . . ." Another possibility is that at the end of the petitions, the leader of prayer may say, "And for what else shall we pray today?" leaving a following silence. Either the leader of prayer or the member of the assembly who speaks out a petition may add the brief phrase that invites the assembly response. Or the leader may let that dialogue wait until all of the congregational bids have concluded. Still, these means of participation may be difficult for very large congregations or for rooms where the acoustics are not good. Another means of enabling direct participation in the day's intercessions is to leave a book of intercessions at the entrance to the assembly's space. People arriving for worship may write a name or a need in this book. The assisting minister who is leading the prayers will then seek to add these names and needs to the prepared intercessions.

The final petition of the prayer may be a thanksgiving for those who have died in faith. People known to the assembly or part of the assembly who have recently died may be named. So may people who are commemorated in the church's calendar on days near to this Sunday. The petition may be framed like this: "We give you thanks for those who have died in faith, especially for [*names from the community*] and for [*names of those on the calendar of commemorations for this day or this week*]; Lord, in your mercy. . . ." The thanksgiving may be this simple. But, however framed, the petition should retain the character of thanksgiving to the God who was the hope and life of these people. Beyond commending them in trust to God at the time of their death and burial, Lutheran assemblies generally do not pray in an intercessory way for the dead, for they are already fully in the hands of God.

Following the hymn of the day, then, or the creed if it is used, the assisting minister who is to lead the prayers of intercession begins. It may be good that this assisting minister is seated next to the presiding minister, functioning as the principal assisting minister of the service. If the place where they are seated is visible to the assembly, then standing in front of those chairs may be a good place from which to lead the prayers. It is possible that the leader of prayer may choose to raise her or his hands in the *orans* posture (Fig. 7.5), the ancient Christian stance of prayer.

If the assisting minister does choose to stand in this way, it would be good for the presiding minister to hold the book containing the prepared intercessions so that both of the assisting minister's hands may be free. That sign of mutual help is profoundly Christian, and it is good if the

Fig. 7.5. Orans posture for prayers of intercession. *The leader of the prayers may choose to use the ancient Christian stance of prayer.*

presider is seen to help another as well as to be helped. Other options are also possible. The assisting minister may stand at the lectern or ambo to lead the prayers. Or she or he may stand in a central place in the aisle of the church. In any case, when the final petition has been prayed, the presiding minister concludes the prayer with a commendation. *Evangelical Lutheran Worship* gives one set of possible words for this concluding prayer. The assembly then assents with their "Amen."

Such praying is a remarkable and rare thing. *Evangelical Lutheran Worship* invites us to the ongoing recovery of this old Christian responsibility, this communal vocation of prayer. But, in order to do so, a local assembly will be especially helped by finding those persons in their midst who have a vocation for such leadership of prayer. Such a person will have a heart that pays attention to the needs of the community and of the world, a humble spirit that is interested in helping others pray, an inviting voice that can be heard in the assembly, and a willingness to continue to learn.

Word: Peace

In the flow of the service, the flow of the pattern for worship used by *Evangelical Lutheran Worship*, the prayers are then finally concluded by the peace. That greeting and gesture can also be regarded as the conclusion of the Word movement of the service and the transition to the Meal movement of the service. Like the prayer of the day, the peace functions as a seam between parts of the service.

As a conclusion to the intercessions, the peace enacts both a prayer and a proclamation. Christians remember the word of Jesus in the Gospel of Mark: "Whenever you stand praying, forgive, if you have anything against anyone; so that your Father in heaven may also forgive you your trespasses." (11:25). The peace functions as a kind of seal on our prayers, a sign that we are serious about our praying. It is as if we were saying, with our gesture, "O God, help the world with the very peace and mutual forgiveness we are trying to show here."

And yet, God has helped and is helping the world with a heart far bigger than our own. The peace is also a proclamation of the presence of a down payment on the very things for which we pray: "The peace of the risen Christ is the answer to our prayer, God's gift to us all" (LE, 21). As Christ stood among the disciples on Sunday, saying "Peace be with you" (John 20:19, 26), so we speak this very same gift to each other. In fact, the presiding minister's words make it very clear that this gift of the risen Christ is the gift that we speak: "The peace *of Christ* be with you always."

The exchange of peace is a ministry, an announcement of grace we make to each other, a summary of the gift given to us in the liturgy of the Word. This ministry we do to each other is far greater than a sociable handshake or a ritual of friendship or a moment of informality. Because of the presence of Jesus Christ, we give to each other what we are saying: Christ's own peace. Then, having been gathered by the Spirit around the Risen One present in the word, we turn to celebrate his meal. That this greeting of peace precedes the offering, the setting of the table, and the communion has sometimes also been interpreted as an enacting of Matthew 5:23-24 and the counsel of Paul in 1 Corinthians 11. The community that comes to this supper prays for and has been given the gift of reconciliation in Christ.

The presiding minister, usually from wherever she or he was standing to conclude the prayers, if that place is visible to the congregation,

Fig. 7.6. Presiding minister announces the peace. *The gesture used for the apostolic greeting may also be used to declare the peace. The assembly responds with "And also with you," and worshipers exchange the peace with one another.*

speaks first. Again, the same gesture (Fig. 7.6) that was used at the greeting at the beginning of the service may be used here.

The assembly responds, extending to the presiding minister this same peace of Christ with the words, "And also with you."

In many places, then, the assembly may turn to greet each other with this same peace as well. It is as if each member of the assembly becomes the risen Christ to his or her neighbor. The gesture itself may vary greatly, each person sensing how the other person chooses. The two people, facing each other, may simply exchange the words or, perhaps, the words and a slight bow. Or the two may speak the words while exchanging a handshake or an embrace or a kiss. Or each person may grasp both of the other person's lower arms, speaking the words in exchange with the other. In a time of contagious disease, some people find this latter practice a useful option.

Congregations also exercise considerable variety in how long this exchange continues and how far from their places people go to make the greeting. The variety is welcome, though it should probably also be monitored. Staying in one's place and ritually greeting all of the people immediately around one's place can express the ministry we all are enacting for each other, without distinction. On the other hand, such a practice can also feel too restrictive for some congregations. Still, moving about the room can easily lead to greeting only one's friends or near acquaintances. Newcomers and strangers can quickly feel left out. It is true that if a member of the assembly knows that across the room stands someone with whom that member has been in disagreement or even against whom that member has sinned, and if the exchange of peace can be a genuine prayer and a genuine gift and not a pretense or an imposition, the word of Christ is rightly enacted by the two people seeking each other out for the exchange of peace at this time. Their genuine reconciliation may begin with this enacted word, this gift of Christ.

In any case, it would be wise for the pastors, from time to time, to find ways to instruct congregations about the meaning and practice of the peace.

With this exchange of Christ's gift, the assembly then turns to the Meal.

CHAPTER EIGHT

Meal

By the mercy of God, the assembly turns to eat and drink the very promise they have been hearing in the scriptures. Or, to say this another way, the word of God is now proclaimed by the assembly eating and drinking these "visible words" (Augustine). Paul writes, "As often as you eat this bread and drink the cup, you proclaim the Lord's death until he comes" (1 Cor. 11:26). This publicly proclaimed, visible, eatable, drinkable word—like the audible word as well—is given by God to bring us to faith and turn us in love and service toward our neighbor. Jesus Christ, whom we have encountered in the heart of the scriptures, here gives himself to us in body and blood as the meal of the church.

We have already seen, in chapter 2, how the New Testament and the Lutheran confessions propose this meal as an every-Sunday event, always as part of a word-meal pattern of worship. We have also seen the many names of the meal and its rich meanings. This event is the giving away of the body and blood of Christ for the sake of forgiveness of sins, life, and salvation *(the sacrament of the altar)*. Thus it is also a feast with the Risen One *(the Lord's supper)*, a *holy communion* with Christ and his people, an open confession of thanksgiving *(eucharist,* from the word *eucharistia)* for all God's acts of creation and redemption, and a dismissal to service *(mass)*. God acts here *(divine service),* making of our public gathering to eat and drink *(liturgy)* the very place of astonishing mercy. And this meal is a trinitarian event. We confess that the Holy Spirit gathers us together and then enlivens the promise of Christ. Eating and drinking Christ's gift, forgiven and fed the gift of life, we stand before the face of the Father. By the power of the Spirit, we become what we eat and turn in mission to the world as the body of Christ, sent as part of the mission of God. Furthermore, we have seen the regular Sunday pattern—Gathering, Word, Meal, Sending—by which *Evangelical Lutheran Worship* means to make this holy communion available to us, Sunday after Sunday.

Christ invites us to the meal each Sunday. There we give thanks, pray, receive the bread and wine, and share this feast in the gathered community. With prayer and with song, we come to the banquet that is prepared for us.

With prayer and with song: it is during the time of this meal that we perhaps see best the various ways communal singing works in the assembly. Four of these ways are partnership, dialogue, unity, and focus. Song involves a *partnership* with the actions of the liturgy, giving the assembly words and music that will accompany the actions of receiving the gifts at the table. Song also facilitates a *dialogue* between the presiding minister and the assembly in giving thanks at the table. At other times assembly song expresses *unity*, joining the assembly and all its individual ministers in one common voice. During the sharing of communion, song may provide *focus* for what is often an extended and flexible time in the service. Communal song is an important way in which the assembly experiences in this time a shared meal that is more than individual nourishment, a communion and not only a distribution.

Now we need to think about the ways in which this Meal part of the service may be practiced.

Diverse Local Meal Practices

The ways of practicing this meal are themselves diverse. The arrangements of the rooms where we gather look different from one another. Different congregations own and use tableware for the meal that is often not quite alike. Differing kinds of bread and wine are used. In some places, this part of the service is an occasion for intense ceremonial practice. In others, the event is uncomplicated and simple. Many pastors face the assembly across the table while proclaiming the great thanksgiving and the promise of Christ—as if to enable us to see the gift and to invite us to join as one body around the table. Some face the front of the church, still using the medieval pattern Lutherans have inherited. Congregations have worked out different ways that people come to the table and receive communion. Some people kneel and some stand. In one place, everyone kneels at an altar rail to eat and drink, waiting to be dismissed group by group or "table" by "table." In another place, there is no group dismissal. In another, everyone comes to the ministers of communion, who stand at a station in the assembly's room to distribute the bread and cup to standing communicants. In one place, very young children receive the supper. In another, those children are blessed at the table until they reach a more mature age.

The urging of *Evangelical Lutheran Worship* is not toward uniformity in all of these things. Rather, it urges that all of us think about the reasons for our practices and consider how they may continue to be renewed. *The Use of the Means of Grace* says:

> Our congregations receive and administer the means of grace in richly diverse ways. This diversity in practice is well grounded in the Confessions: "It is not necessary for the true unity of the Christian church that ceremonies of human institution should be observed uniformly in all places" [Augsburg Confession, Article 7]. We are united in one common center: Jesus Christ proclaimed in Word and sacraments amidst participating assemblies of singing, serving, and praying people. [4b]

Still, it remains important to think about our particular local practices and to inquire about whether they serve or obscure that common center and whether they help or hinder our singing, praying, serving people.

Older liturgical rubrics frequently sounded as if they were regulations and descriptions of a single way. The rubrics in *Evangelical Lutheran Worship* intentionally avoid that tone. As we have seen in chapter 3, they are, rather, instances of wise counsel, compressed experience, invitations to deeper thought about what we do. What follows here, as well, are proposals and discussions for local thinking about good practice, not regulations or requirements. There is no uniform liturgical law among Lutherans in North America. The danger of this approach, however, is that it seems to suggest that worship planning is simply another example of the widespread current phenomenon of personal choice, with worship leaders getting to pick what they like. In fact, there is a widespread consensus among those who have reflected deeply about some of these matters, and we are wise not to ignore that shared wisdom, that common proposal. Again, these proposals are not proposals for uniformity but invitations to thought. Sometimes a practice that at first seems interesting and creative — or simply convenient — may, on further thought, communicate something other than the gospel of Jesus Christ or do something other than build up the assembly.

One of the differences among us, for example, has to do with the table or altar of the meal. Already there is a difference in these names. Both are welcome. Of course, the place where the Lord's supper is set out is a table.

It is a meal we eat at Jesus Christ's invitation, and the food of a meal is set upon a table. We may, however, call that table an *altar* metaphorically, since here Jesus Christ gives us his own sacrifice, the sacrifice that is the end of all sacrifices, amazingly reversing the direction of sacrifice. But the further difference is in the location of the table. In some churches it is against the wall. In other churches it is freestanding.

The freestanding table is the oldest practice, discoverable in the earliest images and architectural remains we have of old church buildings. This practice has been widely recovered today, since it so clearly helps us to see that the Lord's supper celebrates the risen Christ in the midst of an assembly. On the other hand, the east-wall altar has a medieval origin and a continued use into the time of the Reformation and the following centuries. That up-against-the-wall positioning of the table originally carried with it the yet older idea that the east—the place of the sunrise—symbolized the dawn of the resurrection and the promise of the second coming of the Risen One. Most churches were built toward the east, were *oriented* (*orient* meaning east). In prayer together, then, Christians often faced the east as a sign of their faith. As the originally more central table migrated toward the east end of the church, they could see a sign that, in the supper at that table, the Risen One was already coming, already giving a foretaste of the day of promise. But that idea was quickly lost. When the celebration of the supper was made into the medieval sacrifice of the mass, it was as if the priest were holding up the sacrifice of Christ to God, perhaps even sacrificing Christ to God anew. Facing away from the people served that idea.

Even in Lutheran churches, where that idea of sacrifice was rejected, the old practice of facing the wall was maintained, simply because Lutherans were so conservative. In many places, that conservative, medieval practice continues still. Perhaps a very few people think of the idea of the sunrise-orientation of prayer. But for most of us, that front wall in many of our churches is no longer eastward, and in fact many of us do not even ordinarily know where east is. The result is that for the pastor to face away from the assembly during the great thanksgiving feels to many like an act of secrecy, of holy hiddenness, even though the promise of Christ calls for open and public proclamation. One visitor to our congregations was heard to say, "Why does he turn his back to us?" Many more have probably thought that question without receiving a clear answer.

Luther himself wrote in the "German Mass," speaking of the medieval practice he inherited:

> Here [in Wittenberg] we retain the vestments, altar, and candles until they are used up or we are pleased to make a change. But we do not oppose anyone who would do otherwise. In the true mass, however, of real Christians, the altar should not remain where it is, and the priest should always face the people as Christ doubtlessly did in the Last Supper. But let that await its own time. [LW 53:69]

His writing breathes the spirit of humor, freedom, and abhorrence of compulsion, so important to Lutherans. But it also breathes the spirit of thought. Many Lutherans, in concert with many other Christians, think that the time of which Luther spoke has indeed come, and that the pastor should preside at the table facing the people—*versus populum*. The assembly needs to have a sense that it is gathered around that table, sees and hears what happens there, has the promise of Christ clearly addressed to it, participates in the thanksgiving, and is made into a community through God's gift.

In what follows below, a celebration that uses this freestanding table practice will be discussed. Some altar-tables have been built freestanding, with this kind of celebration in mind. But also some currently wall-connected altars can be carefully moved to a new position, can be made to be freestanding. In yet other places, the old wall-altar cannot be moved but can be de-emphasized, becoming perhaps a place of flowers or a table for the vessels for holy communion (a "credence table"), while a significant new table is set up, closer to the people and standing free. Other suggestions will be outlined below, including an idea for using a wall-affixed altar and still facing the people for the thanksgiving. Of course, *Evangelical Lutheran Worship* does not compel this change. But such ancient use, such hearty recommendation by Martin Luther, and such current consensus should really urge us to think about our practice.

Another difference among us has to do with the age of first communion or the communion of young children. After a long study and discussion, both the ELCIC and the ELCA concluded that there are no biblical or confessional grounds for requiring anything else than baptism for admission to the supper. Among Lutherans, in both church bodies, the holy communion is regularly given to the baptized, including baptized children. Holy communion also is regularly accompanied by teaching that is appropriate to the age of the communicants. Furthermore, different congregations make different decisions regarding the age at which children begin to regularly receive communion. The ELCA's statement for guidance and practice in these matters, *The Use of the Means of Grace* (37 and 38) wisely recognizes these things and counsels mutual respect between congregations of varied practice. It also counsels (38d) that communing children and their families, moving from one congregation to another, should be welcomed to the supper in the new congregation, regardless of the local practice, but should respect and participate in the educational processes of their new church community.

This same document (37g) also faces the fact that, in this age of mission, we may sometimes find unbaptized adults among the communicants at our altars. Nobody is to be shamed by this discovery. Many people today may first understand something of Jesus Christ by the words "my body and blood, given and shed for you." Still, such an encounter should lead the congregation to stand beside such people, accompanying them deeper into faith and into baptism.

Words at the Table

Another significant difference among us has to do with the way the great thanksgiving at the table takes place. In fact, these different ways have sometimes been the source of not a little controversy. It is important to remember that these different ways stand side by side among us, part of a common tradition that embraces, if sometimes uneasily, two primary ways of approaching the great thanksgiving. Great care was taken in the preparation of *Evangelical Lutheran Worship* to ensure that neither way would be seen to be privileged. Both are a part of our common life. It may be helpful, however, to describe these patterns and understand both the historic underpinnings and the ongoing developments regarding them.

Many of our pastors and congregations make use, after the preface and "Holy, holy, holy" (Sanctus) and before the Lord's Prayer, of the full text of one of the thanksgivings at the table, of which *Evangelical Lutheran Worship* provides varied and useful examples. Other pastors and congregations instead follow the preface and "Holy, holy, holy" simply with a proclamation of the words of institution and the Lord's Prayer. About this diversity, *The Use of the Means of Grace* says:

The Holy Communion is consecrated by the Word of God and prayer [1 Tim. 4:5]. . . . The biblical words of institution declare God's action and invitation. They are set within the context of the Great Thanksgiving. This eucharistic prayer proclaims and celebrates the gracious work of God in creation, redemption, and sanctification. . . . Our worship books provide several options for giving thanks at the table of the Lord. All of them begin with the dialogue of invitation to thanksgiving and conclude with the Lord's Prayer. Most of them include the preface and the Sanctus after the dialogue. Many continue with an evangelical form of the historic prayer after the Sanctus. The full action, from dialogue through the Lord's Prayer, including the proclamation of the words of institution, is called the Great Thanksgiving. Our congregations, synods, and churchwide organization are encouraged to use these patterns of thanksgiving. [43, 43a]

It remains clear that the patterns themselves are diverse, and *Evangelical Lutheran Worship* provides for this diversity. Again, it is useful for us to know a little more about this diversity. Everyone does not have to do the same thing, but thought about what we are doing is a good idea. Sometimes controversy in this area has been based on too little knowledge.

When the Lutheran Reformation occurred, the only practice for words at the table of the Lord, known and available in the Western church, involved the use of the "Roman canon of the mass"—the list of prayers and petitions that followed the preface and the Sanctus in the Western liturgy. For Luther, that list of prayers was filled with images of sacrifice, as if the Lord's supper were something we were giving to God rather than the other way around. The words of the institution of the supper were found among these petitions and prayers, as if it blended in with the language of sacrifice. On the whole, the conservative and pastoral instincts of the Lutheran Reformation were to "retain the mass," but this sacrifice-idea could not be retained. Happily, all of the "canon" was at the time said silently by the priest, so that simply getting rid of it would hardly be noticed by the assembly. However, what Luther *did* want to be noticed by the assembly were the words and promise of Christ. Indeed, he wanted the whole event to be open and audible, bringing to an end what he regarded as the abomination of the priestly silent mass. Luther was reluctant, however, to publish his ideas about doing the liturgy out of a fear that they would be turned into a new law, a new right way simply replacing the old Roman legalism. When he finally did publish liturgical proposals, the remarkable thing was that there were two of them, and they dealt with the question of the words at the table in two different ways. Furthermore, Luther suggested that there should be a *third* way, different yet and undercutting both of his own proposals, a way that should "await its own time." And he quite seriously urged that if anyone could do better in liturgical proposals, his own work should be set aside.

Nonetheless—and predictably, in spite of his reluctance—Luther's proposals did become the guiding patterns of Lutheran liturgical life. In fact in some geographical areas the Lutheran churches tended to follow the first of the two patterns. In other areas the churches followed more closely the second. In the first pattern, the "Formula for Mass and Communion at Wittenberg" *(Formula Missae),* Luther's solution to the problem of the prayer at table was relatively conservative: Instead of dialogue, sung preface, communal or choral Sanctus, silent canon of the mass (including the silently recited words of institution), and then Lord's Prayer, the Lutheran pastor at the mass should engage in the dialogue and sing aloud the preface, with that simple sung thanksgiving prayer then leading directly into the sung words of institution. Then the choir or the assembly would sing the Sanctus and all would join in the Lord's Prayer. The result was a little prayer of thanksgiving, an open and public use of thanksgiving intertwined with an open and public proclamation of the words of institution as the deepest grounds for thanksgiving. It went like this (using the translation style of *Evangelical Lutheran Worship*):

The Lord be with you.
And also with you.
Lift up your hearts.
We lift them to the Lord.
Let us give thanks to the Lord our God.
It is right to give our thanks and praise.
It is indeed right, our duty and our joy, that we should at all times and in all places give thanks and praise to you, almighty and merciful God, through our Savior Jesus Christ, who in the night in which he was betrayed, took bread, and gave thanks, broke it, and gave it to his disciples, saying: Take and eat; this is my body, given for you. Do this for the remembrance of me.
Again after supper, he took the cup, gave thanks, and gave it for all

to drink, saying: This cup is the new covenant in my blood, shed for you and for all people for the forgiveness of sin. Do this for the remembrance of me.

Holy, holy, holy Lord, God of power and might, heaven and earth are full of your glory. Hosanna in the highest. Blessed is he who comes in the name of the Lord. Hosanna in the highest.

Taught by your saving command and guided by divine institution, we make bold to say: *Our Father in heaven, hallowed be your name, your kingdom come, your will be done, on earth as in heaven. Give us today our daily bread. Forgive us our sins as we forgive those who sin against us. Save us from the time of trial and deliver us from evil. For the kingdom, the power, and the glory are yours, now and forever. Amen.*

For Luther in this pattern, the preface, unlike the canon, was not to be thrown out. Its thanksgiving could be based especially in what God had done in Jesus Christ, made most clear by the words of the supper. Then that thanksgiving could lead into the Sanctus as a further act of thanks and praise. The petitions and the prayers of the canon that used to follow the Sanctus could then be replaced simply by the petitions of the Lord's Prayer.

It is this pattern of the "Formula for Mass at Wittenberg" that the churches of North America have largely followed. The North American "Common Service" of the nineteenth century and the many worship books in which it was used and, more recently, both the *Service Book and Hymnal* and *Lutheran Book of Worship*, were all much influenced by it. Other area churches—for example, in Bavaria, Saxony, Sweden, and Finland—have also based their liturgies in this pattern. In its ongoing use, however—and quite in keeping with Luther's own urging—there has been further development. A variety of prefaces marking the different times of the church year have been kept. The preface has been used to lead directly to the Sanctus, as was the ancient, pre-Reformation practice. And other simple or more extended forms of thanksgiving, with fuller biblical reference to all of the acts of God, have come to surround the words of institution after the Sanctus and before the Lord's Prayer. This continuing creation of "evangelical forms of the historic prayer," as *The Use of the Means of Grace* says, happened already in the sixteenth century in Sweden. Lutherans too joined their Lord in giving thanks over the bread and cup and doing this, as he said to do, for the remembrance of him.

The creation of such prayers has continued to happen in many places in the twentieth and the twenty-first centuries—in Lutheran churches in Germany, Scandinavia, Latin America, Africa, and, beginning in the mid-twentieth century, in North America. Partly, that has happened because of Luther's own urging toward continued work on faithful liturgy in new situations. But partly it has been possible because many Lutherans in this ecumenical time have become persuaded that the sacrificial rhetoric of the Roman canon is not the only way available for Christians praying fully at table. Philipp Melanchthon, in the *Apology of the Augsburg Confession* (24:88, 93), had already approvingly quoted and discussed the principal thanksgiving prayer of Eastern Orthodox liturgy (from the "Liturgy of St. John Chrysostom"), but that Greek text did not seem available for use in sixteenth-century Germany, already struggling to figure out what to do with Latin. In the twentieth and twenty-first centuries, however, the old pattern of the Syrian church in Antioch—the very pattern of the "Greek canon" that Chrysostom used and that the Lutheran confessions approved—came to be more widely and ecumenically known. In that pattern, the words of institution are part of the thanksgiving of the prayer, not part of its petitions, the whole follows a trinitarian outline, using biblical language, and the death of Christ is not presented to God as a sacrifice.

Lutherans and many other Christians throughout the world have begun to use this old pattern in the present time, drafting new texts in this tradition. The thanksgivings at the table in *Evangelical Lutheran Worship*, forms I and III–XI, present such texts. In using these texts, North American Lutherans join their full-communion partners and other churches in a highly significant recent development in ecumenical liturgical renewal: the recovery of biblically-based, gospel-centered prayer at the table of the Lord.

The other proposal that Luther made for celebrating the holy supper was called the "German Mass" *(Deutsche Messe)*. Its prayer at table took a more radical turn. Here Luther proposed that after the sermon there should follow a public admonition for those who want to receive communion, based on a paraphrase of the Lord's Prayer. Then the words of institution were to be sung aloud by the pastor, using the same tone that had been used for proclaiming the gospel earlier in the service. Then the sacrament would be elevated before the whole assembly and the distribution of communion would begin, while the "German Sanctus" ("Isaiah in a

Vision Did of Old," #868) would be sung. Indeed, in this pattern several other liturgical songs besides the Sanctus also were replaced by German chorales or hymns. This pattern was widely used in parts of Northern Germany, in Denmark, and in Norway. In the nineteenth century it came to North America, especially with some Norwegian immigrants, and was used in some Norwegian-American hymnals.

But as Luther himself desired, this second pattern, as well as the first one, also underwent development. Already in Luther's Wittenberg it seems that the actual Lord's Prayer was used and sung, not simply a paraphrase of the prayer. It is as if the whole tradition of prayer at the table, in this pattern, is replaced by the words of the prayer that Jesus gave to his disciples. Furthermore, in many of the churches the dialogue and the preface continued to be beloved, while the elevation sometimes slipped away. The result could sometimes be: dialogue, preface, Sanctus, sung Lord's Prayer, sung words of institution, communion. Then, through much discussion, the Lord's Prayer commonly retook its classic place—just before communion, as the preeminent table prayer of Christians, with its petitions for forgiveness and daily bread. This uniquely Lutheran tradition, not much known by any other group, is represented in *Evangelical Lutheran Worship* by form II after the "Holy, holy, holy." Indeed, the Leaders Edition provides, on page 382, a new version of one of the old Lutheran tones for the words of institution, since this pattern reveals itself most clearly when—after the dialogue, preface, and "Holy, holy, holy" are sung—these words too are sung as a celebration and proclamation of the gospel. This German Mass tradition also is carried on in *Evangelical Lutheran Worship* by the availability there of a variety of paraphrases of classic liturgical songs—world-music versions of such texts, as well as English-language versions of old German chorales (#409–411, 868)—that can be used to sing through the Holy Communion pattern for worship. In that regard, too, both the second canticle of praise in Setting Five and the Kyrie, canticle of praise, and Lamb of God of Setting Ten are like the German Mass.

Both traditions are Lutheran. Neither is required. Pastors and congregations are encouraged, however, to think carefully about these traditions, whichever is used. The choice of the one because it is briefer or the other just because it is there or the choice of either because that is what we have always done are not decisions with good reasons. If one of the thanksgivings at the table is used, it will be best if it is proclaimed gracefully, with understanding, and if the presider encourages the participation of the assembly by their attention and their responses. If the words of institution alone are used, after the "Holy, holy, holy" and before the Lord's Prayer, the presiding minister who is able to sing the dialogue and preface is encouraged to sing also the words of institution so that a fully sung, communal celebration of the great thanksgiving may result.

Pastors and congregations who think carefully about this second pattern for the great thanksgiving may well ask whether the use of this pattern has lost the impact of its original idea of surprising people with a public proclamation of the gospel words of Jesus that had previously been silent and secret. And they may consider whether what began as such a public gospel proclamation may be perceived by worshipers today as a kind of formula whereby the pastor "makes holy" the bread and wine over which it is spoken. That holy-formula misperception may be especially difficult to avoid in places where the pattern is further truncated in ways that go well beyond Luther's counsel or Lutheran tradition, where the words of Jesus are recited alone without dialogue, or preface, or "Holy, holy, holy," or singing, or elevation, or even Lord's Prayer.

In any case, our common counsel to one another in *The Use of the Means of Grace* and in the pattern for worship of *Evangelical Lutheran Worship* is to understand that the whole set of words at the table, regardless of the choice we make, are together a great thanksgiving. Indeed, modern biblical exegesis understands the "do this" of the New Testament stories of the Last Supper to include that we are to have a meal, that is, take bread and wine, give thanks at table, and distribute, receive, and consume the gifts, all in remembrance of Jesus (cf. the "entire action of the sacrament" in the Formula of Concord, Solid Declaration 7:84). This thanksgiving is both a public proclamation of what God has done and a humble prayer, begging God for daily bread for all the world, confidently dependent on the promises of God. The genre "thanksgiving" is a mixed thing, neither prayer nor proclamation alone, but both at once, exactly like the biblical psalms or like the great prayer of Nehemiah 9. It is spoken before God and to God, in thanksgiving and in confession of our need and of God's faithfulness, but it is also spoken publicly, to all in assembly, all who will listen, and all the world.

In the great thanksgiving of *Evangelical Lutheran Worship*, the preface, "Holy, holy, holy," and the first part of the thanksgiving at the table, including the words of institution—or, in form II, the preface, "Holy, holy, holy," and the words of institution alone—are especially thankful proclamation and prayerful confession, like Nehemiah 9:5-31. The second part of the great thanksgiving, including the prayer for the Spirit, and the Lord's Prayer—or, in form II, the Lord's Prayer alone—are the humble and confident petition, like Nehemiah 9:32-37. Once again, this will be the clearer if this great thanksgiving is spoken facing the assembly, across the table or at least across the food. Spoken to the wall, any one of these forms can seem like secret words said by the pastor to God alone and can tend to lead us back to ideas of sacrifice. Rather, all the words at the table—thankful proclamation and humble prayer—are meant to be heard openly in the world.

It would be good for local congregations to try both of these patterns, seeking to do them both well, knowing that they are both richly Lutheran, even if they settle most commonly for one or the other. In any case, it is especially important for congregations and pastors to think about their use, understand a little of their history, and consider how their practice today will be perceived. Finally, it is important for Lutherans to avoid excoriating each other about this historic diversity. The diversity itself is as old as Martin Luther's two patterns. He did not want either of those patterns to be made into binding law. That is part of why he made two proposals and suggested a third. On the contrary, he did want faithful work on the liturgy to continue.

Food, Vessels, Linens

Lutheran congregations also sometimes differ in regards to the exact foods to be used at this table. *The Use of the Means of Grace* counsels:

> In accordance with the words of institution, this church uses bread and wine in the celebration of the Lord's Supper. Communicants normally receive both elements, bread and wine, in the Holy Communion. [44]

It further advises:

> A loaf of bread and a chalice are encouraged since they signify the unity which the sacrament bestows. The bread may be leavened or unleavened. The wine may be white or red. . . . The use of

leavened bread is the most ancient attested practice of the Church and gives witness to the connection between the Eucharist and ordinary life. Unleavened bread underscores the Passover themes which are present in the biblical accounts of the Last Supper. [44a, 44b])

The news of this diversity may be surprising in some congregations, but it too is worthy of some thought.

For a long time, Lutheran congregations have been accustomed to the medieval practice of small pieces of wafer-bread—"hosts," to use the medieval sacrificial name—in the Lord's supper. This bread is indeed unleavened, but its use probably began in the Western church in the ninth century, as the idea of the "sacrifice of the mass" was taking hold and as priests read in the Old Testament that unleavened loaves had been the bread used in scriptural sacrifices. Clergy in the ninth century began to be responsible for baking this new kind of unleavened, sacrificial, sacred bread. Lay persons were not allowed to prepare it. In the Eastern churches, however, such unleavened bread and such Old Testament precedents were never used for the eucharist. Indeed, the oldest Christian practice we can discover, in both East and West, is that of using a loaf or more of regular, leavened bread—the kind of loaves people could bake at home or find in the local market—for the Lord's supper. The change came about only in the Western church. Then, in the Reformation and following, the Lutheran churches, evidencing their usual conservatism, simply continued to use what the Western church ordinarily used: unleavened wafer-bread. Among the Lutherans, however—as among some other Christians—the associations were now no longer with the Old Testament bread of sacrifice, an idea that the Lutherans rejected, but with the passover. Jesus' death was at passover. His Last Supper may have been a passover meal. In any case, he himself is for us the Lamb of God. Christians remembered that among the Jews, unleavened bread was used at passover and for seven days thereafter. To use an unleavened bread in holy communion was thought to connect to that passover meaning, perhaps even to make use of something like the very bread that Jesus used.

Still, this wafer-bread was not really much like passover bread. The truth is, wafers probably continued to be used because they were so convenient: they did not easily spoil and they made few crumbs in their use. In the present time, they can be easily ordered by mail in boxes. The problem is that it has become increasingly difficult for ordinary people to recognize them as bread at all, let alone to understand their passover connections. Many people today do recognize *matzo*, but a loaf of that passover bread—a large piece of *matzo*—does not look like our communion hosts. Furthermore, wafer bread is hard for the people of the congregation to actually make. It has to be purchased from a specialty supplier, away from *here*. And even if members of the congregation do understand the passover connection, they may also remember that unleavened bread was only used for eight days a year. The meal with the risen Christ, from the beginning, was intended for every Sunday throughout the year.

Of course, there can be problems with a regular, leavened loaf of bread as well. Unless the right kind of bread is chosen, it can be difficult to break and can make a mess. That mess can also be true of the use of a loaf or more of *matzo*, an alternative some Christians choose in order to make the passover connections clearer in our time. Nonetheless, a loaf of actual bread certainly is more easily understandable by people in the present time. It can indeed stand for the unity we are given in this supper. It can be beautiful and local. It can taste good, like the goodness of God.

Again, while there is no central requirement in Lutheran practice, we ought to think about what we do. The wafer-bread has been used for a long time and for many people is associated with powerful memories of the life-giving and forgiving grace of God. Still, the older Christian practice of leavened bread may be better for us in this time if it can be gently and carefully introduced and taught. People will understand more clearly the connection between Jesus and our bread, Jesus and our world. And the difficulties can be minimized: the right kind of bread can be locally baked or found and used. Recipes exist that produce a tasty, breakable, relatively crumb-free loaf. If nothing else, a loaf or more of *pita*, purchased at the local grocery store, will work wonderfully. The communion practice can be careful, respectful, using a lined basket to catch and protect the crumbs, showing that we all are willing to be like the Syrophoenician woman who treasured the crumbs from the Lord's table. To use such a loaf may be a little harder, but it will be worth it. (See the bibliography for sources of bread recipes.)

There may be similar surprises with the wine. In the ancient and medieval church, the kind of wine that was used was most likely the wine of the region, whatever its type or color. But in the early Lutheran churches, the most common use was white wine. That may have been because white wine was most common in Germany. But it came to be so, even more, because Lutherans wanted to say that Christ truly gives his blood to us, in, with, and under this cup of wine. It is not that the red of the wine makes us *think* of Christ's blood. It is not that this wine is *like* Christ's blood. But this cup of wine *is* Christ's blood. Lutherans used white wine so that we all would see that this shared cup really is wine, not pretend blood. By Christ's word and promise, not by our pretending or thinking, the wine is also his very blood. When Lutherans came to North America, however, they came under the influence of wider Protestant practice as well as the wide availability of Concord grape wine, and they began to use more and more red wine. There is nothing wrong with that, unless the red wine should subtly influence us to think that our symbolizing rather than Christ's promise grounds this meal. It is certainly true, however, that many people in our congregations think that, because of its similarity to blood, one must use red wine in the holy supper. On the other hand, it is also true that many altar guild members and helpers are deeply grateful when they learn that they do not need to wash out red stains from linen any more. Again, while there is no requirement, it may be wiser in the present time to adopt the older Lutheran practice again, at least for the happiness of altar guilds!

It should be said, however, that specialty breads—say, with lots of raisins and nuts—or specialty wines—sparkling wines or rosé—are probably not wise. The bread and wine should be straightforward, simply beautiful and tasty, basic, recognizable human food, but not things that call attention to themselves.

The bigger question in many Lutheran congregations may be what to do about those people who cannot drink wine or eat wheat bread because of their allergies or their situation of recovery from alcoholism. Again, the counsel of *The Use of the Means of Grace* is wise:

> For pressing reasons of health, individuals may commune under one element. In certain circumstances, congregations might de-cide to place small amounts of non-wheat bread or non-alcoholic wine or grape juice on the altar. Such pastoral and congrega-tional decisions are delicate, and must honor both the tradition

of the Church and the people of each local assembly. Some communicants suffer from allergic reactions or are recovering from alcoholism. . . . [I]t is appropriate for them to receive only one of the elements. Their pastor may assure them that the crucified and risen Christ is fully present for them in, with, and under this one element. [44c, 44d]

So a range of responses to this need is envisioned. In some places and with significant support, a person in recovery may be able to include drinking from the chalice within the disciplines of a healthy life. For other persons, this will be simply impossible. They will need to give up the chalice, waiting for Christ's healing at the end, knowing that others drink for them, and trusting that the whole Christ is there for them in the bread. They may even stand before the person ministering the cup and hear "The blood of Christ, shed for you," knowing that this assertion is true, saying "Amen," perhaps even touching or kissing the chalice, though they do not drink. For other persons, consultation with their pastor will lead the congregation to regularly set out a second cup of grape juice or nonalcoholic wine on the table, intended for use in communion by these persons. Similarly, persons with severe gluten allergies may not receive the bread at all or, on conversation with their pastors, may receive a small piece of non-wheat bread that has been placed on the table, carefully out of contact with the rest of the bread. Perhaps one or more of the assembly's ministers—perhaps the presider herself or himself—will sometimes choose also to receive this non-wheat bread or this nonalcoholic wine to indicate the unity of the assembly in our need and in Christ's gift. Those who are ill are not alone. We are sick together.

While this is the range of diversity that *The Use of the Means of Grace* addresses, the diversity in our congregations is often greater yet. Some assemblies regularly have at least two cups at every station for holy communion, one with wine and one with grape juice, giving everybody a choice, even apart from conversation with their pastor. While such choice is common in North American cultures, deriving in part from a consumer way of life, congregations should probably be careful about its use. Here is yet another place we are invited to think. The unity we are given in Christ and our common identity as assembly in the triune God can be obscured by too great an accent on individual consumer choice. Turning the overwhelming gift of God into an occasion for the kind of choice we are used to at a restaurant or in shopping is at least odd. Any change in this practice, however, will be delicate and will need to be accompanied by respect, teaching, and a great deal of love. And the deepest counsel of *The Use of the Means of Grace* remains: "Common mission among the congregations of this church depends on mutual respect for varied practice in many areas of church life . . ." (Principle 38).

Regardless of what bread and wine are used, however, there is one counsel that is important for all of us. All of the food that is needed for this service should be set out on the table for the great thanksgiving, for the thankful proclamation of Christ's promise, and for our prayer. We will consider below what to do if the food runs out, but—to start with, and as far as we can provide—the ordinary practice is to put all of the food there, before the eyes of the assembly. It should not be in some other room, for example. Of course, our Lord and the Holy Spirit may know what bread and wine will be actually used, but the congregation does not know unless they see it, and one should make it clear, from the outset, that there will be enough for all. "This is done," says *The Use of the Means of Grace*, "so that the gathered assembly may see the full sign of the food it is to share, and so that we may give thanks and proclaim God's promise in conjunction with the use of this very bread and wine" (47a). It will be best if this setting out of the food can be relatively simple: a single plate or basket with all of the bread; a single cup (chalice) together with a pitcher (flagon) or pitchers of the needed wine; perhaps a clean folded cloth holding any nongluten bread; perhaps another flagon or cup with a little grape juice. Other vessels needed for communion—more cups, more baskets—can be brought to the table and filled when the communion begins. The little glasses, if used, can be waiting, unfilled, at a place where the communicants who use them can pick them up as they come. But the table can show forth the single, simple, and unifying gift of this food—centered in one loaf, one cup, signing the one Jesus Christ, given and poured out for the life of the world.

Of course, the vessels used in the holy communion also vary among us. The oldest practice, long maintained in Lutheran congregations, is to use a paten or plate for the bread and a chalice or common cup for the wine. If a loaf of bread is to be used, that plate may need to be larger than it has been in the recent past. Patens or plates from earlier in the church's history (say, the sixth or seventh centuries) show, by their size, that they were used to hold large loaves of bread. Or the paten may need to be replaced by a basket, probably lined with a linen cloth. On the other hand, since the beginning of the twentieth century in North America, some congregations have put their chalices away, replacing them with small glasses, held in trays, sometimes pre-filled, sometimes filled at communion by a cup fitted with a pouring lip. This practice has largely come about because of the growth, in some places, of the societal sense that we ought not share drinking vessels. In fact the evidence seems to be that a cup, carefully used, is the more hygienic, least dangerous of the methods of drinking—at least if you think about the many hands that touch the rims of those small glasses in filling and serving them and if you remember that the least hygienic part of each of us in encountering others, the frequent source of passing pathogens, is our hands, not our mouths. But the sense that has led to the change is probably pre-rational, not liable to be easily addressed by such arguments. If a congregation has decided to use the small glasses, the wisest thing will be to use a pouring cup to fill them at communion, after communicants pick one up themselves on the way to the altar. This practice will maintain the symbol of the cup, make the altar less crowded, make caring for what is left over much easier and more reverent, and actually result in a healthier practice than is possible with the pre-filled glasses.

Another practice in some of our congregations that has arisen out of health concerns and has often continued because of convenience is the practice of intinction—dipping the bread in the cup. Although something like this practice—though administered by the priest with a spoon—has become the normative use of Eastern Orthodox Christianity, it is not wise for Lutherans. Lutherans classically accentuate Christ's invitation and command to eat and to drink, and this dipping is unlike either. The meal character of the Lord's supper is minimized by such a practice, and the supper is even further distanced from our ordinary eating and drinking. Even more, intinction is probably less rather than more healthy than ordinary communion methods. Depending on the way it is done, either many hands reach into the cup, often touching the wine, or the communion minister reaches his or her hand into many mouths. Again, congregations need to think about what they are doing. It is at least partly with this practice in mind that

The Use of the Means of Grace says: "Ordinarily the bread is placed in the communicant's hand and the chalice is guided by the communicant or carefully poured by the minister of communion" (45a).

There has also been a great variety of linens and altar paraments used among us. Leaders in a local congregation may want to trace the history of the practice in their own place (old photographs can be wonderfully interesting and liberating!) and, at the same time, seek out wider information about the history of this variety of textile use. Some congregations have the bread and wine of holy communion at the back of the church, on a cloth on a small table, at the start of the service, bringing them to the altar at the time of the setting of the table. Some congregations place the pre-filled glasses on the altar, covered and under a large white cloth. Other congregations place the bread and wine on the credence table or on the altar itself at the start. The cup and plate, in particular, may be covered with a veil. Most congregations spread a "fair linen"—the medieval Christian tablecloth—on the top or *mensa* of the altar. Some also decorate the altar table with a frontal or similar parament in the color of the season. Lutherans do not regulate this variety.

But useful for all of us are two basic cloths. A large, clean "corporal"—a square linen cloth, large enough for a cup and for all of the bread and the wine to be placed upon it—is spread in the middle of the altar-table, toward the side of the table where the presiding minister will stand. It is the basic tablecloth of the meal, whether or not there is a fair linen. It is the "cloth of the body" (hence its name), the ancient Christian means for catching the crumbs of this precious food. Its outlines delineate the food that is set out here, intended for the holy supper. And several large, linen napkins (purificators)—enough for wiping every cup that will be used, enough to line every bread-basket, plus a few more for emergencies—are set in a small stack at the side of the corporal.

With these reflections on our diversities—on tables and altars and vessels and foods and linens and communicants and words at the table—with this invitation to think about what we are doing, we may be ready to think through some more of the details of the event itself.

Meal: Offering and Setting the Table

As the peace concludes, the assembly is seated. Then two things happen simultaneously: a collection is taken for the mission of the church, including the care of those in need, and the table is set for the celebration of the holy communion. The collection is taken here largely because it came to be associated with going to communion: if God so graciously feeds us, in word and sacrament, we in response should turn toward the needs of our neighbor. We have prayed in faith for those needs. Now we share something of what we have. This is a time in which the good things of the earth, the resources that God has made for the life of all, are celebrated, set out, and shared. Another option might be to take such a collection after we have gone to communion and as we leave the church, in the place indicated by Justin Martyr's second-century report. But we are not used to that placement and could find it confusing. Furthermore, there is a truth in associating the bread and wine of the earth and of human culture, bread and wine that God uses to feed us with the body and blood of Jesus Christ, with the resources of the earth and of our work intended for the church's mission as body of Christ to our neighbors.

We might think carefully about how we can counter the possibility for misperception of the role of this collection. Placed here and called an offering, this action might seem to some as if first we give payment to God and then we receive the communion, like a current enacting of that old malformation of religion: *do ut des;* "I give to you, whatever deity you are, that you may be obligated to give to me." No. We must not mean that by our actions here. We have nothing to give anyway except what God has given us. We have learned again, in listening to the word of God, that we are beggars, side by side with all the beggars of the world. The notes say helpfully:

Actions and accompanying words and music that emphasize a humble and grateful response to all God's gifts will help avoid any sense of transaction or exchange. [LE, 21]

Except, of course, the exchange that Luther and his Augustinian tradition called the "happy exchange," the "wonderful commerce," the *admirabile commercium:* God gives to us so that we may, in turn, give freely to others. What we do here should mean exactly the *opposite* of "we give so God is obligated to us." The whole event of this word and sacrament service, including this simultaneous offering and table setting, is intended to bring us again to see God's great mercy and to turn us therefore toward the world in all its need. What we sing and say here will help bring that to expression.

Congregations have often worked out their own ways of receiving gifts of money, food, and other material goods. Ushers pass baskets or offering plates. Perhaps, if food is regularly brought, a great basket is available at the rear of the church. Some congregations invite people to come in a procession from their places, bringing their gifts. Whatever is done should be done simply, straightforwardly, avoiding ostentation and avoiding making anyone feel ashamed. Still, this collection belongs in our service. Communion is not only about something that is given to us, but about God continually forming us in giving toward our neighbor.

Assembly song during the offering begins with music that has a *partnership* aspect, joining song to the actions of those who bring gifts of bread, wine, and money. The assembly joins in the offering of gifts by thanking God in song for all the gifts presented during this time.

The gathering of the gifts can be a time for offering choral or instrumental music as well. This too is an offering of gifts, a partnership of sorts, as musical gifts are offered to the assembly while other gifts are being received. A choral or instrumental offering need not preclude the assembly's song either. Assembly singing as the gifts are gathered gives a musical reinforcement to the corporate action of giving.

While the collection is being taken, the altar or table is also being set. One or more assisting ministers rise from their place and come to the table. He or she or they unveil the communion vessels, if they are veiled, spread the corporal on the altar-table, and set out on the corporal one cup, put next to the corporal the needed purificators, and, if there is an altar book, see that it is opened to the right page. If the bread and wine needed for communion are also placed near the altar, on a credence table, he or she or they also set all the needed food on the corporal. The presiding minister may also help with this table-setting, but there is something good about assisting ministers — lay people of the congregation — having charge of the table here. The task might ordinarily belong to the person who functions as principal assisting minister: the person, for example, who prays the prayers of intercession and speaks the dismissal. Figure 8.1 shows how the ordinary arrangement on the corporal might look after the table is set.

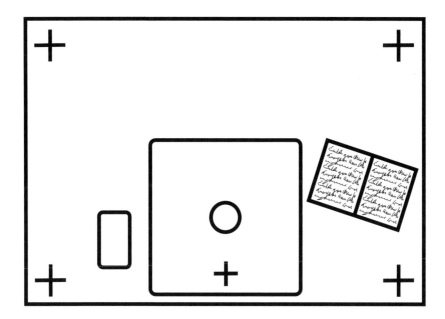

Fig. 8.1. Table set with corporal, book, purificators, and one chalice, awaiting the bread and wine.

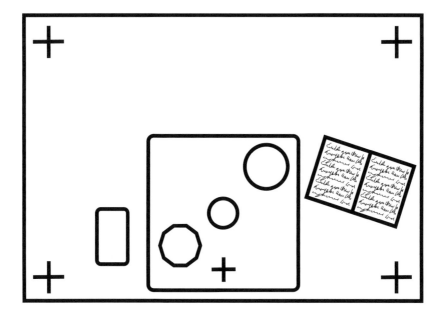

Fig. 8.2. Table set, complete with bread and wine.

If the bread and wine are also already present—or after they have been brought to the table when the gifts of money and other material goods are brought forward—the arrangement might appear as in Figure 8.2.

Of course, all of this table-setting may have already occurred before the service began. Such a practice is also possible. But having before us an empty table, waiting for the supper of the Lord, as we are listening to the word of God, can heighten our sense of expectation. Then having that supper set out in fullness and clarity, followed by us being sent away in faith and service, can help make clear the supper's purpose. In fact, an empty, waiting table, used for no other purpose than the holy communion—not as a shelf for books or flowers, not as a prayer center—can be one of the remarkable symbols of Christianity.

After the offering has been collected, the assembly stands, presenting themselves as well as whatever they have given. Ushers or other lay persons bring forward the collected gifts. They also may bring forward the bread and wine needed for the communion, if these have been set at the rear of the church. All of these, including ourselves and our bodies, are the good things of the earth that God has made and given to be shared. The assisting minister or ministers receive these gifts. As much of the bread and wine as is needed is placed on the corporal. Baskets of food may be placed near the table, perhaps on the floor. The gifts of money may be placed on the side table. All of this is done simply. Any gestures of "offering," of lifting up of the gifts in the air or toward the east wall, would seem to be inconsistent with the spirit of humble response at this moment. Either at this time or after the praying of an offering prayer, the cup may be poured full and the bread may be uncovered or, if it is wafer-bread, taken in sufficient quantity from its vessel (a basket or a pyx or a ciborium) and placed upon the plate. Either an assisting minister or the presiding minister may do this pouring and uncovering.

All of these simultaneous actions are frequently interpreted by music and can be finally interpreted by an offering prayer. The Notes on the Services (LE, 22) make clear the variety of options for the music. A hymn, choral music, instrumental music, a choral setting of a general or seasonal offering song, or one of the old, communal offertories (#181–188), alone or in various combinations, are all welcome. The point is that the music will aim to bring to expression the meaning of the collection and of the setting of the table: the goodness of God in creation; our thankful response to the unearned grace of God; our prayer that God will enable us to make that response in our daily life and work. The old offertory songs can help us to see the point. There is a certain crisis here. We have nothing to give to God except our need and our hopes ("Create in me a clean heart, O God. . ."; "Gather the hopes and dreams of all . . ."), yet we try to make a humble gesture of giving. God, who has given the fruitful vineyards and fields, gives yet more—the bread of life, the joy of salvation, the body and blood of Christ, a foretaste of the all-healing feast—and so turns our giving toward other people, who also have broken hearts and needs and hopes and dreams.

After the offering has been gathered and brought forward and after the table has been set, an assisting minister may pray one of the offering prayers. There may be good reasons not to use prayer here at all: the offering and table-setting actions may have been interpreted enough by the music; silence may be the best interpretation; and the great thanksgiving, remembering God's mercy, is a further interpretation; we do not need to duplicate prayers.

On the other hand, there also may be good reasons to use one of these prayers: many of our congregations are accustomed to a prayer here and, especially, these particular prayers—the three in place in the settings and the six on page 64 (LE, 138–139)—are remarkably well-crafted to say what needs to be said. They articulate in both eloquence and humility a Lutheran doctrine of creation, redemption, and vocation that both expresses and responds to the crisis of the offertory. If one of these prayers is used, it is prayed by an assisting minister standing at the table, perhaps the principal assisting minister of the service. The assisting minister may extend her or his hands in the *orans* position (see p. 177). It is not usually prayed by the presiding minister, who will proclaim the great thanksgiving, nor by the whole assembly. This last suggestion may take a little learning in congregations that have been used to the practice of communally praying the similar prayer in *Lutheran Book of Worship*. In *Evangelical Lutheran Worship*, this collect-like prayer—similar to the prayer of the day and the prayer after communion—is best heard by the assembly, proclaimed by a single voice, so that, having heard the careful articulation of this complex but brief petition, the whole assembly may then assent with its amen. Putting such prayers in the mouth of the whole assembly—especially when they are new texts and there are nine options (including the three printed in all settings in LE and Settings One and Two in AE)—is not a particularly good idea. If another prayer than one of these nine is used, it too should bring something of the same ideas to expression.

Meal: Great Thanksgiving

If the presiding minister has not been at the table, she or he now comes there. If the cup has not yet been poured or if the bread has not yet been uncovered, she or he does these things as well. She or he also checks to see that the book is open to the appropriate page and at a place where it can be easily seen. In some assemblies, an assisting minister may hold the book for the presider and may care for the turning of the pages. The presiding minister should also find the right place to stand. If it is behind the table facing the assembly, then that place may also be centered, but at a little distance from the table—a step back—with the intention of creating the gracious sense that all are welcome here, that the presider is standing as part of a circle around this table, welcoming others to the food. Then, standing and facing the assembly, the presiding minister begins the great thanksgiving. A musician may first give an intonation—the first note or the first three notes of the salutation—if the dialogue and the preface are to be sung. And the presiding minister begins.

The role of assembly song here is *dialogue*, as the presiding minister and assembly share in giving thanks at the table. Following the presider's exhortation, "Lift up your hearts," the assembly responds, "We lift them to the Lord." The presider continues, "Let us give thanks to the Lord our God"; the assembly responds, "It is right to give our thanks and praise." This extended dialogue carries the thanksgiving prayer into the preface, sung by the presiding minister.

The structure of the great thanksgiving is simple and always the same, even though some of the words themselves may differ. The presiding minister who invests the time to learn this structure by heart, learning even some of the words by heart, will find that he or she is able to lead the assembly in this proclamation and prayer with ease and grace. First there is the dialogue itself, with the assembly answering. Then there is the preface. Then, usually, the assembly sings the "Holy, holy, holy"—the Sanctus. Then there is one of the thanksgivings at the table, including the words of institution and several assembly responses, or there are simply the words of institution. Then the assembly prays the Lord's Prayer.

The *dialogue* itself, one of the most ancient and widespread texts in Christian use, consists of the three exchanges. The first enacts, for only the second time in the service, an important greeting between the presiding minister and the assembly. The service began with the apostolic greeting before the prayer of the day. Now the greeting is done in simpler words, words like those with which the angel Gabriel greeted Mary in the Gospel of Luke. Again, the assembly is invited to know of the presence of the risen Christ, in whom they are gathered, who they encountered in the word. The presider is similarly invited, the assurance of Christ's presence being the very grounds on which we can continue at all, the grounds on which the assembly once again asks this pastor to be their presider. The presiding minister then calls upon the assembly to "lift up" their hearts, in which "up" functions as a metaphor for the place where God is. The response of the assembly is a gentle correction: our hearts are there where the risen Christ is—the "Lord" of these first two phrases being the risen Lord. Because of Christ, present here, we can be with God. That is up enough for us. Only then are we all invited to give thanks to God—now the "Lord," in a wonderful layering of meaning, is probably the Father or God as God or the triune God—and we boldly answer that it is right to do so. We have nothing but thanks to bring. Standing with Christ, enlivened by the Spirit poured out from his death and resurrection, we begin to do so.

This ancient Christian dialogue leads directly to the *preface*. The word "preface" can mislead us. This text is the thing itself, the beginning of the thanksgiving at table. It is not like the preface of the book, a little essay on what we are about to do. In fact, preface in this case is an English version of the Latin word *praefatio*, which could be translated as "proclamation," "public speech," "declaration." We might interpret the old latinate word as "initial thanksgiving" or "beginning proclamation of God's mercy." With the preface, we do indeed begin to give thanks, that is to say, we begin to publicly proclaim the merciful and saving acts of God. *Evangelical Lutheran Worship* provides fourteen prefaces—translations and adaptations of old Western Christian texts— all reprinted in each of the ten settings of Holy Communion as these are presented in the Leaders Edition. Which preface is to be used is indicated in the propers of the day. The music for the prefaces, itself of ancient origin, is included in Settings One through Five and in Setting Nine. The texts themselves begin the thanksgiving to God through

Jesus Christ, with an initial recounting or public proclamation of the reasons for doing so.

The "Holy, holy, holy" continues this praise and thanks, now with the whole assembly joining in. The preface brought us to see that even our feeble gestures of thanksgiving are being joined to the praises of all the angels, all the cosmos, and all the church of every time and place. It follows that this text leads us into singing before God in the words of a biblical text for that song, especially the cry of the seraphim in Isaiah 6, but also that of the four living creatures in Revelation 4. With the church's version of these biblical words in our mouths, we find ourselves before the awesome presence of the holy and triune God—the "Thrice Holy One," to use an ancient name. This place of our table has a cosmic location, before the face of God. But then, in one of the unique turns of Christian liturgy, a further biblical text is added. We add the words of Psalm 118—the words the gospels use at the entrance of Jesus into Jerusalem on Palm Sunday—singing of the blessed coming one. We mean Jesus. We mean his coming among us in the world, his death and resurrection and the gift of his presence here. The awesome Holy One remains awesome, terrible, but Jesus Christ comes in God's name, is the Holy One come among us with mercy and self-giving. This table proclaims that coming. Because of his presence, we are able to cry out our need for God to save us: "Hosanna in the highest," that is, "Save now, O high God, save us, save all things!" Thus, the dialogue and preface complete, the presider and assembly join in a song of *unity*, singing the thanksgiving with one voice. Song surrounds the meal's preparation. The scriptural words, the presider's actions, and the liturgical song combine to form the thanksgiving at the table. Actions combined with scriptural words are essential to Luther's understanding of sacramental presence in the meal. Through engagement with song, the entire assembly joins in this thanksgiving. The meal's preparation is thus truly a work of all the gathered community.

Then the presiding minister begins one of the forms for the "thanksgiving at the table," continuing the thanksgiving by proclaiming what God has done in creation and redemption, especially as this is summed up in Jesus and in his words at the supper. It would be good for the presider to study the words of these alternate texts, knowing the diverse forms. Forms I through IV are printed out in full in Settings One and Two in *Evangelical Lutheran Worship*. The other forms are in

Evangelical Lutheran Worship at pages 65–70 (AE). If one of the forms is being used that calls for diverse responses by the assembly, then the assembly should be helped—for example, by a reference in the bulletin or by an announcement before the service begins—to find the needed page. Some of the settings provide assembly music for some of these responses. All eleven of the forms are printed in full within each of the settings in the Leaders Edition.

Form I is a new adaptation of the prayer that first appeared in *Service Book and Hymnal,* 1958, and then again appeared, as prayer III, in *Lutheran Book of Worship*, 1978. Of this prayer, largely drafted in the mid-twentieth century from ancient Christian sources, the French liturgical scholar Louis Bouyer said, "It would be hard to be more ecumenical! But all of these elements, chosen with great discernment, have been molded into a composition that is as moderate as it is natural. In its brief simplicity this prayer has a concise fullness that we are not accustomed to seeing except in Christian antiquity" (*Eucharist;* University of Notre Dame Press, 1968; 441). This prayer represents a continuity between *Service Book and Hymnal, Lutheran Book of Worship*, and *Evangelical Lutheran Worship*.

Form II is simply the words of institution, in the version in which they are used in *Evangelical Lutheran Worship* as well as *Lutheran Book of Worship*, proclaimed as the gift and promise of God, as the deep ground of our thanksgiving. The music for singing this form, as discussed earlier, is at page 382 of the Leaders Edition.

Forms III and IV represent brief thanksgivings, newly drafted for *Evangelical Lutheran Worship*, intended to bring to expression the themes of the two most basic festival cycles of the church year: the Christmas cycle, Advent through Epiphany, and the Easter cycle, Lent through Pentecost. When a presiding minister grows accustomed to these forms and their simple rhetoric, she or he might draw upon the actual lectionary texts of the Sunday being observed to add a line or two to the sections of the proclamation that begin "Blessed are you for/in. . ." or "Praise to you for. . ." The final paragraph of Form IV includes the optional possibility including the name or names of historic witnesses to the Christian faith—perhaps the names of people commemorated in the week following this Sunday (see the Calendar, AE pp. 15–17).

Form V had its origin in the *Occasional Services* of 1982, a companion book to *Lutheran Book of Worship*, as a thanksgiving to be used in the homes of the sick, in hospitals, and in prisons. It was found in that book's "Celebration of Holy Communion with Those in Special Circumstances" (p. 84). The prayer for the Spirit in this version of that thanksgiving has been drawn from a post-communion prayer that had wide use in many Lutheran books in the twentieth century, itself a translation of the old Latin post-communion prayer of Easter. Form V is marked by brevity and simple language for the compassion and healing action of God. It might provide a good text for a beginning use of fuller thanksgivings at the table in congregations that are not used to this practice.

Form VI is rooted in prayers I and II of the *Lutheran Book of Worship*, combining much of their language and making use of their congregational responses. To many congregations, it will be a recognizable and welcoming prayer.

Form VII is drawn from *With One Voice* (it was Prayer V in the leaders edition of that worship supplement). With its use of the elements of earth, air, fire, and water, this thanksgiving celebrates God's gifts in creation. With its fresh language for our need and for God's action in Christ, this form invites us to a new honesty, vigor, and beauty in our words at the table.

Form VIII was first made widely available in *This Far By Faith: An African American Resource for Worship* (1999). It reflects the language of the hymn "Lift Every Voice and Sing" (#841) by James Weldon Johnson, sometimes called the "Black National Anthem." Remembering the suffering ones of all the world, it gathers that memory into a proclamation of the story of the biblical God: "The cry of the poor has become your own cry."

Form IX was prepared as part of the *Evangelical Lutheran Worship* process, though first published, in a slightly different form, in a service of Holy Communion intended for evening, called *Unfailing Light* (GIA Publications, 2004). Music for its responses is available in that resource. It is made up of very brief and evocative phrases, in transparent, even crystalline language. Because of that deceptively simple structure, however, it calls for a presider to practice its use so that its proclamation flows with grace, slowly but also connectedly.

Form X first appeared on the ELCA Web site after the events of September 11, 2001, as a thanksgiving at the table in a time of lament and communal need. Its use of biblical language juxtaposed to human sorrow continues to recommend it for such times, but also for Advent,

Lent, and other times. If a congregation chooses to make the amen responses indicated by the brackets, no further invitation is needed than the words of the presiding minister. The assembly using this prayer will quickly learn to "cry out," "shout," and "plead."

Form XI is a current Lutheran translation of one of the first Christian thanksgivings at table of which we possess a text: the possible third- or fourth-century table prayer found in the ancient Christian church order called *The Apostolic Tradition,* attributed to Hippolytus of Rome. This translation first appeared as prayer IV in *Lutheran Book of Worship* [Ministers Edition, 226] and is only slightly emended here. If this form is used, it can follow immediately upon the dialogue, with the preface and the Sanctus omitted. Such would have been the form of the prayer when it was first used.

It should be noticed that Form I and Forms III–XI all follow a historic form, characteristic of the Antiochan pattern discussed above: the thanksgiving proclamation of the preface and Sanctus is continued, culminating in the proclamation of the gift and promise of Jesus in the words of institution. Then, as those words command, Jesus' death and resurrection are explicitly remembered in a thankful *anamnesis.* Only then does the thanksgiving and proclamation turn to petition and prayer. The turn from public thanksgiving to beseeching prayer can be seen clearly in each of these forms. The assembly prays for the presence and gift of the Spirit, an *epiclesis.* Other prayers for unity and life may then be added. There follows a final doxology and a great amen by the assembly.

Besides these forms, other texts are available in the family of resources around *Evangelical Lutheran Worship*, in print and electronic forms. Lutheran congregations and pastors may also choose to use yet other texts — those published in earlier worship books, those present in provisional materials of the Renewing Worship project, those used by full-communion partners. Helpful guidelines in choosing such texts will include looking for this same trinitarian outline of the thanksgiving, seeking a fresh use of biblical language, and making sure that the text does not deal with the supper as a thing we offer or sacrifice to God.

As *Evangelical Lutheran Worship* thanksgivings at the table are used in local assemblies, it will be wise to consider one form for a season or for at least several Sundays, allowing both presiding minister and assembly to listen to the text and grow accustomed to its use.

When the presiding minister and the assembly, in dialogue, have completed one of these forms, the great thanksgiving is brought to an end by the communal use of the Lord's Prayer. It is as if we have prayed "not as we ought but as we are able" (Form I). But then we come to silence and say again to the risen Christ, through whom we always pray, "Lord, teach us to pray." In the end, by God's great mercy, we are given the words with which to stand before God. The Lord's Prayer functions in many places in the Christian community. But with its petitions for the coming of God's reign and, at the same time, for bread and forgiveness now, it has also been the most traditional prayer before communion used by all the Christian community. The presider may introduce the prayer with one of the introductory sentences printed in the Leaders Edition. Or he or she may simply begin. The Lord's Prayer may be sung. One sung version is found on page 163 of *Evangelical Lutheran Worship*, in Setting Five. With the amen of this prayer, the great thanksgiving is concluded.

Ordinarily, a single person leads this entire great thanksgiving: the presiding minister of this service. Even though the great thanksgiving is made up of several parts, it is not usually wise to split up the leadership of these parts. Such splitting does not help us to see the unity of the whole event. The more important communal sharing in the text is the sharing that a thoughtful presider enables as she or he encourages and invites the participation of the assembly—in responding words, in song, in heart-deep attention, perhaps even in gesture. On the whole, Lutheran congregations and pastors do not participate in "concelebration"—that is, in thanksgiving at the table in which several pastors take different parts of the text and in which the most central parts are recited in choric speech. One presider is enough. Even in ecumenical events, it is wiser for the host pastor to stand aside and yield the leadership at the table to the visiting, ecumenical guest. Furthermore, the accent on one presider leading a participating assembly should not lead to the idea that the whole assembly should recite parts of the great thanksgiving in choric speech. Much of the thanksgiving at table is proclamation, and it is better for us as an assembly to hear the gift of God proclaimed to us—a gift from outside of ourselves to which we then assent in faith. In Christian liturgy, such central proclamation is principally entrusted to our called pastor.

The posture of the assembly through the entire great thanksgiving is standing. It is important that the presiding minister and the assembly, who are in dialogue throughout this Thanksgiving, have the same posture. Furthermore, standing is the posture of the resurrection: Christ has pulled us up together out of death. No wonder that ancient Christian teachers and old conciliar canons, including the resolutions of the Council of Nicaea in the fourth century, forbade kneeling or prostrations on Sunday, the day of the resurrection.

There is a great diversity of practice among us about gestures that may be made during the proclamation of the great thanksgiving. Some presiders make no gestures. Others have an extensive and elaborate repertoire of body postures and hand motions or "manual acts." In other places, members of the congregation join in the *orans* posture during some or all of the great thanksgiving. The habits of pastors

Fig. 8.3: Gesture at great thanksgiving. *The presiding minister may again assume the posture of the apostolic greeting when announcing the opening words of the dialogue: "The Lord be with you." The gesture needs to be visible over the height of the table.*

frequently can be traced to their own seminary formation or to their geographical origins.

But here is one simple way that might be considered by presiding ministers. All of the following gestures will work most clearly and beautifully if the presider has nothing in his or her hands. The book should be on the table or held by an assisting minister. Many of the words involved can be learned by heart. The great thanksgiving begins. The presiding minister may make the greeting gesture (Fig. 8.3), the same gesture used at the greeting with which the service began, when speaking the first words of the dialogue, "The Lord be with you."

As the people respond, the presiding minister may bow toward them, acknowledging their greeting in reply. Then the presider may

Fig. 8.4. Presider acknowledges the assembly's greeting. *As the assembly responds "And also with you," the presiding minister may bow toward them, then, while speaking the following two lines of the dialogue, hold her or his hands, one resting on the other, before the chest.*

Fig. 8.5. Orans posture. *This ancient posture may be used again by the presiding minister during the remainder of the great thanksgiving, including the Lord's Prayer.*

simply hold his or her hands, resting one in the other before the chest, (Fig. 8.4) as she or he speaks the next two lines of the dialogue.

At the beginning of the preface, the presider then assumes the *orans* posture (Fig. 8.5).

This *orans* posture is then the basic posture for all of the rest of the great thanksgiving, including the Lord's Prayer. If that is experienced as too long or too difficult, the hands might be dropped to the rest position during the "Holy, holy, holy" or during other congregational responses. If the bread and wine on the table are clearly visible to everyone in the assembly, they do not need to be handled. Our touch does not make them the body and blood of Christ. The presiding minister may continue to stand in the *orans* posture also through the words of institution. On the other hand, as in most cases in our church buildings, if the bread and wine are not clearly visible, then they may be raised up to be shown to the assembly, in visible association with the word of Jesus Christ. The presiding minister may step forward slightly and pick them up—first the loaf or the basket or paten with all the bread, then the cup containing wine—as each of the words of Jesus are proclaimed in turn. The bread basket or plate may be lifted to about the middle of the presider's chest, not obscuring his or her face. If wafer bread is used, it is good if at least one of the wafers is slightly larger than the others. This larger wafer may be held up by two fingers above the

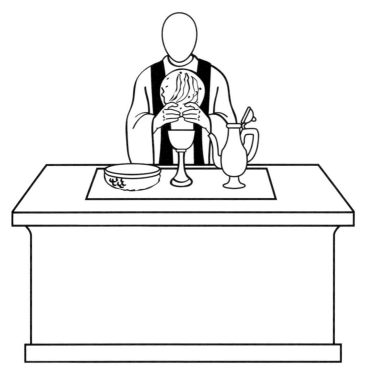

Fig. 8.6. Presenting the bread. *The presiding minister may raise the loaf for all to see.*

paten, while the paten rests on the two open hands. If a single loaf of bread is used, the loaf itself may be held up (Fig. 8.6) for all to see.

The bread should be held peacefully and still, presented to be seen, though the presider may also turn in a single gesture of turning, if that is necessary for people to see. No breaking of the bread occurs here. We are proclaiming Jesus' promise and word, not miming his actions. There need be no pause or further gesture between these words about bread and wine. No manual signs of the cross are needed. The

Fig. 8.7. Raising the cup. *The presiding minister may hold up the cup for all in the assembly to see.*

presiding minister then may pick up the cup, holding it with one hand and resting it on the other (Fig. 8.7), as she or he proclaims the word regarding the cup.

Again, the cup should be held still, peacefully supported to be seen, and, if needed, the presider may make a single gesture of turning to further show the cup. If there is more wine in a pitcher or flagon sitting on the corporal and intended for this communion, this vessel or vessels do not need to be touched. The setting out of the food on the corporal already shows the assembly which food is intended for use here in connection with Christ's promise. When the cup has been replaced, the presiding minister, stepping back again slightly, resumes the *orans* posture (Fig. 8.5 or 8.8), maintaining it through the rest of the thanksgiving at the table and through the Lord's Prayer. No gesture is needed at the prayer for the Holy Spirit. At the amen at the end of the Lord's Prayer, the presider joins his or her hands and then proceeds to prepare for communion.

Fig. 8.8. Orans posture again. *After lowering the raised cup, the presiding minister may assume the orans position for the rest of the thanksgiving at the table and through the Lord's Prayer.*

That description provides one possible, basic model for gestures. It is not required. It is only one simple way. Even within this model there may be variations. At the second line of the dialogue, "Lift up your hearts," some presiders may choose to raise their open hands upward, as if beginning to assume the *orans* posture, returning their hands to a position of rest as the assembly responds and keeping that position of rest through the next exchange. At the "Holy, holy, holy," some presiders may bow deeply at the words from Isaiah 6 and then stand upright again, perhaps making the sign of the cross on her or his body at the words, "Blessed is he who comes in the name of the Lord." This gesture will be the more meaningful if other people standing around the table also make it, if the congregation is used to it, and if its meaning—awe before God's face, then the Christological interpretation of Psalm 118:26—has been taught. Other presiders, following Luther's proposal, may elevate the bread and wine for the assembly to see at the "Holy, holy, holy" and not at the words of institution. On the other hand, some presiders raise up the bread and the cup at the words of institution and then again, side by side or one above the other, at the time of the doxology at the end of the thanksgiving at the table, giving visible accent to the sense that our prayer and praise are all through Jesus Christ, whose presence is signed by this food that he gives us. Still, whatever is done should be thought about, with a concern for how the gestures communicate the meaning of the holy supper.

If, however, the Lord's supper is being celebrated in a church building with the altar against the wall, these proposals will need to be modified yet further. One old practice in Lutheran use was that the presiding minister turned toward the assembly for the dialogue, knowing its words by heart, then turned back toward the altar and the wall for the preface and the rest of the great thanksgiving, lifting up the bread and cup above his or her head—either after each of the words of Jesus or at the doxology or at both places—so that they could be seen by the assembly. Unfortunately, this practice will continue to communicate an air of secrecy and the elevations will too easily be understood as gestures of offering. Another possibility is that the presider faces the wall for the great thanksgiving after the dialogue, except that at the words of Jesus, he or she turns toward the assembly twice, first with the bread and then with the cup in hand, showing these foods as he or she proclaims the words of Jesus, also knowing these words by heart. The problem with this solution is that it breaks the unitary great thanksgiving into fragments. Other proposals have the presiding minister facing the assembly for the great thanksgiving and only turning back toward the altar to get the food when it is mentioned. The resultant table-prayer, with the leader's back turned toward the food—indeed, with his or her back turned toward the gift of Christ—seems odd, even jarring, as if the physical food did not matter.

Short of actually providing a freestanding table, the most creative solution seems to be the following: The altar against the wall is set for the holy communion. Several assisting ministers then join the presiding minister at the altar. One takes the breadbasket. One takes the cup and the flagon. All of the food is so held. Another assisting minister takes the book. They all turn toward the assembly, the assisting ministers flanking the presiding minister, as shown in Figure 8.9. The presiding

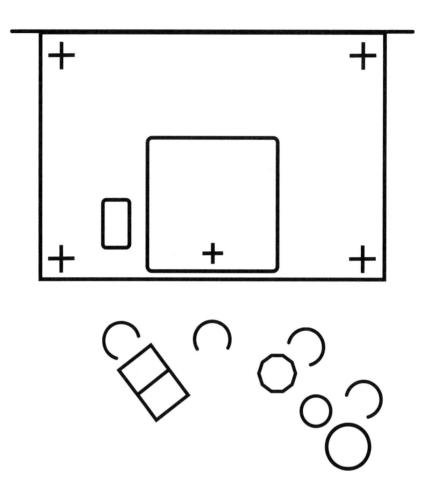

Fig. 8.9. Great Thanksgiving when the altar is against the wall. *The presiding minister and one or more assisting ministers take the bread, the wine, and the book from the altar, turn, and present them to the assembly.*

minister then leads the great thanksgiving, from the dialogue through the Lord's Prayer, facing the people, with hands free and with the book held by an assisting minister where she or he can see it. If desired, the gestures outlined above can be made. Or, if needed, the assisting minister holding the bread can raise it slightly during the proclamation of the word of Jesus about the bread. The assisting minister holding the cup can do the same at the word about the cup. When the Lord's Prayer is finished, all of these vessels are replaced on the corporal.

In whatever way these words at the table are proclaimed, the assembly then proceeds to the communion.

Meal: Communion

The presiding minister now may speak one of the invitations to the table, both of them drawn from biblical texts: Psalm 34:8 (cf. 1 Peter 2:3) or Luke 14:17. Another invitation may be used as well, perhaps one in the tradition of the local congregation. The assembly is then seated. If loaf bread is being used, it may now begin to be broken. Such other vessels as are needed for communion—additional baskets for the bread or additional cups for the wine—are now brought to the table. The wine may be poured into these cups and the bread broken into these baskets. Some congregations have the ministers of communion break all the bread into fragments for communion at this time. Others only break the loaves into such larger pieces as are needed for each basket. If wafer-bread is used, it does not need to be broken at all. Then the baskets and the cups are placed into the hands of the communion ministers. It is a good idea to have several ministers of communion, most of whom can be lay people from the congregation. The Notes on the Services say:

> Having a sufficient number of communion ministers reinforces the sense that the assembly is communing together. Even when the assembly is small, having at least one assisting minister is helpful. [LE, 23]

Usually, the presiding minister is among these communion ministers, serving the bread. In any case, she or he oversees the process of communion, caring for the well-being of the assembly. It would be good for all of the communion ministers to have spent some time together in one or more training sessions, thinking about the importance of their ministry and practicing the manner of communion in this assembly.

While the final preparations are made for the communion, the communion song may begin. The first song during these preparations and at the beginning of communion has traditionally been "Lamb of God." Echoing both John 1:29 and Revelation 5:6, this song addresses the risen Christ giving himself away at this table as the true Lamb. See below and see the Notes on the Services (24) for further suggestions about communion song.

When the vessels are in the hands of the communion ministers, the communion itself begins. We have already discussed several of the diverse patterns and practices possible for the administration of communion. Whether the practices of this assembly include kneeling or standing, communion station or altar rail, continuous procession or dismissal by group, some matters involved in communion are common to all of us. Echoing *The Use of the Means of Grace* (45a), the Notes on the Services say:

> Ministers with the bread ordinarily place it in the person's cupped hands. Ministers with the cup present it in such a way that people may naturally guide it to their mouths. [LE, 23]

Thus, if loaf bread is used and the loaf has not yet been broken into small fragments, the communion minister who serves the bread must hold the bread above the basket, holding that basket by the same hand that holds the bread and using the other hand to break off one appropriately sized fragment after another to place into each communicant's open hands. Careful practice with this gesture can lead to a gracious confidence and a care against scattering crumbs on the floor. Similarly, the minister of the chalice will usually hold the middle or node of the chalice stem by one hand, presenting the cup near the person's mouth and allowing the communicant to tip the chalice to his or her lips by holding on to its base. Then the communion minister uses the purificator, held in the other hand, to wipe the outside and the inside of the lip of the chalice while, at the same time, rotating the cup to present it to the next communicant. In assemblies using small glasses, the minister with the cup must pour carefully into the small glass, afterward touching the spout of the chalice with the purificator to catch any stray drops. Sometimes this works best if the hand holding the purificator is placed gently underneath the hand of the communicant holding the small glass, in order to steady the glass and have some gracious contact with the communicant. While these gestures are occurring, the words of the communion—"The body of Christ, given for you" or "The blood of Christ, shed for you"—are spoken by the communion minister to each person. And each person may respond "Amen" to each of these words and to the gift itself.

But it is never quite so simple. Communion ministers must be prepared to graciously respond if someone does not hold out his or her hands for the bread or does not touch or guide the cup or, on the contrary, seems to wish to take the cup into his or her own hands. Sometimes the bread must be placed in the communicant's mouth, the cup must be gently tipped without assistance to the communicant's lips, or the cup must be briefly surrendered into the communicant's hands. Sometimes, even if it is not the regular practice of the assembly, the cup must be so held that a communicant may dip the bread. Furthermore, the communion ministers need to be prepared to respond graciously to someone who stands or kneels before them and is not communing. If a child who is not yet communing is there, it is probably wisest that the minister of the bread—usually the presiding minister—will speak a blessing, while touching this child's head (perhaps these or similar words: "May Jesus Christ hold you forever in grace and love"). If the communion minister does not know whether the child communes, it is gracious simply to ask an accompanying adult ("Does your child commune?"). Some ecumenical guests, indicating that they are not communing with arms crossed over their breast, might be similarly blessed (perhaps: "Almighty God bless you and, by the Spirit, bring us to unity in Christ"). The minister of the cup, then, needs to note the persons who have been so blessed in order not to present the cup to them. On the other hand, some people who can receive communion in only one kind may still need to hear the promise of the other gift—as discussed above—even though they do not eat or drink that gift. The body and blood of Christ *is* given and shed for them. Or the communicant who is receiving nonwheat bread or nonalcoholic wine will need the communion minister to know this and to be able to get this food from the altar without fuss or display. Furthermore, should either a communicant or a communion minister drop the bread or spill the wine, communion ministers will need to know how to recover without shaming or embarrassing anybody. A new fragment can be presented to the communicant, and then the fallen fragment can be quickly picked up and either eaten by the minister or put on the side in the basket. For small spills of wine, the purificators are helpful. While our manifest intention should be to handle and serve this holy food with deep reverence, protecting the least crumb, God is not angered by spills. The earth itself is beloved by God and redeemed by Christ's blood, the very blood that was on the ground at Calvary. Furthermore, the body of Christ that is this brother or sister communicant is also to be encountered and cared for with reverence. All of these cases help to make it clear that the ministry of the bread and the cup calls for wisdom, sensitivity, and care.

The words spoken during the distribution of communion, the words about the bread and about the cup, may be spoken aloud. They do not need to be whispered. Said aloud, they also may evoke a strong, clear "Amen" from the communicant. Indeed, the *you* in "given for you" and "shed for you," quoting the words of institution again, is to be understood as plural—"given for you all"—while it is also addressed to this particular person. Each one receives the gift given to all, and that reception is a public, open event, not a secret. Those words, said clearly and graciously, are also quite enough. Nothing else needs to be said. It is probably also wise not to add the person's name to these words. Anxiety about remembering everyone's name correctly or hurt about not having yourself named when others are or a sense of alienation on the part of visitors who are not known or a sense of unwarranted intimacy when the name is combined with the whisper—these things do not need to be added to the communion ritual. There are already enough delicate issues for communion ministers to negotiate.

During educational processes in the congregation—communion formation, confirmation classes, adult forums, adult preparation for baptism—people can be gently and graciously helped to know how to come to communion. People do not automatically know what to do. One old help for this teaching is the proposal made by the fourth-century bishop Cyril of Jerusalem in his addresses to newly baptized men and women, called *Mystagogical Catecheses*. In those addresses he suggested that we make of our hands a throne to receive the Lord of life, first given into our open hands, one hand on top of the other, and then brought by those open hands up and into our mouth, heart, and life. Further help can be given by suggesting that the cup can be easily guided through using its base, while the communion minister holds the center of its stem or its node.

As the cup empties, the minister with the cup needs to return to the altar to further fill the cup from the flagon there. Or, another assisting minister may be charged with the task of carrying the flagon to the ministers with the cup in order to supply them. If the flagon itself empties, a good solution is to have a small pitcher of water nearby on the credence table. As soon as it is clear that there will be a shortage, water can be added to the wine remaining in the chalice, thinning it for the last communicants and yet still allowing everybody to drink from the wine that was originally on the table. Similarly, the best solution to the discovery that not enough bread remains is simply to break the remaining pieces smaller, even to the size of crumbs, giving everybody to eat from the bread that was originally on the table, the sign of our unity. The question of repeating the great thanksgiving or any part of it does not need to arise. In the extreme possibility of needing yet more bread and wine, however, one should see the Notes on the Services (LE, 24).

The ministers themselves may commune either after or before the communion of the whole assembly. The counsel of the Notes on the Services (23), however, is wise. In ancient times, it was hospitable to eat or drink first, indicating to other guests that the food was good, not poisoned. Today, it is hospitable to eat or drink last. The assisting ministers may commune each other or the presiding minister may commune them. Then an assisting minister may commune the presiding minister last of all. This communion of the ministers may take place at the communion stations or behind or before the altar, as the communion process is coming to an end. If the presiding minister or other ministers should be exercising leadership roles in more than one service of Holy Communion on a Sunday, they should commune at each of these services (see *The Use of the Means of Grace* 46).

When the communion is complete, the remaining food is brought back to the corporal. If communion ministers are to be sent with this communion to people who are absent, then the needed amount of bread and wine may be at this time placed into the containers of a communion kit that lies ready on the credence table. In some assemblies, the yet remaining food is then covered and removed to the credence table. The corporal is also folded and placed with the remaining bread and wine, leaving the altar once again empty. In other assemblies, the veiled cup and plate, other cups, each covered with a purificator, the covered baskets and the closed flagon or flagons are left on the table. Whatever the local practice, the counsel of *The Use of the Means of Grace* should be followed: "Any food that remains is best consumed by the presiding minister and assisting ministers and by others present following the service." [47b]

Of course, if there is simply too much wine and too few people for that counsel to be followed safely, the wine might be reverently poured upon the ground. A variety of local customs exist if there is too much bread remaining to be consumed after the service: a remaining loaf may be given to someone who needs bread or broken fragments may be scattered on the grass for birds or other animals. In any case, the remaining food is dealt with reverently but without anxiety. This cleaning up best takes place after the service, not during the service while the assembly waits.

Meal: Communion Song

Singing during communion distribution is an opportunity for assembly song that provides *focus*. Because this is a flexible time in the service and involves the assembly's movement, singing can enable a centering focus amidst the movement and variety of activity. Some will use this time for personal prayer. Assembly singing surrounds those praying with the community's songs of faith. Others will be communing. Singing also surrounds them. Singing can be continuous, even as individuals drop in and out of the song. Singing focuses the assembly as it accompanies the actions of those walking, sitting, communing, and praying.

For all these reasons, selecting music that will continue even when only a portion of the assembly is singing is important. Choosing simple songs during communion allows the assembly to join in as they wait in line to commune, to pray, or to silently listen as they commune. In some assemblies, worshipers may even take printed communion songs with them to the table. In any case, planners should make choices that will allow the song to continue during this flexible and open time.

A further consideration here is the potential to develop and choose song that doesn't depend on having a service folder or book in hand. Memorized songs allow an assembly to continue singing during communion and eliminates the need to use the service folder or worship book to sing, allowing the assembly to focus more on the song itself. It also encourages an assembly to develop and expand its memory.

What can an assembly memorize? The loss of memorization as a learning tool today makes this question an honest and important one. While initially it may seem that there is little today that assemblies know by memory, looking deeper may prove to be worth the trouble. What better to build community than to share songs from memory! Building an assembly's capacity for memorized song will take time and can grow only incrementally. The effort may well be worth it as an assembly grows into a greater and more diverse body of song. This song can enrich and deepen the assembly in its singing; it can also enrich and deepen the individual lives of those who sing.

Memorized song also goes out from the assembly in the mind and heart of the worshiper. That song continues through the week, reminding individuals of their place in the assembly and nourishing each one in their own spiritual need. The benefits of memorized song continue to multiply over the weeks and months and through the assembly's life as songs take on their own life inside and outside of the Sunday liturgy.

Musical song types particularly conducive to memory include repetitive choruses, refrain and verse-style songs, call-and-response songs, and stanza-based hymns. All of these types commend themselves for memorization by their use of repetition and their simplicity.

Repetitive choruses or refrains are a good place to begin to develop memorized singing. "Take, Oh, Take Me As I Am" (#814) is an example of such a simple refrain. This hymn is intended to be sung multiple times, and can be lengthened or shortened as needed. It can be sung in unison or in four-part harmony, allowing for variety from one repetition to another. The musical structure also encourages singing in a loop, as the final chord of the song leads naturally again to the first chord. After singing a few times, an assembly can easily sing this without the music or the words in front of them. Other examples of this style of song include:

472 Eat This Bread
473 Holy, Holy, Holy / *Santo, santo, santo*
481 Come to the Table
486 God Extends an Invitation / *Nuestro Padre nos invita*
616 Jesus, Remember Me
642 Ubi caritas et amor / *Where True Charity and Love Abide*
643 We Are All One in Christ / *Somos uno en Cristo*
682 To God Our Thanks We Give / *Reamo leboga*
721 Goodness Is Stronger than Evil
741 Your Will Be Done / *Mayenziwe*
794 Calm to the Waves

Refrain and verse-style songs can also be effective during communion. In a song like "Eat This Bread, Drink This Cup" (#492), all can memorize and sing the refrain. The choir or those seated in the pews can continue singing the verses, with everyone joining again at the refrain. This sets up a natural alternation, allows people to drop in and out or continue at will, and keeps the song alive in the assembly. Other examples of this style of song include:

423 Shall We Gather at the River
465 As the Grains of Wheat
466 In the Singing
469 By Your Hand You Feed Your People
471 Let Us Break Bread Together
474 Bread of Life from Heaven
477 I Received the Living God
483 Here Is Bread
484 You Satisfy the Hungry Heart / *Gift of Finest Wheat*
485 I Am the Bread of Life
489 Soul, Adorn Yourself with Gladness / *Vengo a ti, Jesús amado*
493 Taste and See
496 One Bread, One Body
498 United at the Table / *Unidos en la fiesta*
500 Now We Remain
581 You Are Mine
591 That Priceless Grace
592 Just As I Am, without One Plea
595 Jesus Loves Me!
596 My Hope Is Built on Nothing Less
614 There Is a Balm in Gilead
622 Neither Death nor Life
625 Come, We That Love the Lord / *We're Marching to Zion*
633 We've Come This Far by Faith
638 Blessed Assurance
649 Behold, How Pleasant / *Miren qué bueno*
653 Where True Charity and Love Abide / *Ubi caritas et amor*
674 Let Us Talents and Tongues Employ
708 Jesu, Jesu, Fill Us with Your Love
720 We Are Called

733 Great Is Thy Faithfulness

780 Shepherd Me, O God

785 When Peace like a River / *It Is Well with My Soul*

787 On Eagle's Wings

815 I Want to Walk as a Child of the Light

Call-and-response hymns set up an alternation between two groups of singers. The response either remains the same or is cued by the leader(s), allowing the entire assembly to sing the response. A cantor, a small group of singers, or a choir can lead the call. Examples of this type of song include:

464 Bread of Life, Our Host and Meal

491 Come, Let Us Eat

677 This Little Light of Mine

744 Lord, Be Glorified

846 Amen, We Praise Your Name / *Amen siakudumisa*

860 I'm So Glad Jesus Lifted Me

869 We Have Seen the Lord / *Nimemwona Bwana*

Some assemblies may be able to sing **stanza-based hymns** from memory. Ultimately, these hymns are more difficult to sing memorized, because their text changes from stanza to stanza. Well-loved hymns can often find a place in the heart and the assembly's memory, despite their difficulty. Here it is critical to know the assembly's traditions, its most familiar hymnody, and its penchant for passing its musical treasures to the next generation. Some hymns to consider are:

608 Softly and Tenderly Jesus Is Calling

638 Blessed Assurance

742 What A Friend We Have in Jesus

769 If You But Trust in God to Guide You

773 Precious Lord, Take My Hand

779 Amazing Grace, How Sweet the Sound

781 Children of the Heavenly Father / *Tryggare kan ingen vara*

782 My Shepherd, You Supply My Need

789 Savior, like a Shepherd Lead Us

838 Beautiful Savior

839, 840 Now Thank We All Our God

856 How Great Thou Art

Developing a group of memorized songs and hymns like this, then alternating them during communion, gives the assembly an opportunity to free itself from the printed song, and to engage one another more directly while they sing.

The number of hymns and songs to learn by memory will vary with each assembly. Factors such as size of the worshiping assembly, history and tradition of the local assembly, and vitality of congregational singing will all affect the outcome. Many assemblies could learn more from memory than they currently do. Increasing an assembly's quantity of memorized song is a worthy endeavor. Memorization can strengthen assembly singing as it places significant texts and tunes into the hearts and minds of the worshipers.

Developing an assembly's love of assembly song is essential at all points in the liturgy, and especially during the meal. Connecting to the community's life and faith will strengthen the meal's celebration, building up the assembly as it strengthens individuals' faith lives.

Meal: Prayer after Communion

After the table has been cleared (or the remaining food veiled) and after all in the assembly have returned to their places, the assembly stands. The presiding minister and the assisting ministers may also have returned to their places, or some of them may have done so, leaving the presiding minister and one assisting minister to lead the remaining parts of the service from the table. If the chairs of the presider and the principal assisting minister are clearly visible, however, that may be the best place from which to lead the conclusion, the direct table service now completed. If it is the custom of the congregation, the presider now may speak one of the table blessings included at this place in each of the settings in the Leaders Edition, but these final words about communion, themselves a version of the medieval words at the distribution, are not necessary. After the assembly stands and, if it is used, after this blessing, the assembly may sing "Now, Lord, you let your servant go in peace" (the Nunc dimittis). Alternatively, this song may be sung as the last of the songs during communion, perhaps while the ministers are communing or the table is being cleared. Or it may be sung during the Sending, as the sending song after the blessing. The song itself, one of the canticles from the infancy narrative in the Gospel of Luke (2:29-32), is remarkably appropriate to these places in the liturgy. It came into several early Lutheran liturgies in the sixteenth century and has continued in Lutheran use until now, with the result that it is one of the most characteristic marks of Lutheran liturgical practice. As the story says that old Simeon took the child Jesus into his arms, finally seeing the promised Light of God, so in communion we have received Christ into our hands and lives. As Simeon was then willing to go to a peaceful death, we sing with him that we now are willing to go to witness and service. This Christ is for all the nations.

While all these things—how the communion exactly ends, where the ministers then stand, the use of the table blessing, and the location and use of "Now, Lord"—are optional, the prayer that follows at this point should be used. Like the prayer of the day and the peace, it is one of the three transitional moments of the pattern for worship in *Evangelical Lutheran Worship*. It leads us from the Meal to the Sending. The prayer is now prayed by the principal assisting minister, from the place before his or her chair or from the table. The assisting minister may use the *orans* posture for this prayer (see Fig. 7.5/page 171 for the posture), and, so that his or her hands may be free, the presiding minister may help by holding the book with the text of the prayer in a way that the assisting minister may see it. Three optional texts are given in place in each of the settings in the Leaders Edition and in Settings One and Two in the Assembly Edition. Six more options, including seasonal choices, are given (LE, 139; AE p. 65). All of these options bring us to prayer before God that the wonderful sacrament we have received will turn us toward a needy world in mission and service. We are coming to the Sending.

CHAPTER NINE

Sending

Like the Gathering, the time of the Sending is flexible, adaptable to the community and the day. Also like the gathering, it is a forming of the assembly. This time, however, the forming is for the assembly's life in the world as this local expression of the body of Christ disperses. Sending is a time for again recalling our baptism; this time for taking our baptismal calling with us into our daily vocation. It is a time for sending and being sent; a time to thank God for the gifts of this assembly and prepare to extend them into the community. It is a time to gather up the gifts of bread and wine so that they can be sent to those who were absent that day; a final time to thank God for those gifts.

In the sending movement of the pattern, we hear for a final time the multiple voices of assembly leadership. The presider's voice pronounces the blessing or benediction, God's good word, over the gathering. The assisting minister's voice announces the assembly's dismissal. The assembly's voice gives assent to both, and may also add its own voice in sending song. In sending, as in the three movements that precede it, we hear the assembly and its leaders in dialogue with one another.

Sending reminds us that every assembly gathering is a cycle, existing for a time and then dispersing. We arrive at the sending after traveling from the rite of gathering to the word and meal. We heard and proclaimed the Word; we were nourished at the Meal; and now we complete the cycle, returning to the church's entrance, the place of Gathering.

At the time of the sending, we are no longer the same individuals who earlier crossed the threshold of the worship space. We are now a community who has encountered the living Christ in this place, and has been empowered for ministry through the sending. Like Jesus on the Mount of Transfiguration, we can't remain forever in the assembly. Our vocation sends us to a world in need, to live amidst the pains and struggles of our world. Just as the gathering empowers the community by forming itself that day, the sending empowers the community by calling each one to their service and ministry in the world. Sending also reminds the assembly that the church is not contained within its walls, but extends as the body of Christ throughout the world.

At a festive service, the sending might take a more elaborate and extensive treatment than an ordinary Sunday morning. At the Easter Vigil, for example, the sending is more than a short dismissal. After the Word and Meal, it is time for rejoicing and a joyful sending. There might be a procession to the back of the church singing a joyful hymn like "Good Christian Friends, Rejoice and Sing!" (#385). There the assembly can gather and continue the feasting with food and conversation. Gifts might be presented to the newly-baptized and newly-confirmed that night. Such a great sending matches the rejoicing and delight in the festival.

Usually, though, the sending is not so elaborate. In fact, it is normally the briefest of the four sections. It serves to turn us from the meal we have received and point us back toward our life and ministry extending from this gathering into the world. In the sending, we may affirm our vocation as baptized Christians; we hear the final blessing; we may sing a sending hymn. When it is finished, we say with gratitude, "Thanks be to God!" It is enough to sustain us for the journey ahead.

The cross leads the way out of the assembly. In sending, the assembly follows the cross into the world, leading each worshiper to encounter Christ in all the places life leads. Sending, then, is *movement:* from the communion table to the cross in the world. Finding ourselves between the table and the cross orients us to leave. We are sent; the liturgy is complete.

But the cycle continues. The sending inevitably leads again to the gathering. We disperse as a community sent into the world; we will gather again the following Sunday, in a never-ending cycle. This cycle has deep resonances in the biblical notion of sabbath, obeying God's command to honor a day each week for worship and rest, in an ever-repeating cycle that originates in God's action and always returns again.

Sunday, for Christians, both completes and begins the weekly cycle in a celebration of Christ's resurrection. Unlike Jewish tradition, which honors sabbath as the last day of the week, Christians gather on the first day of the week, the day of Christ's resurrection. This is a day for meeting, a gathering for hearing the word of God and for encountering the Risen One in the Lord's supper. It is more a day for meeting than for rest, though the word of God at the heart of our meeting is intended to bring us to deep rest (Heb. 4:3-12). Yet there is more to this weekly cycle. Sunday is not only the first day of the week; it is also the eighth day of creation, the day on which Christians recognize that God completes creation, bringing salvation in Jesus' resurrection.

So there is the weekly cycle of first day to eighth day, which again becomes the first day in a continuous cycle. This cycle (Fig. 9.1) returns us each week from the sending we left on the previous Sunday to the gathering on the next Sunday. We may recall the account in Luke 10 of the seventy disciples Jesus sent out, who later "returned with joy" (v. 17) to report on the success of their mission experience—and to again be fed in word and meal.

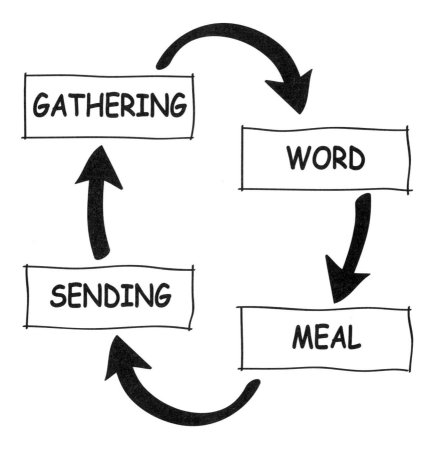

Fig. 9.1. Christian cycle of worship and life. *There's a cycle within the Sunday assembly but also an eight-day cycle of gathering-word-meal-sending-gathering . . . that continues from Sunday to Sunday.*

This piece of the cycle, from sending back to gathering, is important in several respects. It connects all of our life in an integrated fashion to and from our life in Christ and in and out of the Sunday assembly. It also connects to God's faithfulness, both in sending us out and in bringing us back again to gather each week.

It is not always possible to return each week to the assembly. Illness, distance, or any number of other factors may hinder anyone from attending. Even so, the cycle continues, inviting and gathering again and again.

There have also been times in history when the return to the gathering has been interrupted for a long period. Returning to gathering after an absence is not new. We can see already in the Old Testament how this pattern gets interrupted. In the time following the Babylonian exile, the people of Israel returned to their homes in Jerusalem and Judah. During the exile they had forgotten their great gatherings. Psalm 137 recounts how the people had lost their ability to sing the songs of Zion they had previously known. "How could we sing the Lord's song in a foreign land?" (v. 4). Once they returned to their home and land, they forgot this great cycle of gathering for their festivals and no longer called themselves together to worship and pray together.

Nehemiah, though, remembered God's promise and command, and called all the people into the public square to listen to Ezra read the book of the law of Moses. By reading them the entire book of the law of God, he reminded them that God was still calling them to celebrate. "This day is holy to our Lord; and do not be grieved, for the joy of the Lord in your strength" (Nehemiah 8:10).

Nehemiah led the people in celebrating the festival of booths; they kept the festival for seven days, restoring their pattern of gathering. He begins the plan to build again the walls of Jerusalem, a physical sign of the regathering of the Israelites. Stone by stone, Nehemiah oversaw the building of Jerusalem, amidst criticism even by many Israelites. Indeed, even after the exile of hundreds of years, Nehemiah's rebuilding stood as a sign that God had not abandoned the people, and that they could freely return and enter again into the great sabbath cycle.

In our own times, many Christians live in oppressive circumstances or under political regimes that don't allow for public gathering. Others find it difficult or impossible to gather with the assembly for personal reasons and circumstances. Even when gathering is not possible, this cycle reminds us that God does not abandon us in the time between sending and gathering. Just as Nehemiah tells the Israelites, God awaits our return, rejoicing with us when we gather again to celebrate the festival in word and meal, and to rejoice in God's presence and strength.

No matter how long we stay away, no matter how far we have strayed, we return again to the gathering and find that we are still connected to the body of Christ gathered there. Whether we have been gone a week or most of a lifetime, the gathering welcomes all to the feast each week. The cycle continues with each new gathering.

Sending Song

Singing at the sending strengthens the assembly as it prepares to disperse. Along with the dismissal, singing at the sending gives voice one more time to the entire assembly, enabling their final praises and response to God for all the gifts received. Sending song may give thanks for the meal just shared, may acknowledge gratitude for the assembly, or may empower the assembly for its mission in the world. At times it may do all of these.

Sending song can also connect us again to our vocations in the world. Remembering Jesus' words that "just as you did it to one of the least of these who are members of my family, you did it to me" (Matthew 25:40), we see our own vocation to the world in relation to the church's sending. Though scattered throughout the community and world during the week, the source of our daily work comes from our Sunday assembly. Sending songs which carry these themes include:

535 Hallelujah! We Sing Your Praises / *Haleluya! Pelo tsa rona*
538 The Lord Now Sends Us Forth / *Enviado soy de Dios*
540 Go, Make Disciples
542 O Living Bread from Heaven
543 Go, My Children, with My Blessing
546 To Be Your Presence
547 Sent Forth by God's Blessing
548 Rise, O Church, like Christ Arisen
551 The Spirit Sends Us Forth to Serve
663 Spread, Oh, Spread, Almighty Word
670 Build Us Up, Lord
672 Signs and Wonders
710 Let Streams of Living Justice

808 Lord Jesus, You Shall Be My Song / *Jésus, je voudrais te chanter*
809 Send Me, Lord / *Thuma mina*
810 O Jesus, I Have Promised
866 We Are Marching in the Light / *Siyahamba*
886 Oh, for a Thousand Tongues to Sing

Being Sent

Sending also reminds us whose actions determine our worship. This portion is not called Going, which we would do, but Sending, which God does. God sends us from this place to live our vocation in the world. We simply respond with gratitude and acknowledgment that we are sent. The Affirmation of Christian Vocation (AE p. 84) is useful as part of the sending rite. It says:

> Sisters and brothers, both your work and your rest are in God.
> Will you endeavor to pattern your life on the Lord Jesus Christ,
> in gratitude to God and in service to others, at morning and
> evening, at work and at play, all the days of your life?
> **I will, and I ask God to help me.**

This affirmation provides the assembly with a means for connecting the sending rite to a baptismal life in the world. By acknowledging the desire to live in the pattern of Jesus' life, the assembly declares its own intention to live in the world as baptized Christians.

Then comes the blessing. The presiding minister proclaims God's blessing on this assembly in this time of sending. It is a time of benediction, literally hearing God's good words, this final time in the gathering. The presiding minister announces the blessing of God and may make the sign of the cross over the assembly (see pp. 119–120, Fig. 6.5). The assembly may make the sign of the cross along with the presiding minister as a final reminder of their baptism in Christ.

There are several options for the final blessing. Pages 114-15 (AE) show three of these options. In each case the presiding minister proclaims the blessing (Fig. 9.2); the assembly receives God's blessing with the response "Amen." The assembly assents to the blessing God gives in sending us back into our daily lives.

Sending song may follow the blessing. During the song, the cross may lead the ministers back to the entrance of the space for the final

Fig. 9.2. The blessing. *The presiding minister may raise his or her arms to give the final blessing. The assembly responds with "Amen!"*

dismissal. The assembly turns to follow the cross, may bow in reverence as it passes, then faces toward the world where it will live out its vocation. The cross leads us back into the world.

Finally comes the dismissal. The assisting minister's voice announces this final declaration. This is a voice the assembly has heard throughout the liturgy; perhaps leading the canticle of praise, praying the prayers, assisting during the meal. Now this voice announces that the assembly is sent from this gathering for its various work in the world.

There are several options for wording the dismissal. Four are listed on page 115. "Go in peace" begins each one. The final statement can make a connection to the theme of the day, season of the church year, or readings for the day. "Remember the poor," "Share the good news," or "Christ is with you" are recommended here. If alternate sentences are composed locally, they are most likely to function successfully if they copy the brevity of these examples, three or four words, and if they are focused on sending into mission. In each case the assembly responds, "Thanks be to God."

We live in gratitude to God in and away from the Sunday assembly. God provides us with the means to live gratefully in all of our lives, strengthening us ever new with the word of God and the sacramental meal. We live in the continual cycle of gathering, sending, and gathering again. Truly we respond as we are sent, "Thanks be to God!"

CHAPTER TEN

Service of the Word

The Service of the Word in *Evangelical Lutheran Worship* provides an alternate resource for the Sunday assembly. It remains true that Holy Communion is the normal weekly service in Lutheran congregations. Lutherans confess that they celebrate the Holy Communion on every Sunday and festival (Apology of the Augsburg Confession, 24), and they mean by this confession that they gather on Sundays and festivals both for the full reading and preaching of the appointed scriptures and for the full celebration of the meal of Jesus Christ. Both the Evangelical Lutheran Church in America and the Evangelical Lutheran Church in Canada have encouraged local congregations to recover this weekly practice, and *Evangelical Lutheran Worship* has been published with that encouragement in mind. But it also remains true that this recovery—like all change among Lutherans related to worship—ought not take place by compulsion, but by teaching, encouragement, and reasoned, loving invitation.

Many Lutherans in North America have grown up with a less frequent celebration of the Lord's supper, and, if for no other reason than what they have been taught, some of these congregation members do not feel prepared to commune every Sunday. A longstanding practice among us is that Lutherans do not finish the communion service if there are no communicants prepared to share in the holy supper, if the pastor would be the only communicant. For our congregations, at this time, there needs to be an alternative service in *Evangelical Lutheran Worship*. The double commitment of confessional Lutherans—to weekly celebration of a service of both word and table and to avoiding a thanksgiving over bread and wine and a proclamation of Jesus' promise without the assembly eating and drinking—has led to a uniquely Lutheran creation: Holy Communion without communion; mass without meal, *missa brevis*.

We have seen (chapter 2) how, under a variety of pressures, Sunday communion became less frequent in the history of Lutheran churches. We have also seen that the twentieth and twenty-first centuries have been marked by a steady return of Lutheran congregations to the original practice of every-Sunday communion. Still, many congregations have not yet adopted this practice. While the work of teaching and encouragement continues, those congregations need a service for their Sunday celebration. The Service of the Word provides an important option.

The idea of the Service of the Word is that the pattern of the full communion service — the pattern for worship of *Evangelical Lutheran Worship* (92–93) — is to be followed, except that here a thanksgiving for the word of God replaces the Meal in the Gathering–Word–Meal–Sending pattern. The sense is that the full shape of the historic service — all its scripture readings from the lectionary, its sermon, its intercessions for the needs of the world, its collection, and its sending in mission — is needed in the local congregation on Sunday. But if, because of long practice and piety, the people here are not ready to receive holy communion, the meal should not be forced on them; nor should it be celebrated in their presence with only one or two communicants, as if it were a medieval private mass; nor should it be held after the service for a few people who remain. The holy communion, in such a situation, is begun but not finished. The meal itself—the taste of the promise heard in these scriptures, the visible word proclaiming the same thing these audible words proclaim—will be held at an announced time: next Sunday or the first Sunday in the month or some other approaching time. That invitation is what Lutherans have classically meant by this practice of part of the Sunday pattern for worship.

By this understanding, our congregations are indeed free to celebrate Sunday without distributing communion. But if they do so, it is important that three other things are true as well. They should be announcing when the full service of communion will be held. They should be regularly checking to see if it is still true that there are no communicants besides the pastor prepared to receive communion Sunday after Sunday. And their pastor or pastors should be preaching and teaching the meaning of the supper, to encourage and welcome people to more frequent participation, to help them to trust the words "for you." This accent on teaching and this refusal of compulsion were at the heart of Martin Luther's own pungent and still timely advice to pastors in both the Small Catechism and the Large. For example, Luther wrote:

We should preach in such a way that the people make themselves come without our law and just plain compel us pastors to administer the sacrament to them. . . . For if they believed that they had so much evil and needed so much good, they would not neglect the sacrament, in which help against such evil is provided and in which so much good is given. It would not be necessary to compel them with any law to receive the sacrament. Instead, they would come on their own, rushing and running to it; they would compel themselves to come and would insist that you give them the sacrament. For these reasons you do not need to make any law concerning this, as the pope did. Only emphasize clearly the benefit and the harm, the need and the blessing, the danger and the salvation in this sacrament. Then they will doubtless come on their own without any compulsion. . . . However, if you either do not urge such participation or make it into a law or poison, then it is your fault if they despise the sacrament. How can they help but neglect it, if you sleep and remain silent? [Small Catechism, Preface 22-24]

The Service of the Word is, thus, a service of Holy Communion that is waiting for another time to celebrate the Meal. It is the classic Lutheran option for a Sunday on which the sacrament of the altar cannot be celebrated. It is the service used by a congregation that is still teaching and inviting to a greater frequency in communion, still working on coming to the celebration of the Lord's supper as the principal, full-congregational service every Sunday. Indeed, the outline of this service intends that the centrality of the word of God will be so strongly celebrated—the presence of the risen Christ so clearly known in the word that is read, preached, and sung—that the assembly almost begins to taste the promise of God in their ears!

Unfortunately, this reason for using the Service of the Word on Sunday has sometimes been forgotten. It has become easier, quicker, more convenient, less trouble to have holy communion less frequently, while the Lutheran confessional commitment and the urgency of Luther's advice have been set aside. As a congregation chooses to use this service on Sunday, it will be good for the proposal of the Lutheran confessions to be revived and for the leadership of the congregation to undertake anew the very teaching and preaching, encouraging, exhorting, and loving that Luther recommended so heartily. Indolence about such urging of frequent communion on the part of church leadership — "sleep," Luther calls it — is not helpful and lets the vigorous and beautiful Service of the Word simply become a "half-service" and a customary practice, instead of an invitation to the supper, an invitation ultimately to taste the same Word whom we have heard.

In recent times, some congregations have chosen other kinds of services for non-communion Sundays. Simple patterns of hymn-singing and preaching have been tried in some places. In others, a sermon has been appended to patterns drawn from daily prayer: Morning Prayer (or Matins) and Sermon, for example. In the late twentieth century, North American Lutherans experimented with creating another kind of service of the word, one that had strong, communally sung parts and was based on another pattern than that found in the Holy Communion service. One problem with these solutions is that they are not as open to being interpreted, in the old Lutheran way, as invitations to and preparations for the supper. But another problem is that the assembly will easily lose the rich range of materials available for the service of Holy Communion — a three-reading lectionary and a sermon related to those readings, a variety of other propers, a hymn of the day, a strong intercessory prayer — materials all intended also to be used in the Service of the Word of *Evangelical Lutheran Worship*. Yet another problem is this: the services of daily prayer work wonderfully to mark the flow of the day with praise and prayer, circling around the central Sunday service of a congregation. They work less well as that central service. There is certainly room for reflection on the scriptures that have been read during Morning Prayer, for example, but probably not such clear room for the kind of full sermon our congregations need to have in the Sunday assembly. Furthermore, over the long run, many people found the pattern of the Service of the Word in *Lutheran Book of Worship,* one of the most important of the alternate experiments, to be lacking for Sunday use, to miss the logic of the pattern for worship.

Of course, these services of daily prayer or these devotional patterns of hymnody, preaching, and prayer have a place among us, especially in schools and congregations that are able to schedule more services through the week than the main service on Sundays and festivals. And the Service of the Word may also have a role on weekdays, in schools and congregations or at meetings and gatherings of the wider church. For a weekday use of the Service of the Word, planners should consult the Notes on the Services (LE, 25), especially regarding the possible use of the daily lectionary (AE pp. 1121–53) and the appropriate adaptations of the service if a lay person presides.

But if a local assembly decides to use *Evangelical Lutheran Worship*'s Service of the Word as its principal service on Sundays when there is not communion, then the following notes, based on the Notes on the Services (LE, 25–27), might be observed:

- The propers appointed for the day, including especially the lectionary (but not including the preface), belong to this service.
- Any of the settings for Holy Communion, through the peace — as well as any of the service music that might replace some parts of those settings — can be used by the assembly in celebrating this service.
- For the Gathering, Word, and Sending sections of the service, see the notes above, in chapters 5, 6, and 8.
- The order for confession and forgiveness is printed in the service (AE pp. 211–12), but the order for thanksgiving for baptism (AE p. 97) could be used instead.
- A sermon is integral to this service. Without a sermon, one of the services of daily prayer would be a better choice. Given the discussion above, it is important for one part of the sermon to encourage people toward communion, to show how the gospel proclaimed in the texts of the day is given for us to eat and drink through the gift of Jesus Christ in the supper. Preaching can awaken the hunger and thirst to come to communion.
- Along with texts familiar from the Holy Communion service, another optional dismissal, to be spoken by an assisting minister, is included in the sending rite here. This text calls us to discipleship in our daily lives. Also included in the Ash Wednesday service (AE p. 255), it is a revised version of a text widely used in Presbyterian liturgy and found in the *Book of Common Worship*.

Service of the Word: Gathering

Musical choices abound in a Service of the Word and can unfold in a myriad of ways. Because this service is derived from the Holy Communion service, much of the music from the settings of Holy Communion can be useful here as well. The Gathering, Word, and Sending sections in the Service of the Word are clearly patterned after the Holy Communion service. Musical portions of the service from those portions of Holy

Communion may be equally useful in the Service of the Word. Word is the central focus of this service and thus deserves special attention.

While there is always great flexibility for song in the time of gathering, here the gathering song may take on a weightier portion of the service. An extended gathering can serve the purpose of preparing to hear God's word and can itself begin the day's proclamation. Songs and psalms of praise, canticles, hymns, praise choruses, and more, can fill this time of gathering the assembly.

Gathering is a time to musically reflect the church's day and season. "Lord, have mercy" conveys our longing for God's mercy and peace in a more reflective time. "Glory to God" gives the assembly angelic words to sing in a festival season. (An option for "This is the feast" is not included in the Service of the Word since the meal is omitted.) Psalms too can reflect and help set the tone for the Sunday celebration in praise, lament, and thanksgiving. Consider the possibility of a series of psalms as a way to extend the gathering.

The gathering in a Service of the Word prepares the assembly for hearing and reflecting on God's word. This service, with its focus on proclaimed and interpreted word, can invite the assembly to deepen its own hearing and proclamation of the word. One way a gathering could prepare for this kind of hearing would be the practice of silence. Practicing silence together during the gathering would challenge most assemblies. A considered use of silence, however, may deepen and strengthen an assembly's gathering. Caution and care is warranted here if this is a new practice for an assembly. For many, it may simply not be practical, with a variety of ages and needs of worshipers. Over time, however, gathering together in the simple silence of God's presence can be a powerful experience in a community.

Likewise, singing psalms during the gathering can also be a way to introduce silence into a gathering. Especially during reflective and penitential times of the church year, an extended time of silence, punctuated with psalm singing may be effective and provide a means to introduce silence into the gathering.

Singing the songs of the Taizé community can also deepen an assembly's gathering. Their extended, repetitive style invites an assembly to settle into them, singing them continuously. Such singing releases an assembly from a hurried atmosphere and invites them to simply enter into this extended time period. Skillful leadership can make repetitions seamless. Musical leaders can give the simple cues needed for the assembly to know how long to continue singing. Examples of Taizé songs useful for the gathering time include:

262 Wait for the Lord
388 Be Not Afraid
406 Veni Sancte Spiritus / *Holy Spirit, Come to Us*
528 Come and Fill Our Hearts / Confitemini Domino
175 Alleluia

Service of the Word: Word

The time of hearing, proclaiming, interpreting, and responding to the word of God is the center of this service. Thus, its importance can be highlighted by expanding this section, varying it with the season, and giving the assembly a prominent voice.

Using all the readings for the day, complete with musical responses, is one way to highlight this section. Singing the psalm can vary from week to week. Using psalm tones, metrical psalms, refrain and verse psalms, and other forms of psalmody will enrich the practice of singing the psalms. See chapter 7 for a full discussion of psalm singing.

Singing the gospel acclamation, with or without its proper verse, prepares the assembly to hear the gospel, and gives them a communal response to hearing the word. There are two acclamations printed in the service (AE p. 216). Other options include the settings of Holy Communion and the service-music section, #168–177. Keep this acclamation rich, sung by all, and prominent.

The gospel reading and sermon follow. The assembly attends to the word and its interpretation at this center of the service. Following the sermon there is a time for silence. Here is another opportunity to allow the proclaimed word to deepen in the hearts of the assembly, through shared silence. Allowing a generous silence here can grow as an assembly adapts to the use of this time.

The assembly now voices its own proclamation, singing the hymn of the day. This is the assembly's response to the word heard, proclaimed, and interpreted. The assembly itself speaks, in its full communal voice, proclaiming God's goodness in Jesus Christ. (See chapter 7 for a full discussion of the hymn of the day.)

Choirs and other ensembles could also take a part in proclaiming the word. In all cases, careful attention to the texts presented is essential so that the proclamation is clear. Interpretive reading or drama is another way the word might be proclaimed in the assembly. Any of these artistic forms are possible vehicles for the word and can be considered in their relation to the assembly.

Only the full text of the Apostles' Creed is presented within the Service of the Word. Although the Nicene Creed is also an option, congregations may well consider whether at least during the seasons of Advent, Christmas, and Easter, and on festivals—the times when the Nicene Creed is suggested for use—the full service of word and meal might be celebrated weekly.

Service of the Word: Thanksgiving and Sending

During the time of thanksgiving, the assembly gives thanks through offering, song, and prayer. This is a time to focus on the church's mission, its care for those in need, and to gather monetary gifts. The canticle "Salvation belongs to our God" is one possibility for song during this time. Other hymns and songs include:

458 Praise and Thanksgiving Be to God
679 For the Fruit of All Creation
682 To God Our Thanks We Give / *Reamo leboga*
683 The Numberless Gifts of God's Mercies
689 Praise and Thanksgiving
730 Lord Our God, With Praise We Come
783 Praise and Thanks and Adoration
791 We Sing to You, O God
829 Have You Thanked the Lord?
837 Many and Great, O God / *Wakantanka taku nitawa*
839, 840 Now Thank We All Our God
884, 885 Praise God, from Whom All Blessings Flow

Likewise, sending songs that focus on sending into mission, on gratitude for the word, and for vocation in the world will bring the assembly from the Service of the Word to service in the world. Appropriate sending hymns include:

201, 202 Now, Lord
537 On Our Way Rejoicing
538 The Lord Now Sends Us Forth / *Enviado soy de Dios*
540 Go, Make Disciples

Throughout Lutheran history, many of the Sunday services of the word that were held when communion could not be celebrated and distributed began and ended with prayer. The prayer at the end of the service was a thanksgiving for the word of God that had been read and preached in this service. The Service of the Word of *Evangelical Lutheran Worship* continues this tradition. Just as the full Holy Communion service brings the whole assembly, after the Word part of the service, to join together in dialogue with the presiding minister, giving thanks for all of Gods' deeds of mercy, so now this service invites us all into thanksgiving. After the peace, an offering is gathered. As a way to bring the meaning of that collection to expression and to appropriately end the service, the assembly then sings a vigorous canticle or hymn of thanksgiving, and the presiding minister prays a prayer that praises the triune God for the gift of the word—the very word we have heard here—and pleads for the Spirit, trusting that God will continue to act through the word, as we now turn toward a world in need. The longer prayer, with congregational responses, echoes the biblical pattern of prayers like that in Nehemiah 9. The shorter prayer, based on the collect form, carries the sense that this Service of the Word is part of God's action to bring us and all the world to the great feast. Both conclude with the Lord's Prayer before the Sending.

Within a Service of the Word, itself an invitation to the Meal of Jesus Christ, that meal which continually feeds us with forgiveness and life and turns us toward our neighbor, it is right for us to pray "renew our faith, increase our hope, and deepen our love, for the sake of a world in need," or to pray "give us the light we need, awaken us to the needs of others, and at the end bring all the world to your feast."

That deep-red-colored book now lies closed on the desk. The tabs that marked the book's organization are now faint markings on the left-side of the book's closed pages. What has transpired since it was opened?

It is the writers' hope that in looking deeply at the contents of *Evangelical Lutheran Worship*, assemblies will find new and enlivening practices for their own Sunday worship life. The hope for renewal that drove much of the planning process for this family of worship resources now is on the desk and in the pews of local parishes, chapels, and seminaries. *The Sunday Assembly* is intended as a guide for examining Lutheran practice as it has been handed to us by generations that preceded us, in the hope that it will continue to shape the generations of faithful Christians, gathering in assembly, who will follow us.

As *Evangelical Lutheran Worship* is opened again in each local place, may it guide and challenge us as we plan and lead worship for the people of God gathered in the Sunday assembly.

Appendixes

Glossary

A

acclamation

brief sung or spoken response; see *gospel* and *eucharistic acclamation*

acolyte

assisting minister who serves roles such as crucifer, torchbearer, bookbearer, candlelighter, and server

Advent

season of the church year beginning four Sundays before December 25; a time of preparation for celebrating the birth of Christ

affirmation of baptism

rite in which previously baptized persons make public affirmation of their baptismal promises and the church affirms God's baptismal gift

Agnus Dei (ahn-yoos DEH-ee)

"Lamb of God"; threefold prayer or litany often sung at the breaking of bread

alb

white robe worn by liturgical leaders; may be worn by newly baptized; see p. 100

alleluia

Latin spelling of Hebrew exclamation hallelujah: "praise the Lord"

altar

the table, the Lord's table

ambo

single reading stand for the proclamation of the readings and preaching

anointing

marking the head or body with oil

anthem

choral music based on scripture, hymn text, poem, or free text

antiphon (AN-tih-fon)

brief verse sung before and after a psalm or canticle, often but not always drawn from the main text; may be sung by a different voice or voices; see *refrain*

antiphonal (an-TIH-fun-ul)

singing of verses in alternation between two groups of singers

assembly

the people gathered for worship

assisting minister

liturgical leader who assists the assembly in worship, preferably a layperson

B

baptismal garment

white robe with which the newly baptized may be clothed; see *alb*

Benedictus

see Blessed Are You, Lord

bidding prayer

prayer form used at the Good Friday liturgy, among other times, in which each bid (invitation to prayer for particular needs) is followed by silent prayer and then a leader's prayer summing up the assembly's prayers

Blessed Are You, Lord

canticle from Luke 1:68-79; song of Zechariah; Benedictus; traditional canticle at morning prayer

brazier

a container for holding a fire, especially the "new fire" at the Vigil of Easter

C

canon

a type of song in which the singing group is divided into multiple sections which begin and end the song sequentially, at evenly-spaced intervals

canticle

liturgical song, usually based on a scriptural text, typically without rhyme or poetic meter

canticle of praise

canticle or hymn sung in the gathering rite; see *Glory to God, This Is the Feast*

cantor

a leader of song; the person who oversees the worship music in a congregation

carol

seasonal song, often in refrain form and with roots in folk song or dance

catechumen (cat-eh-CUE-men)

youth or adult preparing for baptism and first communion

catechumenate (cat-eh-CUE-men-ut)

process through which youth or adults may prepare for baptism and first communion

catholic

the universal church—"holy, catholic church"

chalice (CHAL-iss)

see *cup*

chancel

section of the worship space where altar, ambo/pulpit, leaders' chairs are located

chasuble (CHA-zuh-bul)

poncho-like vestment often worn over an alb and stole by presiding minister at the communion service; sometimes the stole is worn on top of the chasuble; see p. 103

chorus

see *refrain*

chrism

oil used for anointing at baptism

Christmas

a twelve-day time of rejoicing over the birth of Christ; also the Nativity of Our Lord (December 25) and its vigil, Christmas Eve (December 24), which begin the Christmas season

collect (KOL-lect)

short prayer in liturgy; see *prayer of the day*

commemorations

days on the calendar celebrating persons or events, sometimes distinguished from the more important lesser festivals

common meter

a hymn meter with the pattern of 8, 6, 8, and 6 syllables per phrase; see *meter* (poetic)

communion song

assembly singing during the communion of the people; may include "Lamb of God," communion hymn(s), and post-communion canticle

complementary

within the Revised Common Lectionary, an option for the first reading and psalm in the time after Pentecost in which the first reading is selected to coordinate in some way with the gospel reading; see *semicontinuous*

compline (COM-plun)

see *night prayer*

confirmation

see *affirmation of baptism*

crèche

manger within a nativity scene, or the nativity itself

crucifer

the acolyte who carries the processional cross

cup

primary vessel used for serving the wine of Holy Communion

D

daily prayer

a form of prayer service, originating in monastic worship, including morning prayer (matins), evening prayer (vespers), night prayer (compline, prayer at the close of the day)

dialogue

brief phrases or sentences used responsively between leader and assembly; especially, the three-part dialogue that begins the great thanksgiving; also, the two-part dialogue that precedes the prayer over the water in holy baptism

doxology

a trinitarian ascription of praise

E

Easter

a fifty-day time of rejoicing over the resurrection of Christ; also the festival of the Resurrection of Our Lord, the beginning of Easter

Easter proclamation

prayer of joy and thanksgiving sung during the Vigil of Easter; also known as the Exsultet, from the Latin meaning "rejoice," the first word of the text

Easter Vigil

see *Vigil of Easter*

entrance hymn

see *gathering song*

Epiphany

festival of Christ's incarnation on January 6

eucharist (YOU-ca-rist)

the celebration of the word of God and the eucharistic meal

eucharistic acclamations

sung or spoken responses within the great thanksgiving; they may include the "Holy, holy, holy"; another response (such as "Christ has died . . .") within the eucharistic prayer; the great amen at the conclusion of the eucharistic prayer

eucharistic prayer

see *thanksgiving at the table*

evening prayer

a form of daily prayer designed for and prayed in the evening, traditionally near sunset; vespers

Exsultet

see *Easter proclamation*

F

feast

a day on which Christ's death and resurrection is celebrated; includes every Sunday as well as principal and lesser festivals of the church year

festivals

see *feast;* also, particular celebrations of God's saving action in Christ, often focused on events in the life of Christ or on the lives and witnesses of apostles and other followers

font

place where the water for baptism is kept and/or from which it is applied during baptism

G

gathering rite

beginning section of communion liturgy, including the greeting and the prayer of the day, and often also confession and forgiveness, thanksgiving for baptism, and gathering song

gathering song

section of singing during the gathering rite, which may include one or more of: hymns, songs, psalms, Kyrie or other litany, Trisagion, and canticle of praise such as "Glory to God" or "This is the feast"

Gloria in excelsis (ek-SHEL-sees)

see *"Glory to God"*

Gloria Patri (gloh-ree-ah PAH-tree)

trinitarian doxology ("Glory to the Father . . .") sometimes used to conclude canticles, responsories, and psalms

Glory to God

canticle often used in gathering rite, expanding on the song of the angels in Luke 2; Gloria in excelsis

gospel acclamation

brief sentence, usually scriptural, sung before the gospel reading; includes beginning and concluding "Alleluia" and proper or general verse; Lenten acclamation omits alleluia; see *gospel responses*

gospel canticle

songs from the gospels traditionally sung within daily prayer: "Blessed Are You, Lord," "My Soul Proclaims the Greatness of the Lord," "Now, Lord"

gospel responses

acclamations, "Glory to you, O Lord" or "Praise to you, O Christ," spoken or sung after the announcement and the conclusion to the gospel reading

great amen

closing acclamation, usually sung, often concluding the eucharistic prayer

great thanksgiving

in the communion service, the body of actions and words beginning with the dialogue and concluding with the Lord's Prayer

greeting

apostolic greeting; opening biblical greeting by the presiding minister

H

hallelujah

Hebrew for "praise the Lord"

Holy, holy, holy

acclamation during the great thanksgiving, expanding on the song of the seraphim in Isaiah 6 and the cry of the crowds in Matthew 21

hosanna

interjection meaning "Save us"

hymn

song sung by the assembly; more specifically, a song with a consistent metrical pattern, often in strophic form (multiple stanzas sung to the same tune), sometimes with a refrain

hymn of light

hymn of praise to Christ the light in evening prayer; "Joyous light"; Phos hilaron

hymn of the day

principal hymn in the communion service, following the sermon, responding to and proclaiming the word

hymnody

a body of assembly song, usually distinguished from service music

I

intercessions

see *prayers of intercession*

intinction

method of distributing communion in which the bread is dipped into the wine and then eaten

introit (IN-tro-it)

in medieval and later liturgies, a whole or partial psalm sung at the entrance; generally a prescribed text

invitation to communion

minister's invitation to the table spoken immediately after the Lord's Prayer

K

Kyrie (KIH-ree-ay)

shortened form of Kyrie eleison (eh-LEH-ee-zon) (Greek for "Lord, have mercy"); a usually sung prayer in gathering rite

Kyrie litany

form of Kyrie consisting of brief petitions with the response "Lord, have mercy"

Kyrie, threefold

"Lord, have mercy; Christ, have mercy; Lord, have mercy." Also sixfold (L, L, C, C, L, L) or ninefold (L, L, L, C, C, C, L, L, L)

L

Lamb of God

threefold prayer or litany often sung as the first song during the communion

lay

a person who is not ordained to the public ministry of the church

leader

one who leads a service such as daily prayer; may be either lay or ordained

lectern

reading stand, sometimes distinguished from pulpit; see *ambo*

lectionary

book containing the full texts of scripture readings for proclamation in the liturgy; or list of scripture readings appointed for proclamation in the liturgy; also a system of enumerating the sets of readings used in the time after Epiphany and the time after Pentecost (e.g., Lectionary 23)

lector

see *reader*

Lent

the season of the church year beginning on Ash Wednesday and concluding with the Three Days (or Maundy Thursday)

lesser festivals

days in the church year that fall in importance between the principal festivals such as Christmas, Ascension, and Pentecost, and commemorations

lessons

see *readings*

light hymn

see *hymn of light*

litany

prayer, often sung, consisting of brief petitions and fixed assembly responses

liturgy

the words and actions that form the worship of the Christian assembly

liturgy of the meal

in the communion service, offering, setting the table, great thanksgiving, and the communion of the assembly; the meal section of the service

liturgy of the word

scripture readings with psalm, gospel acclamation, sermon, hymn of the day, creed, prayers of intercession, and peace; the word section of the service

long meter

a hymn meter with four phrases of eight syllables per phrase; see *meter* (poetic)

M

Magnificat (mahn-YEE-fee-kaht)

see *My Soul Proclaims the Greatness of the Lord*

matins

see *morning prayer*

meter (musical)

pattern of beats within a piece or section of music, normally indicated by time signature

meter (poetic)

in reference to hymns, the rhythmic pattern of the poetry; catalogued in a metrical index by the number of syllables per musical line

metrical psalm

a psalm that is paraphrased to fit a hymn form, usually with several stanzas

ministers of communion from the assembly

laypersons who bring the body and blood of Christ to those who are absent from the assembly

morning prayer

a form of daily prayer designed for and prayed in the morning; matins

My Soul Proclaims the Greatness of the Lord

canticle from Luke 1:46–55; song of Mary; Magnificat; canticle at evening prayer

N

narthex

gathering space, foyer, entryway to the worship space

nave

main section of the worship space, where the assembly is located

new fire

the bonfire kindled at the beginning of the Easter Vigil

night prayer

daily prayer service for use at the end of the day, just prior to retiring for the night; compline; prayer at the close of the day

Now, Lord

canticle from Luke 2:29–32; song of Simeon; Nunc dimittis; used as a last communion song or sending song in communion service and as gospel canticle in night prayer

Nunc dimittis

see *Now, Lord*

O

O antiphons

traditional refrains sung with canticles of daily prayer during the final days of Advent, beginning with various addresses to Christ ("O Emmanuel," "O Dayspring")

offering

collection of money and other gifts for the mission of the church

office hymn

traditional name for the principal hymn within daily prayer, usually concluding the psalmody section

Oh, Come, Let Us Sing

Psalm 95:1-7a; Venite; one of the primary choices for first psalm at morning prayer

ordained

a person who has been publicly set aside for particular ministry by and within the church

order

way in which the parts of the service are arranged; a section within a full service, such as order for baptism, order for gathering; rite

ordinary

in traditional communion liturgy forms, the unchanging parts, e.g., Kyrie, "Glory to God," creed; sometimes refers to the "green Sundays" as those in "ordinary time," meaning numbered or counted Sundays

ordo

order of worship; essential shape and elements of a service, such as gathering, word, meal, and sending; can also mean church calendar

ostinato

melodic figure and/or brief verse, repeated continuously; commonly used in songs from the Taizé community

P

pall

a large covering draped over a coffin while it is in the church (funeral pall); linen-covered square placed atop a communion cup when it is not in use

Palm Sunday

see *Sunday of the Passion*

paschal (PAS-kul)

in Christian use, the passage of Jesus Christ from death to life

paschal candle

tall, white candle lit at the Easter Vigil, during the Easter season, and at baptisms and funerals

paten (PAT-un)

see *plate*

peace, the

moment in the service when those in the assembly greet one another with the peace of the risen Christ

Pentecost

the third of the great festivals of the church year, celebrating the giving of the Holy Spirit; occurs fifty days after Easter Sunday, and is the last day of Easter

Phos hilaron
> see *hymn of light*

plainsong
> rhythmically free, nonharmonic melody; Gregorian chant, plainchant

plate
> vessel often used to hold communion bread for distribution; paten

postlude
> optional music, usually instrumental, concluding the sending rite

prayer after communion
> brief prayer after all have communed

prayer at the close of the day
> see *night prayer*

prayer of the church
> see *prayers of intercession*

prayer of the day
> appointed opening prayer of the communion liturgy

prayers of intercession
> prayers of the assembly during the word section of the service

preface
> introductory section of the great thanksgiving, following the dialogue and leading into the Holy, holy, holy; see *proper preface*

preface dialogue
> three versicles and responses that begin the great thanksgiving; often just dialogue

prelude
> music, usually instrumental, preceding the gathering rite; also, a hymn introduction (may also be referred to as hymn or chorale prelude)

presiding minister

the ordained minister who presides and preaches at the communion service

proper preface

introductory section of thanksgiving within the great thanksgiving, appointed for a particular day, season, or occasion; see *preface*

propers, the

the liturgical texts appointed for a given day, e.g., readings, prayer of the day, gospel acclamation

psalm paraphrase

psalm text generally adapted to metrical form for use with hymn tune or other melody

psalm tone

melodic formula to carry the singing of a psalm verse or pair of verses (double tone)

psalmody

a section of psalms and other assembly song, especially in daily prayer

pulpit

reading stand, sometimes distinguished from lectern and used for preaching; see *ambo*

pyx

an alternative container for distributing the bread of communion, usually taking the form of a small, cylindrical covered box

R

RCL

see *Revised Common Lectionary*

reader

the assisting minister or other person, usually lay, appointed to read from scripture in worship

readings

the scripture texts appointed for public reading in the liturgy

refrain

brief sentence or phrase (usually an excerpt from the psalm) sung before, after, and at intervals during a psalm; see *antiphon*; repeated portion of a hymn, song, or canticle, sometimes called a chorus, sung in alternation with stanzas or verses

responsive

singing or speaking of psalm verses in alternation by any two groups within an assembly

responsorial

singing of psalm verses by choir or cantor in alternation with an assembly refrain

responsory

response to the reading within daily prayer; in classical form, two versicles and the Gloria Patri sung by a leader alternating with a repeated assembly response

Revised Common Lectionary

three-year set of Sunday and festival readings for worship shared (with some variations) among many church bodies worldwide

rite

liturgical orders or sections that take place within a full assembly service, e.g., baptism rite, ordination rite, gathering rite; may be used synonymously with order

ritual

a symbolic action or grouping of actions, with or without words

round

a type of canon in which the melody, in each voice, begins again after finishing (a "perpetual canon")

S

sacrament of the altar

Holy Communion

salutation

greeting sometimes preceding prayer: "The Lord be with you. / And also with you."

semicontinuous

within the Revised Common Lectionary, an option for the first reading and psalm in the time after Pentecost in which the first reading is taken somewhat sequentially from books of the Old Testament; see *complementary*

sanctuary

technically, the area immediately surrounding the altar

Sanctus

see *Holy, holy, holy*

sending song

singing in the sending rite just before or after the dismissal; departure/recessional hymn

sending rite

in communion liturgy, concluding rite with blessing and dismissal

sequence hymn

appointed hymn that may follow or replace the verse as a gospel acclamation

service

full liturgical order; communion service, baptism service, service of morning prayer

service music

musical setting(s) of the regularly recurring texts of the liturgy

setting

music for the recurring sung texts of a whole service; the accompaniment for a tune; a choral or instrumental interpretation of a text or melody

short meter

a hymn meter with the pattern of 6, 6, 8, and 6 syllables per phrase; see *meter* (poetic)

sign of the cross

tracing the cross on the forehead or over the body

song

assembly singing; sometimes used interchangeably with hymn; when used in distinction from hymn, assembly music characterized by refrains and metrically irregular, ballad-like stanzas

stanza

largest poetic sub-unit of a hymn or song, with each stanza often sung to the same melody

stations of the cross

devotional form usually involving a set of images from Jesus' passion

stole

long fabric band worn by ordained ministers over the shoulders; see p. 102

Sunday of the Passion

beginning of Holy Week and last Sunday in Lent; often called Palm Sunday because of the entrance with palms traditionally used on that day

T

Te Deum laudamus (teh DEH-oom lou-DAH-moos)

see *We praise you, O God*

tenebrae (TEN-eh-bray)

a Holy Week liturgy involving increasing darkness

Thankful Hearts and Voices Raise

post-communion canticle based on Ps. 105

thanksgiving at the font

prayer at holy baptism preceding the baptism of a candidate

thanksgiving at the table

prayer at Holy Communion that includes Jesus' words of institution; often also includes thanksgiving to God for acts of salvation and prayer to the Holy Spirit; eucharistic prayer

thanksgiving for baptism

service element, often part of the gathering rite in the communion service, that may include a prayer of thanksgiving for baptism coupled with a visible reminder of baptism

This Is the Feast

canticle used usually in gathering rite, based on Revelation 5 and 19

Three Days, the

the Three Days of Maundy Thursday (evening) through the Resurrection of Our Lord (Easter Day, sometimes including evening); triduum

thurible

censer; vessel in which incense is burned

time after Epiphany

variable number of weeks after the Epiphany of Our Lord (January 6) and before Ash Wednesday

time after Pentecost

variable number of weeks after the Day of Pentecost and before the First Sunday of Advent

time of the church, the

the nonfestival part of the church year, including the time after Pentecost and often the time after Epiphany

triduum

see *the Three Days*

Trisagion (tris-ah-gee-on)

"Holy God, holy and mighty, holy and immortal" / "Have mercy on us"; traditional sung prayer, may be used in the gathering rite of the communion service, as a response to the Good Friday reproaches, or at other times

V

veil

a cloth placed over the communion vessels before and after the communion service

Venite

see *Oh, come, let us sing*

verse, the

see *gospel acclamation*

versicle

a short verse or sentence said or sung by a leader, followed by a response by the assembly

vespers

see *evening prayer*

Vigil of Easter

celebration of the resurrection on the night before Easter; first celebration of Easter

W

We Praise You, O God

Te Deum laudamus; traditional canticle associated with morning prayer

worship space

entire area in which the assembly worships; may encompass chancel, nave, and gathering space

Hymn of the Day

A Table of Suggested Usage for the Church Year

L*utheran Book of Worship* reintroduced to Lutherans in America the idea of a list of hymns of the day that would remain fixed—that is, a given hymn would recur each time a certain Sunday or festival appeared in the church year. The idea was rooted in the practice of the early church (a hymn cycle was developed as early as the sixth century) as adapted by Martin Luther and his followers in the Reformation. Luther's substitution of a vernacular hymn for the Gradual between the second reading and gospel soon developed into a list of Gradual Hymns for the various Sundays, a list that was quite consistent from one church order to another. That same list was easily moved from the Gradual position to the hymn of the day following (or before) the sermon.

With the development of the three-year lectionary, some found it harder to accept a list that served for all three years, especially in those seasons when the readings for a given day (say, July 10–16, Lectionary 15) have little in common. Others have still found value in attempting to maintain a common, single-year list.

The following hymn of the day selections follow the liturgical season and relate to the Revised Common Lectionary. The first hymns listed reflect generally the day and the season of the church year. The hymns that follow, with designations A, B, and C, are also useful as hymn of the day selections, but are more directly related to the readings of the day in the lectionary year indicated than the first hymns in the list. While there is sometimes a direct relationship between the day's gospel and the hymn of the day, at other times the first or second readings or the psalm may have a more direct relationship to the hymn.

The hymns span a wide range of musical styles and time periods. The representation of global, multicultural, folk, and early-American hymns has been expanded, while many of the chorale choices in long-standing Lutheran practice also remain. When used for worship planning, this list may offer new ways to expand the assembly's proclamation, even as it retains its original and traditional common core of hymnody.

This is only a suggested list arranged numerically; others are available. See, for example, the listings in *Indexes to Evangelical Lutheran Worship*.

First Sunday of Advent
263 Savior of the Nations, Come
436 Wake, Awake, for Night Is Flying
241 O Lord, How Shall I Meet You (A)
720 We Are Called (A)
435 Lo! He Comes with Clouds Descending (B)
438 My Lord, What a Morning (B)
245 Creator of the Stars of Night (C)
246 Hark! A Thrilling Voice Is Sounding! (C)

Second Sunday of Advent
247 Come Now, O Prince of Peace / *Ososŏ, ososŏ*
249 On Jordan's Bank the Baptist's Cry
250 Blessed Be the God of Israel (A)
254 Come, Thou Long-Expected Jesus (A)
256 Comfort, Comfort Now My People (B)
266 All Earth Is Hopeful / *Toda la tierra* (B)
255 There's a Voice in the Wilderness (C)
264 Prepare the Royal Highway (C)

Third Sunday of Advent
244 Rejoice, Rejoice, Believers
246 Hark! A Thrilling Voice Is Sounding!
710 Let Streams of Living Justice (A)
264 Prepare the Royal Highway (A, B)
267 Joy to the World (B)
532 Gather Us In (C)
239 Hark, the Glad Sound! (C)

Fourth Sunday of Advent
257 O Come, O Come, Emmanuel
573 My Soul Now Magnifies the Lord
245 Creator of the Stars of Night (A)
266 All Earth Is Hopeful / *Toda la tierra* (A)
265 The Angel Gabriel from Heaven Came (B)
251 My Soul Proclaims Your Greatness (B, C)
258 Unexpected and Mysterious (C)

Nativity of Our Lord (A, B, C) – I

272 Lo, How a Rose E'er Blooming
280 Midnight Stars Make Bright the Skies /
     Mingxing canlan ye wei yang

Nativity of Our Lord (A, B, C) – II

268 From Heaven Above
296 What Child Is This

Nativity of Our Lord (A, B, C) – III

267 Joy to the World
295 Of the Father's Love Begotten

First Sunday of Christmas

287 Let All Together Praise Our God
288 Good Christian Friends, Rejoice
275 Angels, from the Realms of Glory (A)
272 Lo, How a Rose E'er Blooming (B)
313 O Lord, Now Let Your Servant (B)
648 Beloved, God's Chosen (C)
718 In a Lowly Manger Born (C)

Second Sunday of Christmas (A, B, C)

295 Of the Father's Love Begotten
510 Word of God, Come Down on Earth

Epiphany of Our Lord (A, B, C)

306 Come, Beloved of the Maker
308 O Morning Star, How Fair and Bright!

Baptism of Our Lord • Lectionary 1

304 Christ, When for Us You Were Baptized
305 When Jesus Came to Jordan
311 Hail to the Lord's Anointed (A)
314 Arise, Your Light Has Come! (A)
671 Shine, Jesus, Shine (B)
673 God, Whose Almighty Word (B)
442 All Who Believe and Are Baptized (C)
581 You Are Mine (C)

Second Sunday after Epiphany • Lectionary 2

309 The Only Son from Heaven
310 Songs of Thankfulness and Praise
307 Light Shone in Darkness (A)
336 Lamb of God / *Your Only Son* (A)
574 Here I Am, Lord (B)
799 Come, Follow Me, the Savior Spake (B)
312 Jesus, Come! For We Invite You (C)
688 Lord of Light (C)

Third Sunday after Epiphany • Lectionary 3

866 We Are Marching in the Light / *Siyahamba*
726 Light Dawns on a Weary World (A)
696 Jesus Calls Us; o'er the Tumult (A, B)
798 Will You Come and Follow Me / *The Summons* (A, B)
709 When Our Song Says Peace (C)
710 Let Streams of Living Justice (C)

Fourth Sunday after Epiphany • Lectionary 4

514 O Word of God Incarnate
655 Son of God, Eternal Savior
728 Blest Are They (A)
665 Rise, Shine, You People! (B)
737 He Comes to Us as One Unknown (C)

Fifth Sunday after Epiphany • Lectionary 5

507 O God of Light
715 Christ, Be Our Light
688 Lord of Light (A)
610 O Christ, the Healer, We Have Come (B)
798 Will You Come and Follow Me / *The Summons* (C)

Sixth Sunday after Epiphany • Lectionary 6

310 Songs of Thankfulness and Praise
806 O God, My Faithful God
802 Let us Ever Walk with Jesus (A)
617 We Come to You for Healing, Lord (B)
726 Light Dawns on a Weary World (C)
728 Blest Are They (C)

Seventh Sunday after Epiphany • Lectionary 7

604 O Christ, Our Hope

631 Love Divine, All Loves Excelling (A)

708 Jesu, Jesu, Fill Us with Your Love (A)

657 Rise, O Sun of Righteousness (B)

605 Forgive Our Sins As We Forgive (B, C)

Eighth Sunday after Epiphany • Lectionary 8

665 Rise, Shine, You People!

871 Sing Praise to God, the Highest Good

858, 859 Praise to the Lord, the Almighty (A)

584 The Son of God, Our Christ (B)

506 The Word of God Is Source and Seed (C)

652 Built on a Rock (C)

Transfiguration of Our Lord

316 Oh, Wondrous Image, Vision Fair

317 Jesus on the Mountain Peak

671 Shine, Jesus, Shine

Ash Wednesday

321 Eternal Lord of Love, Behold Your Church

600 Out of the Depths I Cry to You

601 Savior, When in Dust to You

First Sunday in Lent

319 O Lord, throughout These Forty Days

325 I Want Jesus to Walk with Me

503–505 A Mighty Fortress Is Our God

322 Oh, Love, How Deep (A)

740 God of the Sparrow (B)

766 Lord of Our Life (B)

326 Bless Now, O God, the Journey (C)

Second Sunday in Lent

323 God Loved the World

750 Lord, Thee I Love with All My Heart

448 This Is the Spirit's Entry Now (A)

667 Take Up Your Cross, the Savior Said (B)

566 When Twilight Comes (C)

735 Mothering God, You Gave Me Birth (C)

Third Sunday in Lent

324 In the Cross of Christ I Glory
333 Jesus Is a Rock in a Weary Land
658 O Jesus, Joy of Loving Hearts (A)
777 Come to Me, All Pilgrims Thirsty (A)
772 Oh, That the Lord Would Guide My Ways (B)
806 O God, My Faithful God (B)
481 Come to the Table (C)

Fourth Sunday in Lent

593 Drawn to the Light
714 O God of Mercy, God of Light
779 Amazing Grace, How Sweet the Sound
452 Awake, O Sleeper, Rise from Death (A)
323 God Loved the World (B)
715 Christ, Be Our Light (B)
594 Dear Christians, One and All, Rejoice (C)
606 Our Father, We Have Wandered (C)

Fifth Sunday in Lent

330 Seed That in Earth Is Dying
343 My Song Is Love Unknown
333 Jesus Is a Rock in a Weary Land (A)
886 Oh, for a Thousand Tongues to Sing (A)
485 I Am the Bread of Life (B)
329 As the Sun with Longer Journey (B)
793 Be Thou My Vision (C)
810 O Jesus, I Have Promised (C)

Sunday of the Passion/Palm Sunday (A, B, C)

340 A Lamb Goes Uncomplaining Forth
342 There in God's Garden
343 My Song Is Love Unknown

Monday in Holy Week (A, B, C)

338 Beneath the Cross of Jesus
357 Lamb of God, Pure and Sinless

Tuesday in Holy Week (A, B, C)

324 In the Cross of Christ I Glory
431 O Christ, What Can It Mean for Us

Third Sunday of Easter

389 Christ Is Alive! Let Christians Sing

391 This Joyful Eastertide

374 Day of Arising (A)

635 We Walk by Faith (A)

646 The Peace of the Lord / *La paz del Señor* (B)

744 Lord, Be Glorified (B)

817 You Have Come Down to the Lakeshore /
Tú has venido a la orilla (C)

846 Amen, We Praise Your Name / *Amen siakudumisa* (C)

Fourth Sunday of Easter

502 The King of Love My Shepherd Is

778 The Lord's My Shepherd

780 Shepherd Me, O God

789 Savior, like a Shepherd Lead Us

790 Day by Day (A)

645 Christ Is Made the Sure Foundation (B)

764 Have No Fear, Little Flock (B)

619 I Know That My Redeemer Lives! (C)

Fifth Sunday of Easter

362 At the Lamb's High Feast We Sing

389 Christ Is Alive! Let Christians Sing

645 Christ Is Made the Sure Foundation (A)

758 You Are the Way (A)

403 Like the Murmur of the Dove's Song (B)

447 O Blessed Spring (B)

377 Alleluia! Jesus Is Risen! (C)

777 Come To Me, All Pilgrims Thirsty (C)

Sixth Sunday of Easter

367 Now All the Vault of Heaven Resounds

631 Love Divine, All Loves Excelling

641 All Are Welcome (A)

737 He Comes to Us as One Unknown (A)

539 Abide, O Dearest Jesus (B)

708 Jesu, Jesu, Fill Us with You Love (B)

381 Peace, to Soothe Our Bitter Woes (C)

815 I Want to Walk as a Child of the Light (C)

Ascension of Our Lord (A, B, C)

392 Alleluia! Sing to Jesus

393 A Hymn of Glory Let Us Sing!

821 Shout to the Lord

857 Lord, I Lift Your Name on High

Seventh Sunday of Easter

247 Come Now, O Prince of Peace / *Ososŏ, ososŏ*

322 Oh, Love, How Deep

655 Son of God, Eternal Savior

517 Lord, Keep Us Steadfast in Your Word (A)

579 Lord, You Give the Great Commission (A)

323 God Loved the World (B)

482 I Come with Joy (B)

496 One Bread, One Body (C)

Vigil of Pentecost (A, B, C)

401 Gracious Spirit, Heed Our Pleading /
Njoo kwetu, Roho mwema

403 Like the Murmur of the Dove's Song

577, 578   Creator Spirit, Heavenly Dove

Day of Pentecost

395 Come, Holy Ghost, God and Lord

407 O Living Breath of God / *Soplo de Dios viviente*

627 O Day Full of Grace

643 We Are All One in Christ / *Somos uno en Cristo* (A)

400 God of Tempest, God of Whirlwind (B)

404 Come, Gracious Spirit, Heavenly Dove (C)

The Holy Trinity

410 All Glory Be to God on High

414 Holy God, We Praise Your Name

577, 578   Creator Spirit, Heavenly Dove

412 Come, Join the Dance of Trinity (A)

540 Go, Make Disciples (A)

413 Holy, Holy, Holy, Lord God Almighty! (B)

396 Spirit of Gentleness (B, C)

845 Voices Raised to You (C)

Sunday, May 24–28 • Lectionary 8

687 Come to Us, Creative Spirit

743 Now to the Holy Spirit Let Us Pray

806 O God, My Faithful God (A)

757 All My Hope on God Is Founded (A, B)

523 Let Us Go Now to the Banquet / *Vamos todos al banquete* (B)

508 As Rain from the Clouds (C)

524 What Is This Place (C)

Sunday, May 29–June 4 • Lectionary 9

521 O Day of Rest and Gladness

633 We've Come This Far by Faith

596, 597   My Hope Is Built on Nothing Less (A)

862 Praise, Praise! You Are My Rock (A)

526 God Is Here! (B)

530 Here, O Lord, Your Servants Gather /
     Sekai no tomo to te o tsunagi (C)

651 Oh, Praise the Gracious Power (C)

Sunday, June 5–11 • Lectionary 10

584 The Son of God, Our Christ

607 Come, Ye Disconsolate

617 We Come to You for Healing, Lord

610 O Christ, the Healer, We Have Come (A, C)

670 Build Us Up, Lord (B)

612 Healer of Our Every Ill (C)

621 Jesus Lives, My Sure Defense (C)

Sunday, June 12–18 • Lectionary 11

580 How Clear Is Our Vocation, Lord

598 For by Grace You Have Been Saved

575 In Christ Called to Baptize (A)

576 We All Are One in Mission (A)

635 We Walk by Faith (B)

663 Spread, Oh, Spread, Almighty Word (B)

328 Restore in Us, O God (C)

587, 588   There's a Wideness in God's Mercy (C)

Sunday, June 19–25 • Lectionary 12

709 When Our Song Says Peace

766 Lord of Our Life
796 How Firm a Foundation (A)
755 Jesus, Savior, Pilot Me (B)
761 Evening and Morning (B)
611 I Heard the Voice of Jesus Say (C)
843 Praise the One Who Breaks the Darkness (C)

Sunday, June 26–July 2 • Lectionary 13

684 Creating God, Your Fingers Trace
714 O God of Mercy, God of Light
641 All Are Welcome (A)
719 Where Cross the Crowded Ways of Life (A)
617 We Come to You for Healing, Lord (B)
733 Great Is Thy Faithfulness (B)
584 The Son of God, Our Christ (C)
798 Will You Come and Follow Me / *The Summons* (C)

Sunday, July 3–9 • Lectionary 14

396 Spirit of Gentleness
675 O Christ, Our Light, O Radiance True
777 Come to Me, All Pilgrims Thirsty (A)
606 Our Father, We Have Wandered (A, B)
576 We All Are One in Mission (B, C)
579 Lord, You Give the Great Commission (B, C)
735 Mothering God, You Gave Me Birth (C)

Sunday, July 10–16 • Lectionary 15

506 The Word of God Is Source and Seed
513 Listen, God Is Calling / *Neno lake Mungu*
512 Lord, Let My Heart Be Good Soil (A)
518 We Eat the Bread of Teaching (A)
645 Christ Is Made the Sure Foundation (B)
717 Let Justice Flow like Streams (B)
708 Jesu, Jesu, Fill Us with Your Love (C)
712 Lord, Whose Love in Humble Service (C)

Sunday, July 17–23 • Lectionary 16

648 Beloved, God's Chosen
786 O Holy Spirit, Enter In
604 O Christ, Our Hope (A)

693 Come, Ye Thankful People, Come (A)

654 The Church's One Foundation (B)

789 Savior, like a Shepherd Lead Us (B)

711 O Day of Peace (C)

725 When the Poor Ones / *Cuando el pobre* (C)

Sunday, July 24–30 • Lectionary 17

515 Break Now the Bread of Life

775 Jesus, Priceless Treasure

622 Neither Death nor Life (A)

464 Bread of Life, Our Host and Meal (B)

469 By Your Hand You Feed Your People (B)

746, 747   Our Father, God in Heaven Above (C)

887 This Is My Song (C)

Sunday, July 31–August 6 • Lectionary 18

655 Son of God, Eternal Savior

464 Bread of Life, Our Host and Meal (A)

469 By Your Hand You Feed Your People (A)

461 All Who Hunger, Gather Gladly (B)

485 I Am the Bread of Life (B)

678 God, Whose Giving Knows No Ending (C)

734 God, Whose Farm Is All Creation (C)

Sunday, August 7–13 • Lectionary 19

400 God of Tempest, God of Whirlwind

793 Be Thou My Vision

755 Jesus, Savior, Pilot Me (A)

794 Calm to the Waves (A)

474 Bread of Life from Heaven (B)

804 Come Down, O Love Divine (B)

683 The Numberless Gifts of God's Mercies (C)

764 Have No Fear, Little Flock (C)

Sunday, August 14–20 • Lectionary 20

759 My Faith Looks Up to Thee

813 Faith of Our Fathers

733 Great Is Thy Faithfulness (A)

735 Mothering God, You Gave Me Birth (A)

498 United at the Table / *Unidos en la fiesta* (B)

518 We Eat the Bread of Teaching (B)
666 What Wondrous Love Is This (C)
788 If God My Lord Be for Me (C)

Sunday, August 21–27 • Lectionary 21

620 How Sweet the Name of Jesus Sounds
795 God, My Lord, My Strength
652 Built on a Rock (A)
717 Let Justice Flow like Streams (A)
849 Yours, Lord, Is the Glory / *Tuya es la gloria* (A, B)
474 Bread of Life from Heaven (B)
757 All My Hope on God Is Founded (B)
581 You Are Mine (C)
625 Come, We That Love the Lord / *We're Marching to Zion* (C)

Sunday, August 28–September 3 • Lectionary 22

507 O God of Light
804 Come Down, O Love Divine
510 Word of God, Come Down on Earth (A)
667 Take Up Your Cross, the Savior Said (A)
772 Oh, That the Lord Would Guide My Ways (B)
806 O God, My Faithful God (B)
523 Let Us Go Now to the Banquet / *Vamos todos al banquete* (C)
532 Gather Us In (C)

Sunday, September 4–10 • Lectionary 23

716 Lord of All Nations, Grant Me Grace
722 O Christ, Your Heart, Compassionate
470 Draw Us in the Spirit's Tether (A)
603 God, When Human Bonds Are Broken (A)
612 Healer of Our Every Ill (B)
719 Where Cross the Crowded Ways of Life (B)
667 Take Up Your Cross, the Savior Said (C)
799 Come, Follow Me, the Savior Spake (C)
801 Change My Heart, O God (C)

Sunday, September 11–17 • Lectionary 24

605 Forgive Our Sins As We Forgive
834 Immortal, Invisible, God Only Wise
482 I Come with Joy (A)

776 What God Ordains Is Good Indeed (A)

733 Great Is Thy Faithfulness (B)

806 O God, My Faithful God (B)

779 Amazing Grace, How Sweet the Sound (C)

789 Savior, like a Shepherd Lead Us (C)

Sunday, September 18–24 • Lectionary 25

587, 588 There's a Wideness in God's Mercy

589 All Depends on Our Possessing

678 God, Whose Giving Knows No Ending (A)

686 We Give Thee but Thine Own (A)

397 Loving Spirit (B)

659 Will You Let Me Be Your Servant (B)

710 Let Streams of Living Justice (C)

717 Let Justice Flow like Streams (C)

Sunday, September 25–October 1 • Lectionary 26

712 Lord, Whose Love in Humble Service

801 Change My Heart, O God

416 At the Name of Jesus (A)

772 Oh, That the Lord Would Guide My Ways (A)

607 Come, Ye Disconsolate (B)

800 Spirit of God, Descend upon My Heart (B)

621 Jesus Lives, My Sure Defense (C)

750 Lord, Thee I Love with All My Heart (C)

Sunday, October 2–8 • Lectionary 27

769 If You But Trust in God to Guide You

796 How Firm a Foundation

447 O Blessed Spring (A)

727 Lord Christ, When First You Came to Earth (A)

648 Beloved, God's Chosen (B)

876 Let the Whole Creation Cry (B)

633 We've Come This Far by Faith (C)

635 We Walk by Faith (C)

Sunday, October 9–15 • Lectionary 28

646 The Peace of the Lord / *La paz del Señor*

833 Oh, That I Had a Thousand Voices

488, 489 Soul, Adorn Yourself with Gladness /
Vengo a ti, Jesús amado (A)
523 Let Us Go Now to the Banquet / *Vamo todos al banquete* (A)
506 The Word of God Is Source and Seed (B)
678 God, Whose Giving Knows No Ending (B)
617 We Come To You for Healing, Lord (C)
829 Have You Thanked the Lord? (C)

Sunday, October 16–22 • Lectionary 29
745 Lord, Teach Us How to Pray Aright
580 How Clear Is Our Vocation, Lord
581 You Are Mine (A)
686 We Give Thee but Thine Own (A)
416 At the Name of Jesus (B)
712 Lord, Whose Love in Humble Service (B)
517 Lord, Keep Us Steadfast in Your Word (C)
742 What a Friend We Have in Jesus (C)

Sunday, October 23–29 • Lectionary 30
790 Day by Day
820 O Savior, Precious Savior
708 Jesu, Jesu, Fill Us with Your Love (A)
729 The Church of Christ, in Every Age (A)
612 Healer of Our Every Ill (B)
673 God, Whose Almighty Word (B)
581 You Are Mine (C)
606 Our Father, We Have Wandered (C)

Sunday, October 30–November 5 • Lectionary 31
360 Love Consecrates the Humblest Act
631 Love Divine, All Loves Excelling
510 Word of God, Come Down on Earth (A)
709 When Our Song Says Peace (A, B)
648 Beloved, God's Chosen (B)
590 Salvation unto Us Has Come (C)
779 Amazing Grace, How Sweet the Sound (C)

Sunday, November 6–12 • Lectionary 32
436 Wake, Awake, for Night Is Flying
724 All Who Love and Serve Your City

638　Blessed Assurance (A)

710　Let Streams of Living Justice (A)

686　We Give Thee but Thine Own (B)

725　When the Poor Ones / *Cuando el pobre* (B)

339　Christ, the Life of All the Living (C)

619　I Know That My Redeemer Lives! (C)

Sunday, November 13–19 • Lectionary 33

438　My Lord, What a Morning

645　Christ Is Made the Sure Foundation

670　Build Us Up, Lord (A)

678　God, Whose Giving Knows No Ending (A)

434　Jesus Shall Reign (B)

596, 597　My Hope Is Built on Nothing Less (B, C)

757　All My Hope on God Is Founded (B, C)

Christ the King • Sunday, November 20–26 • Lectionary 34

430　Rejoice, for Christ Is King!

431　O Christ, What Can It Mean for Us

719　Where Cross the Crowded Ways of Life (A)

826　Thine the Amen (A)

408　Come, Thou Almighty King (B)

435　Lo! He Comes with Clouds Descending (B)

343　My Song Is Love Unknown (C)

432　The Head That Once Was Crowned (C)

The Use of the Means of Grace

A Statement on the Practice of Word and Sacrament

Adopted for guidance and practice by the Fifth Biennial Churchwide Assembly of the Evangelical Lutheran Church in America, August 19, 1997.

PREFACE: THE TRIUNE GOD AND THE MEANS OF GRACE

The Triune God acts in the means of grace
Principle 1

Jesus Christ is the living and abiding Word of God. By the power of the Spirit, this very Word of God, which is Jesus Christ, is read in the Scriptures, proclaimed in preaching, announced in the forgiveness of sins, eaten and drunk in the Holy Communion, and encountered in the bodily presence of the Christian community. By the power of the Spirit active in Holy Baptism, this Word washes a people to be Christ's own Body in the world. We have called this gift of Word and Sacrament by the name "the means of grace." The living heart of all these means is the presence of Jesus Christ through the power of the Spirit as the gift of the Father.

Background 1A

"We believe we have the duty not to neglect any of the rites and ceremonies instituted in Scripture, whatever their number. We do not think it makes much difference if, for purposes of teaching, the enumeration varies, provided what is handed down in Scripture is preserved. For that matter, the Fathers did not always use the same enumeration."[1]

Background 1B

In Christ's flesh, in his death and resurrection, all people are invited to behold and to receive the fullness of God's grace and truth.[2]

The Triune God creates the Church
Principle 2

God gives the Word and the sacraments to the Church and by the power of the Spirit thereby creates and sustains the Church among us.[3] God establishes the sacraments "to awaken and confirm faith."[4] God calls the Church to exercise care and fidelity in its use of the means of grace, so that all people may hear and believe the Gospel of Jesus Christ and be gathered into God's own mission for the life of the world.

Background 2A

In a world of yearning, brokenness, and sin, the Church's clarity about the Gospel of Jesus Christ is vital. God has promised to come to all through the means of grace: the Word and the sacraments of Christ's institution. While the Church defines for itself customary practices that reflect care and fidelity, it is these means of grace that define the Church.

Background 2B

Yet even the Church itself is threatened should it fail to claim the great treasures of the Gospel. Either careless practice or rigid uniformity may distort the power of the gift. This statement is one way in which we, in the Church, can give counsel to one another, supporting and sustaining one another in our common mission.

Background 2C

We are people whose lives are degraded by sin. This estrangement from God manifests itself in many ways, including false values and a sense of emptiness. Many in our time are deprived or depriving, abusing or abused. All humanity, indeed all creation, is threatened by sin that erupts in greed, violence, and war. In the midst of isolation, lovelessness, and self-absorption, the Church is tempted to turn in on itself, its own needs, and preferences. As a church in this time, we seek to give and receive God's Word and sacraments as full and reliable signs of Christ.

What is the Church?
Principle 3

"It is also taught among us that one holy Christian church will be and remain forever. This is the assembly of all believers among whom the Gospel is preached in its purity and the holy sacraments are administered according to the Gospel."[5]

Background 3A

The Evangelical Lutheran Church in America is committed by its statement of purpose to "worship God in proclamation of the Word and administration of the sacraments and through lives of prayer, praise, thanksgiving, witness, and service."[6] The Scriptures and our Confessions establish this purpose. We believe that "through the Word and the sacraments, as through means, the Holy Spirit is given, and the Holy Spirit produces faith, where and when it pleases God, in those who hear the Gospel."[7]

This statement encourages unity amid diversity
Principle 4

The gift of Word and Sacrament is from God. This statement on sacramental practices seeks to encourage unity among us in the administration of the means of grace and to foster common understanding and practice. It does not seek to impose uniformity among us.

Background 4A

This statement grows out of this church's concern for healthy pastoral action and strong congregational mission. It does not address our practice of Word and Sacrament out of antiquarian or legalistic interests but rather to ground the practice of our church in the Gospel and to encourage good order within our church.

Application 4B

Our congregations receive and administer the means of grace in richly diverse ways. This diversity in practice is well grounded in the Confessions. "It is not necessary for the true unity of the Christian church that ceremonies of human institution should be observed uniformly in all places."[8] We are united in one common center: Jesus Christ proclaimed in Word and sacraments amidst participating assemblies of singing, serving, and praying people.

PART I: PROCLAMATION OF THE WORD AND THE CHRISTIAN ASSEMBLY

What is the Word of God?
Principle 5

Jesus Christ is the Word of God incarnate. The proclamation of God's message to us is both Law and Gospel. The canonical Scriptures of the Old and New Testaments are the written Word of God.[9] Through this Word in these forms, as through the sacraments, God gives faith, forgiveness of sins, and new life.

Application 5A

Proclamation of the Word includes the public reading of Scripture, preaching, teaching, the celebration of the sacraments, confession and absolution, music, arts, prayers, Christian witness, and service. The congregation's entire educational ministry participates in the proclamation of the Word.

Sunday provides a day for assembly around Word and Sacrament
Principle 6

Sunday, the day of Christ's resurrection and of the appearances to the disciples by the crucified and risen Christ, is the primary day on which Christians gather to worship. Within this assembly, the Word is read and preached and the sacraments are celebrated.

Application 6A

Sunday is the principal festival day of Christians. The Holy Communion is one name for the Sunday service of Word and Sacrament in which the congregation assembles in God's presence, hears the word of life, baptizes and remembers Baptism, and celebrates the Holy Supper. The service of Word and Sacrament is also celebrated on other great festivals of the year, according to the common Christian calendar received in our churches. The Christian community may gather for proclamation and the Lord's Supper at other times as well, as, for example, on other days of the week, and when the services of marriage or of the burial of the dead are placed within the context of the Holy Communion.[10]

The Scriptures are read aloud

Principle 7
The public reading of the Holy Scriptures is an indispensable part of worship, constituting the basis for the public proclamation of the Gospel.

Application 7A
The use of ELCA-approved lectionaries serves the unity of the Church, the hearing of the breadth of the Scriptures, and the evangelical meaning of the church year. The Revised Common Lectionary and the lectionaries in Lutheran Book of Worship make three readings and a psalm available for every Sunday and festival.

Application 7B
The use of a Bible or lectionary of appropriate size and dignity by those who read the Scriptures aloud, the use of this book in liturgical processions, and its placement on the reading desk or pulpit may bring the centrality of the Word to visible expression.

The baptized people proclaim God's Word
Principle 8

All the baptized share responsibility for the proclamation of the Word and the formation of the Christian assembly.

Application 8A
One of the ways lay people exercise the public proclamation of the Word is as assisting ministers. Among these assisting ministers will be readers of Scripture and also cantors and leaders of prayer.[11]

Application 8B

Musicians serve the assembly by illuminating the readings and the sacraments, by the congregation's participation in song.

Application 8C

There are varieties of ways beyond the assembly in which the public ministry of the Word is exercised. Some of these include the work of catechists, evangelists, and teachers.

God's Word is preached
Principle 9

The preaching of the Gospel of the crucified and risen Christ is rooted in the readings of the Scriptures in the assemblies for worship. Called and ordained ministers bear responsibility for the preached Word in the Church gathered for public worship.[12]

Application 9A

Preaching is the living and contemporary voice of one who interprets in all the Scriptures the things concerning Jesus Christ.[13] In fidelity to the readings appointed for the day, the preacher proclaims our need of God's grace and freely offers that grace, equipping the community for mission and service in daily life. "Only under extraordinary circumstances would the sermon be omitted" from the Sunday and festival service of Holy Communion.[14]

Application 9B

While other persons may sometimes preach, the called pastor of a congregation has responsibility for this preaching, ordinarily preparing and delivering the sermon and overseeing all public ministry of the Word in the congregation. In congregations without a called pastor, the synodical bishop assumes this responsibility, often by providing an interim pastor. All Christians, however, bear responsibility to speak and teach the Gospel in daily life.

The common voice of the assembly speaks the Word
Principle 10

The assembled congregation participates in proclaiming the Word of God with a common voice. It sings hymns and the texts of the liturgy. It confesses the Nicene or Apostles' Creed.[15]

Application 10A

Hymns, the liturgy, and the creeds are means for the community itself to proclaim and respond to the Word of God.[16] This witness should be valued, taught, and taken to heart.

The treasury of music is ever expanding with new compositions and with songs from the churches of the world.

The arts serve the Word
Principle 11

Music, the visual arts, and the environment of our worship spaces embody the proclamation of the Word in Lutheran churches.

Application 11A

Music is a servant of the Gospel and a principal means of worshiping God in Lutheran churches. Congregational song gathers the whole people to proclaim God's mercy, to worship God, and to pray, in response to the readings of the day and in preparation for the Lord's Supper.

Application 11B

In similar ways the other arts also are called to serve the purposes of the Christian assembly. The visual arts and the spaces for worship assist the congregation to participate in worship, to focus on the essentials, and to embody the Gospel.

Application 11C

In these times of deeper contact among cultures, our congregations do well to make respectful and hospitable use of the music, arts, and furnishings of many peoples. The Spirit of God calls people from every nation, all tribes, peoples, and languages to gather around the Gospel of Jesus Christ.[17]

Confession and Absolution proclaim the Word
Principle 12

The Gospel also is proclaimed in Confession and Absolution (the Office of the Keys) and in the mutual conversation and consolation of the brothers and sisters.[18] Our congregations are called to make faithful use of corporate and individual confession of sins and holy absolution.

Application 12A

Absolution is a speaking and hearing of the Word of God and a return to Baptism. The most important part of confession and forgiveness is the "work which God does, when he absolves me of my sins through a word placed in the mouth" of a human being.[19] Liturgical patterns for corporate and individual confession and forgiveness are given in Lutheran worship books.

On other occasions Christians assemble around the Word
Principle 13

Assemblies for worship are not limited to Sunday or to celebrations of Word and Sacrament. Christians gather for worship on other days of the week, for morning or evening prayer, for services of the Word or devotions, to mark local and national festivals, and for important life occasions such as weddings and funerals. Christians also gather in their own homes for prayer, Bible reading, and devotions.

Application 13A

Every opportunity for worship is valued and encouraged. The communal observance of morning and evening prayer and the celebration of weddings and funerals within services of Word and Sacrament in the congregation are appropriate traditions. Morning and evening prayers and mealtime blessings in the household are also an extension of corporate worship.

PART II: HOLY BAPTISM AND THE CHRISTIAN ASSEMBLY

What is Baptism?
Principle 14

In Holy Baptism the Triune God delivers us from the forces of evil, puts our sinful self to death, gives us new birth, adopts us as children, and makes us members of the body of Christ, the Church. Holy Baptism is received by faith alone.

Background 14A

By water and the Word in Baptism, we are liberated from sin and death by being joined to the death and resurrection of Jesus. In Baptism God seals us by the Holy Spirit and marks us with the cross of Christ forever.[20] Baptism inaugurates a life of discipleship in the death and resurrection of Christ. Baptism conforms us to the death and resurrection of Christ precisely so that we repent and receive forgiveness, love our neighbors, suffer for the sake of the Gospel, and witness to Christ.

Application 14B

Baptism is for the sake of life in Christ and in the body of Christ, the Church. It also may be given to those who are close to death, and is a strong word of promise in spite of death. Individuals are baptized, yet this Baptism forms a community. It is for children. It is for adults. It is done once, yet it is for all of our life.

Jesus Christ has given Holy Baptism
Principle 15

Baptism was given to the Church by Jesus Christ in the Great Commission, but also in his own baptism by John and in the baptism of the cross.

Background 15A

One great source of the teaching and practice of the Church regarding Baptism is the Great Commission: "Go therefore and make disciples of all nations, baptizing them in the name of the Father and of the

Son and of the Holy Spirit, and teaching them to obey everything that I have commanded you. And remember, I am with you always, to the end of the age."[21]

Background 15B

Other passages are also part of the biblical tradition of the origin and meaning of Baptism. Another source is the account of Jesus' own baptism at the River Jordan. While Jesus is the eternal Son of God, all who are baptized into him are adopted as beloved children of God. With Jesus all the baptized are anointed by the outpoured Spirit. Because of Jesus we are, through Baptism, gathered and included in the life of the Triune God.

Background 15C

In two places in the New Testament where Jesus speaks of his own baptism,[22] he refers not to his being washed in the Jordan River, but to his impending death.[23] It is that death to which we are joined in Baptism, according to the witness of Paul.[24]

Baptism is once for all
Principle 16

A person is baptized once. Because of the unfailing nature of God's promise, and because of God's once-for-all action in Christ, Baptism is not repeated.

Background 16A

Baptism is a sign and testimony of God's grace, awakening and creating faith. The faith of the one being baptized "does not constitute Baptism but receives it. . . ." "Everything depends upon the Word and commandment of God. . . ."[25]

Application 16B

Rebaptism is to be avoided[26] since it causes doubt, focusing attention on the always-failing adequacy of our action or our faith. Baptized persons who come to new depth of conviction in faith are invited to an Affirmation of Baptism in the life of the congregation.[27]

Application 16C

There may be occasions when people are uncertain about whether or not they have been baptized. Pastors, after supportive conversation and pastoral discernment, may choose to proceed with the baptism. The practice of this church and its congregations needs to incorporate the person into the community and its ongoing catechesis and to proclaim the sure grace of God in Christ, avoiding any sense of Baptism being repeated.

Baptism involves daily dying and rising
Principle 17

By God's gift and call, all of us who have been baptized into Christ Jesus are daily put to death so that we might be raised daily to newness of life.[28]

Background 17A

Believers are at the same time sinners and justified. We experience bondage to sin from which we cannot free ourselves and, at the same time, "rebirth and renewal by the Holy Spirit."[29] The baptismal life is expressed each time the baptized confess their sins and receive forgiveness. "Repentance, therefore, is nothing else than a return and approach to Baptism. . . ."[30]

Application 17B

There are many ways to encourage this daily dying to sin and being raised to live before God. They include confession and absolution, the reading of the Scriptures, preaching, the mutual comfort and consolation of the sisters and brothers,[31] daily prayer and the sign of the cross, the remembrance of the catechism, and the profession of the creed.

Application 17C

Christians continue in the covenant God made with them in Baptism by participation in the community of faith, by hearing the Word and receiving Christ's Supper, by proclaiming the good news in word and deed, and by striving for justice and peace in all the world.[32]

Baptism is for all ages
Principle 18

God, whose grace is for all, is the one who acts in Baptism. Therefore candidates for Baptism are of all ages. Some are adults and older children who have heard the Gospel of Jesus Christ, declare their faith, and desire Holy Baptism. Others are the young or infant children of active members of the congregation or those children for whom members of the congregation assume sponsorship.

Application 18A

Since ancient times, the Christian Church has baptized both infants and adults.[33] Our times require great seriousness about evangelization and readiness to welcome unbaptized adults to the reception of the faith and to Baptism into Christ. Our children also need this sign and means of grace and its continued power in their lives. In either case, Baptism is God's gift of overwhelming grace. We baptize infants as if they were adults, addressing them with questions, words, and promises that their parents, sponsors, and congregation are to help them know and believe as they grow in years. We baptize adults as if they were infants, washing them and clothing them with God's love in Christ.

Baptism includes catechesis
Principle 19

Baptism includes instruction and nurture in the faith for a life of discipleship.

Application 19A

When infants and young children are baptized, the parents and sponsors receive instruction and the children are taught throughout their development. With adults and older children, the baptismal candidates themselves are given instruction and formation for faith and ministry in the world both prior to and following their baptism. The instruction and formation of sponsors, parents, and candidates prior to Baptism deals especially with faith in the triune God and with prayer. In the case of adults and older children this period of instruction and formation is called the catechumenate.

Occasional Services includes an order for the enrollment of candidates for Baptism.[34]

Application 19B

The parish education of the congregation is part of its baptismal ministry. Indeed, all of the baptized require lifelong learning, the daily reappropriation of the wonderful gifts given in Baptism.

Sponsors assist those being baptized
Principle 20

Both adults and infants benefit from having baptismal sponsors. The primary role of the sponsors is to guide and accompany the candidates and, so far as possible, their families in the process of instruction and Baptism. They help the baptized join in the life and work of the community of believers for the sake of the world.

Application 20A

Congregations are encouraged to select at least one sponsor from among the congregational members for each candidate for Baptism.[35] Additional sponsors who are involved in the faith and life of a Christian community may also be selected by parents of the candidate or by the candidate. Choosing and preparing sponsors requires thoughtful consideration and includes participation by pastors or other congregational leaders.

Background 20B

The sponsors of children are often called godparents. They may fulfill a variety of social roles in certain cultures. The roles may be regarded as an elaboration of the central baptismal role they have undertaken. Such sponsors take on a lifelong task to recall the gifts of Baptism in the life of their godchild.

Background 20C

The sponsor provided by the congregation is, in the case of the baptism of an infant, especially concerned to accompany the family as it prepares for Baptism and, as a mentor, to assist the integration of the child into the community of faith as it grows in years. In the case of the baptism of an adult, this sponsor accompanies the candidate throughout the catechumenate, in prayer and in mutual learning, assisting the newly baptized adult to join in the ministry and mission of this community.

Application 20D

The entire congregation prays for those preparing for Baptism, welcomes the newly baptized, and provides assistance to sponsors.

Baptism takes place in the assembly
Principle 21

Candidates for Holy Baptism, sponsors, and an ordained minister called by the Church gather together with the congregation for the celebration of Baptism within the corporate worship of the Church.

Application 21A

When pastoral considerations require Baptism to take place outside of corporate worship, if at all possible representatives of the congregation gather for Baptism. In such a case a public announcement of the baptism is made at the service the following Sunday.

Application 21B

Baptism may take place at varying points in the worship service. When the Baptism follows the Liturgy of the Word, it helps to emphasize Baptism's connection to the promise of the Gospel and faith in that promise and leads the baptized to the altar. When infants are baptized in a service where adults are not, the Baptism may be part of the entrance rite. This emphasizes that their instruction is to follow and reminds the whole congregation of the baptismal nature of the order for Confession and Forgiveness. At the Vigil of Easter, baptisms are placed between the Service of Readings and the proclamation of the Easter texts. This helps Christians to remember their burial with Christ into death, and rising with him to new life.

A pastor presides at Baptism
Principle 22

An ordained minister presides at Holy Baptism.[36]

Application 22A

God is the one who acts in Baptism. The pastor, congregation, candidates, and sponsors gather around the font to administer the sacrament. The pastor presides in the midst of a participating community. Ordinarily this presider is the pastor of the congregation where the Baptism is being celebrated. The pastor acts as baptizer, but does so within a congregation of the Church which actively assents and responds.

Baptism may occur before an imminent death
Principle 23

In cases of imminent death, a person may be baptized by any Christian. Should sudden death prevent Baptism, we commend the person to God with prayer, trusting in God's grace.

Application 23A

Counsel for such a baptism at the time of imminent death may be found in Occasional Services and should be widely known in the Christian community.[37] A dead person, child or adult, is not baptized. Prayers at such a death may include naming, signing with the cross, anointing for burial, and commendation to God. Prayers and commendations may be offered in the event of a stillbirth or of the early loss of a pregnancy.

Application 23B

When a person who was baptized in imminent danger of death survives, Occasional Services provides for a Public Recognition of the Baptism at corporate worship.[38]

We baptize in the name of the Triune God
Principle 24

Holy Baptism is administered with water in the name of the triune God, Father, Son, and Holy Spirit. Baptism into the name of the triune God involves confessing and teaching the doctrine and meaning of the Trinity. The baptized are welcomed into the body of Christ. This is the community which lives from "the grace of the

Lord Jesus Christ, the love of God, and the communion of the Holy Spirit . . . ."[39]

Background 24A

The Church seeks to maintain trinitarian orthodoxy while speaking in appropriate modern language and contexts. While a worldwide ecumenical discussion is now underway about such language, we have no other name in which to baptize than the historic and ecumenically received name.[40]

Background 24B

It is in the crucified Jesus that we meet the God to whom he entrusted all, who raised him from the dead for us, and who poured out the Spirit from his death and resurrection. Washing with water in this name is much more than the use of a formula. The name is a summary of the power and presence of the triune God and of that teaching which must accompany every Baptism. Without this teaching and without the encounter with the grace, love, and communion of the triune God, the words may be misunderstood as a magic formula or as a misrepresentation of the one God in three persons, "equal in glory, coeternal in majesty."[41] What Father and Son mean, in biblical and creedal perspective, must also be continually reexamined. The doctrine of God teaches us the surprising theology of the cross and counters "any alleged Trinitarian sanction for sinful inequality or oppression of women in church and society."[42]

Application 24C

Some Christians, however, are received into our congregations from other churches in which they were baptized "in the name of Jesus Christ."[43] There are some whose Baptisms were accompanied by trinitarian examination and confession of faith,[44] and whose Baptisms have occurred within the context of trinitarian life and teaching. We will do well to avoid quarrels over the validity of these Baptisms.

Application 24D

Outside the context of trinitarian life and teaching no Christian Baptism takes place, whatever liturgical formula may be used.

Baptism is a public sign
Principle 25

We seek to celebrate Baptism in such a way that the celebration is a true and complete sign of the things which Baptism signifies.[45]

Background 25A

"The pedagogical force of practice is considerable."[46] A strong baptismal theology calls for a strong baptismal practice, teaching and showing forth the meaning of Baptism and inviting Christians to discover continually its importance for their daily lives. Those who plan baptisms attend to the use of faithful words and gracious actions, to including the event within the Sunday service, to the architectural or natural setting, to the regular preparation of candidates, sponsors, parents, and congregation for Baptism, to post-baptismal teaching that strengthens us for mission, and to the possibility of great festivals as times for Baptism.

Application 25B

"It is appropriate to designate such occasions as the Vigil of Easter, the Day of Pentecost, All Saints' Day, and the Baptism of Our Lord for the celebration of Holy Baptism. Baptismal celebrations on these occasions keep Baptism integrated into the unfolding of the story of salvation provided by the church year."[47] The Vigil of Easter is an especially ancient and appropriate time for Baptism, emphasizing the origin of all baptism in Christ's death and resurrection.

Water is used generously
Principle 26

Water is a sign of cleansing, dying, and new birth.[48] It is used generously in Holy Baptism to symbolize God's power over sin and death.

Application 26A

A variety of modes may be used; for example, both immersion and pouring show forth God's power in Baptism. Immersion helps to communicate the dying and rising with Christ. Pouring suggests cleansing from sin. We have taught that it is not the water which does such great things, but the Word of God connected with the water.[49] God can use whatever water we have. Yet, with Martin Luther, we wish to make full use of water, when it is possible. "For baptism . . . signifies that the old man [self] and the sinful birth of flesh and blood are to be wholly drowned by the grace of God. We should therefore do justice to its meaning and make baptism a true and complete sign of the thing it signifies."[50]

A font is located in the assembly
Principle 27

A baptismal font filled with water, placed in the assembly's worship space, symbolizes the centrality of this sacrament for faith and life.

Application 27A

As congregations are able, they may consider the creation of fonts of ample proportions filled with flowing water, or baptismal pools which could allow immersion. "The location of the font within the church building should express the idea of entrance into the community of faith, and should allow ample space for people to gather around."[51]

Other signs proclaim the meanings of Baptism
Principle 28

The laying on of hands and prayer for the Holy Spirit's gifts, the signing with the cross, and the anointing with oil help to appropriate the breadth of meanings in Baptism. Other symbolic acts also are appropriate such as the clothing with a baptismal garment and the giving of a lighted candle.

Background 28A

These interpretive signs proclaim the gifts that are given by the promise of God in Baptism itself. Some keys to their interpretation are given in the Holy Scriptures. The laying on of both hands with the prayer for the gifts of the Holy Spirit is a sign of the pouring out of the Spirit of God to empower the people of God for mission. The sign of the cross marks the Christian as united with the Crucified. The use of oil is a sign of anointing with the Spirit and of union with Jesus Christ, the anointed one of God.

Baptism incorporates into the Church
Principle 29

In Baptism people become members not only of the Church universal but of a particular congregation. Therefore all baptisms are entered into the permanent records of the congregation and certificates are issued at the time of the administration of the sacrament.

Application 29A

The time of the presentation of this certificate may be at the Baptism itself or at a post-baptismal visit or during post-baptismal formation. The Evangelical Lutheran Church in America keeps a roster from the baptismal ministry of its military chaplains.

Baptism is repeatedly affirmed
Principle 30

The public rite for Affirmation of Baptism may be used at many times in the life of a baptized Christian. It is especially appropriate at Confirmation and at times of reception or restoration into membership.

Application 30A

"When there are changes in a Christian's life, rites of affirmation of Baptism and intercessory prayer could mark the passage."[52] "Moving into a nursing home, beginning parenthood or grandparenthood, choosing or changing an occupation, moving out of the parental home, the diagnosis of a chronic illness, the end of one's first year of mourning, the ending of a relationship, and retirement are all examples of life's transitions that could be acknowledged by these rites."[53] Other examples include adoption and the naming of an already baptized child, release from prison, reunion of an immigrant family, and new life after abuse or addiction.

Application 30B

Every Baptism celebrated in the assembly is an occasion for the remembrance and renewal of baptism on the part of all the baptized. The Easter Vigil especially provides for a renewal of baptism.[54]

PART III: HOLY COMMUNION AND THE CHRISTIAN ASSEMBLY

What is Holy Communion?
Principle 31

At the table of our Lord Jesus Christ, God nourishes faith, forgives sin, and calls us to be witnesses to the Gospel.

Background 31A

Here we receive Christ's body and blood and God's gifts of forgiveness of sin, life, and salvation to be received by faith for the strengthening of faith.[55]

Jesus Christ has given the Holy Communion
Principle 32

The Lord's Supper was instituted by Jesus Christ on the night of his betrayal.[56]

Background 32A

In numerous places in the Gospels, the early Church also recognized the eucharistic significance of other meals during Christ's ministry and after his resurrection.[57]

Jesus Christ is truly present in this sacrament
Principle 33

In this sacrament the crucified and risen Christ is present, giving his true body and blood as food and drink. This real presence is a mystery.

Background 33A

The Augsburg Confession states: "It is taught among us that the true body and blood of Christ are really present in the Supper of our Lord under the form of bread and wine and are there distributed and received."[58] The Apology of the Augsburg Confession adds: "We are talking about the presence of the living Christ, knowing that 'death no longer has dominion over him.' "[59]

Background 33B

"The 'how' of Christ's presence remains as inexplicable in the sacrament as elsewhere. It is a presence that remains 'hidden' even though visible media are used in the sacrament. The earthly element is . . . a fit vehicle of the divine presence and it, too, the common stuff of our daily life, participates in the new creation which has already begun."[60]

The celebration of Holy Communion includes both Word and sacramental meal
Principle 34

The two principal parts of the liturgy of Holy Communion, the proclamation of the Word of God and the celebration of the sacramental meal, are so intimately connected as to form one act of worship.

Application 34A

Our congregations are encouraged to hold these two parts together, avoiding either a celebration of the Supper without the preceding reading of the Scriptures, preaching, and intercessory prayers or a celebration of the Supper for a few people who remain after the dismissal of the congregation from a Service of the Word. The Holy Communion is not simply appended to the offices of Morning or Evening Prayer.

Application 34B

The simple order of our liturgy of Holy Communion, represented in the worship books of our church, is that which has been used by generations of Christians. We gather in song and prayer, confessing our need of God. We read the Scriptures and hear them preached. We profess our faith and pray for the world, sealing our prayers with a sign of peace. We gather an offering for the poor and for the mission of the Church. We set our table with bread and wine, give thanks and praise to God, proclaiming Jesus Christ, and eat and drink. We hear the blessing of God and are sent out in mission to the world.

The Holy Communion is celebrated weekly
Principle 35

According to the Apology of the Augsburg Confession,[61] Lutheran congregations celebrate the Holy Communion every Sunday and festival. This confession remains the norm for our practice.

Background 35A
The Church celebrates the Holy Communion frequently because the Church needs the sacrament, the means by which the Church's fellowship is established and its mission as the baptized people of God is nourished and sustained.[62] This practice was reaffirmed in 1989 by the Evangelical Lutheran Church in America. We continue to need "consistent pastoral encouragement and instruction relating to Holy Communion . . . pointing up Christ's command, his promise, and our deep need."[63] For a variety of historical reasons, Lutherans in various places moved away from the weekly celebration of the sacrament.

Application 35B
All of our congregations are encouraged to celebrate the Lord's Supper weekly, but not every service need be a Eucharist.

Application 35C
Participation in the sacramental meal is by invitation, not demand. The members of this church are encouraged to make the sacrament a frequent rather than an occasional part of their lives.

The Holy Communion has a variety of names
Principle 36

A variety of names demonstrate the richness of Holy Communion. Those names include the Lord's Supper, Holy Communion,

Eucharist, Mass, the Sacrament of the Altar, the Divine Liturgy, and the Divine Service.

Background 36A

Each name has come to emphasize certain aspects of the sacrament. The "Lord's Supper" speaks of the meal which the risen Lord holds with the Church, the meal of the Lord's Day, a foretaste of the heavenly feast to come. "Holy Communion" accentuates the holy *koinonia* (community) established by the Holy Spirit as we encounter Christ and are formed into one body with him and so with each other. "Eucharist" calls us to see that the whole meal is a great thanksgiving for creation and for creation's redemption in Jesus Christ. "Divine Liturgy" says the celebration is a public action, carried out by a community of people. Yet, "Divine Service" helps us to see that the primary action of our gathering is God's astonishing service to us; we are called to respond in praise and in service to our neighbor. The term "Mass" is probably derived from the old dismissal of the participants at the end of the service and the sending away of the bread and the cup to the absent: it invites us into mission. "Sacrament of the Altar" invites each one to eat and drink from the true altar of God, the body and blood of Christ given and shed "for you."[64]

The Holy Communion is given to the baptized
Principle 37

Admission to the Sacrament is by invitation of the Lord, presented through the Church to those who are baptized.[65]

Application 37A

When adults and older children are baptized, they may be communed for the first time in the service in which they are baptized. Baptismal preparation and continuing catechesis include instruction for Holy Communion.

Background 37B

Customs vary on the age and circumstances for admission to the Lord's Supper. The age for communing children continues to be discussed and reviewed in our congregations. When "A Report on the Study of Confirmation and First Communion"[66] was adopted, a majority of congregations now in the Evangelical Lutheran Church in America separated confirmation and reception of Holy Communion and began inviting children to commune in the fifth grade. Since that time a number of congregations have continued to lower the age of communion, especially for school age children. Although A Statement on Communion Practices[67] precluded the communion of infants, members and congregations have become aware of this practice in some congregations of this church, in historical studies of the early centuries of the Church, in the Evangelical Lutheran Church in Canada, and in broader ecumenical discussion.

Application 37C

Baptized children begin to commune on a regular basis at a time determined through mutual conversation that includes the pastor, the child, and the parents or sponsors involved, within the accepted practices of the congregation. Ordinarily this beginning will occur only when children can eat and drink, and can start to respond to the gift of Christ in the Supper.

Application 37D

Infants and children may be communed for the first time during the service in which they are baptized or they may be brought to the altar during communion to receive a blessing.

Application 37E

In all cases, participation in Holy Communion is accompanied by catechesis appropriate to the age of the communicant. When infants and young children are communed, the parents and sponsors receive instruction and the children are taught throughout their development.

Background 37F

Catechesis, continuing throughout the life of the believer, emphasizes the sacrament as gift, given to faith by and for participation in the community. Such faith is not simply knowledge or intellectual understanding but trust in God's promises given in the Lord's Supper ("for you" and "for the forgiveness of sin") for the support of the baptized.

Application 37G

When an unbaptized person comes to the table seeking Christ's presence and is inadvertently communed, neither that person nor the ministers of Communion need be ashamed. Rather, Christ's gift of love and mercy to all is praised. That person is invited to learn the faith of the Church, be baptized, and thereafter faithfully receive Holy Communion.

The age of first Communion may vary
Principle 38

Common mission among the congregations of this church depends on mutual respect for varied practice in many areas of church life including the ages of first Communion.

Background 38A

"In faithful participation in the mission of God in and through this church, congregations, synods, and the churchwide organization— as interdependent expressions of this church—shall be guided by the biblical and confessional commitments of this church. Each shall recognize that mission efforts must be shaped by both local needs and global awareness, by both individual witness and corporate endeavor, and by both distinctly Lutheran emphases and growing ecumenical cooperation."[68]

Background 38B

There is no command from our Lord regarding the age at which people should be baptized or first communed. Our practice is defined by Christ's command ("Do this"), Christ's twin promises of his presence for us and for our need, and the importance of good order in the Church. In all communion practices congregations strive to avoid both reducing the Lord's Supper to an act effective by its mere performance without faith and narrowing faith to intellectual understanding of Christ's presence and gifts. Congregations continually check their own practices and statements against these biblical and confessional guides.

Application 38C

Congregations of this church may establish policies regarding the age of admission to Holy Communion. They also may grant pastoral exceptions to those policies in individual cases which honor and serve the interdependence (koinonia) of congregations of this church.

Application 38D

Out of mutual respect among congregations, children who are communing members of a congregation of this church who move to a congregation with a different practice should be received as communing members (perhaps as a pastoral exception to the congregation's general policy). They and their parents also should be respectful of the traditions and practices of their new congregation. Even if transferring children have received education appropriate to their age in a former parish, the new congregation's program of instruction is also to be followed.

The Holy Communion takes place in the assembly
Principle 39

The gathered people of God celebrate the sacrament. Holy Communion, usually celebrated within a congregation, also may be celebrated in synodical, churchwide, and other settings where the baptized gather.

Application 39A

Authorization for all celebrations of Communion in a parish setting where there is a called and ordained minister of Word and Sacrament is the responsibility of the pastor in consultation with the Congregation Council.

Application 39B

In established centers of this church—e.g., seminaries, colleges, retreat centers, charitable institutions, and administrative centers— authorization for the celebration of Holy Communion shall be given, either for a limited or unlimited time, by the presiding bishop of this church or, where only one synod is concerned, by the bishop of that synod.

Application 39C

In institutions not formally associated with this church—e.g., hospitals, retirement homes, colleges and universities, or military bases—where there is a called pastor or chaplain, authorization for the celebration of Holy Communion rests with the pastor in consultation with the appropriate calling-sending expression of this church.[69]

Background 39D

The authorizing role of bishops is a sign of our interconnectedness. This church provides for ministry in many settings. Chaplains, for example, bring the means of grace to people in institutions on behalf of the whole Church.

A pastor presides at the Holy Communion
Principle 40

In witness that this sacrament is a celebration of the Church, serving its unity, an ordained minister presides in the service of Holy Communion and proclaims the Great Thanksgiving. Where it is not possible for an extended period of time to provide ordained pastoral leadership, a synodical bishop may authorize a properly trained lay person to preside for a specified period of time and in a given location only.[70]

Background 40A

"In the celebration of the eucharist, Christ gathers, teaches and nourishes the church. It is Christ who invites to the meal and who presides at it. He is the shepherd who leads the people of God, the prophet who announces the Word of God, the priest who celebrates the mystery of God. In most churches, this presidency is signified by an ordained minister. The one who presides at the eucharistic celebration in the name of Christ makes clear that the rite is not the assembly's own creation or possession; the eucharist is received as a gift from Christ living in his church. The minister of the eucharist is the ambassador who represents the divine initiative and expresses the connection of the local community with other local communities in the universal Church."[71]

Lay assisting ministers serve in many roles
Principle 41

Designated and trained lay persons serve in a variety of leadership roles in the Eucharist. Among these assisting ministers will be readers, interpreters, cantors, musicians and choir members, servers of communion, acolytes, leaders of prayer, those who prepare for the meal, and those who offer hospitality.[72]

Background 41A
"The liturgy is the celebration of all who gather. Together with the pastor who presides, the entire congregation is involved. It is important, therefore, that lay persons fulfill appropriate ministries within the service."[73]

Preparation is recommended
Principle 42

Forms of preparation for Holy Communion focus the community of faith both on the breadth of creation's need for redemption and the depth of God's redemptive actions. Such forms of preparation are recommended, but not required, for that person "is worthy and well prepared who believes these words, 'for you' and 'for the forgiveness of sins.'"[74]

Application 42A
Opportunities for corporate and individual confession and absolution, including the use of the Brief Order for Confession and Forgiveness, are especially appropriate. Helpful forms of personal preparation may include self-examination, prayer, fasting, meditation, and reconciliation with others through the exchange of peace.

Background 42B
In considering preparation for Holy Communion many people in our congregations have turned for counsel to Paul's admonition to the Corinthians: "Examine yourselves, and only then eat of the bread and drink of the cup. For all who eat and drink without discerning the body eat and drink judgment against themselves."[75] Paul's words are addressed to those in the community who are eating

and drinking while excluding from the meal others who belong to Christ. "Do you show contempt for the church of God," he says, "and humiliate those who have nothing?"[76] The body that Christians need to discern is the body of Christ which is the Church[77] and that is the body which is being ignored by the exclusions in Corinth.

The Holy Communion is consecrated by the Word of God and prayer
Principle 43

The biblical words of institution declare God's action and invitation. They are set within the context of the Great Thanksgiving. This eucharistic prayer proclaims and celebrates the gracious work of God in creation, redemption, and sanctification.

Application 43A

Our worship books provide several options for giving thanks at the table of the Lord. All of them begin with the dialogue of invitation to thanksgiving and conclude with the Lord's Prayer. Most of them include the preface and the Sanctus after the dialogue. Many continue with an evangelical form of the historic prayer after the Sanctus. The full action, from dialogue through the Lord's Prayer, including the proclamation of the words of institution, is called the Great Thanksgiving. Our congregations, synods, and churchwide organization are encouraged to use these patterns of thanksgiving.[78]

Bread and wine are used
Principle 44

In accordance with the words of institution, this church uses bread and wine in the celebration of the Lord's Supper. Communicants normally receive both elements, bread and wine, in the Holy Communion.

Application 44A

A loaf of bread and a chalice are encouraged since they signify the unity which the sacrament bestows. The bread may be leavened or unleavened. The wine may be white or red.

Background 44B

The use of leavened bread is the most ancient attested practice of the Church and gives witness to the connection between the Eucharist and ordinary life. Unleavened bread underscores the Passover themes which are present in the biblical accounts of the Last Supper.

Application 44C

For pressing reasons of health, individuals may commune under one element. In certain circumstances, congregations might decide to place small amounts of non-wheat bread or nonalcoholic wine or grape juice on the altar. Such pastoral and congregational decisions are delicate, and must honor both the tradition of the Church and the people of each local assembly.

Background 44D

Some communicants suffer from allergic reactions or are recovering from alcoholism. As suggested by the 1989 Evangelical Lutheran Church in America *A Statement on Communion Practices,*[79] it is appropriate for them to receive only one of the elements. Their pastor may assure them that the crucified and risen Christ is fully present for them in, with, and under this one element. While our confessions speak against Communion "in one form,"[80] their intent is to protest the practice of withholding the cup from the whole assembly. The confessional concern is to make both the bread and the wine of the sacrament available to the faithful, and not to inhibit them.

Communion practices reflect unity and dignity
Principle 45

Practices of distributing and receiving Holy Communion reflect the unity of the Body of Christ and the dignity and new life of the baptized.

Application 45A

The promise of Christ is spoken to each communicant by those distributing the Sacrament: "The Body of Christ given for you;" "The Blood of Christ shed for you." Ordinarily the bread is placed in the communicant's hand and the chalice is guided by the communicant or carefully poured by the minister of communion.

Application 45B

Continuous communion of the whole congregation, with the post-communion blessing given after all have communed, underscores the aspects of fellowship and unity in the sacrament. Either standing or kneeling is appropriate when receiving Communion.[81] Ministers of Communion will need to facilitate the communion of those who have difficulty moving, kneeling, standing, holding the bread, or guiding the chalice.

Application 45C

Common devotion during the distribution of Communion is served both by music and by silence.

Leaders commune at each service
Principle 46

As a sign of unity, and out of their own need for grace, the presiding minister and assisting ministers may commune at each Eucharist.

Application 46A

"It is appropriate within the Lutheran tradition that the presiding minister commune himself/herself or receive the Sacrament from an assistant."[82] This reception may be before or after the congregation communes.

The bread and wine are handled with reverence
Principle 47

The bread and wine of Communion are handled with care and reverence, out of a sense of the value both of what has been set apart by the Word as a bearer of the presence of Christ and of God's good creation.

Application 47A

The food needed for the sacramental meal is placed on the table before the Great Thanksgiving. This is done so that the gathered assembly may see the full sign of the food it is to share, and so that we may give thanks and proclaim God's promise in conjunction with the use of this very bread and wine. Nonetheless, in the rare event that more of either element is needed during distribution, it is not necessary to repeat the words of institution.[83]

Application 47B
Any food that remains is best consumed by the presiding and assisting ministers and by others present following the service.

Congregations provide Communion for the absent
Principle 48

Congregations provide for communion of the sick, homebound, and imprisoned.

Application 48A
Occasional Services provides an order for the Distribution of Communion to Those in Special Circumstances. As an extension of the Sunday worship, the servers of Communion take the elements to those unable to attend.[84]

Application 48B
When pastors celebrate a service of Word and Sacrament in a home, hospital, or other institution, the corporate nature of the gift is strengthened by including others from the congregation. Occasional Services provides an order for the Celebration of Holy Communion with Those in Special Circumstances.[85]

We practice eucharistic hospitality
Principle 49

Believing in the real presence of Christ, this church practices eucharistic hospitality. All baptized persons are welcomed to Communion when they are visiting in the congregations of this church.

Application 49A
Admission to the sacrament is by invitation of the Lord, presented through the Church to those who are baptized.[86] It is a sign of hospitality to provide a brief written or oral statement in worship

which teaches Christ's presence in the sacrament. This assists guests to decide whether they wish to accept the Lord's invitation. In the exercise of this hospitality, it is wise for our congregations to be sensitive to the eucharistic practices of the churches from which visitors may come.

Application 49B

When a wedding or a funeral occurs during a service of Holy Communion, communion is offered to all baptized persons.

Lutherans long for unity at Christ's table
Principle 50

Because of the universal nature of the Church, Lutherans may participate in the eucharistic services of other Christian churches.

Background 50A

This church's ongoing ecumenical dialogues continue to seek full communion with other Christian churches.

Application 50B

When visiting other churches Lutherans should respect the practices of the host congregation. A conscientious decision whether or not to commune in another church is informed by the Lutheran understanding of the Gospel preached and the sacraments administered as Christ's gift.

Application 50C

For Lutheran clergy to be involved as presiding or assisting ministers in the celebration of Holy Communion in other churches, a reciprocal relationship between the denominations involved should prevail.[87]

PART IV: THE MEANS OF GRACE AND CHRISTIAN MISSION

The means of grace lead the Church to mission
Principle 51

In every celebration of the means of grace, God acts to show forth both the need of the world and the truth of the Gospel. In every gathering of Christians around the proclaimed Word and the holy sacraments, God acts to empower the Church for mission. Jesus Christ, who is God's living bread come down from heaven, has given his flesh to be the life of the world.[88] This very flesh, given for the life of all, is encountered in the Word and sacraments.

Background 51A

Baptism and baptismal catechesis join the baptized to the mission of Christ. Confession and absolution continually reconcile the baptized to the mission of Christ. Assembly itself, when that assembly is an open invitation to all peoples to gather around the truth and presence of Jesus Christ, is a witness in the world. The regular proclamation of both Law and Gospel, in Scripture reading and in preaching, tells the truth about life and death in all the world, calls us to faith in the life-giving God, and equips the believers for witness and service. Intercessory prayer makes mention of the needs of all the world and of all the Church in mission. When a collection is received, it is intended for the support of mission and for the concrete needs of our neighbors who are sick, hurt, and hungry. The holy Supper both feeds us with the body and blood of Christ and awakens our care for the hungry ones of the earth. The dismissal from the service sends us in thanksgiving from what we have seen in God's holy gifts to service in God's beloved world.

Application 51B

In the teaching and practice of congregations, the missional intention for the means of grace needs to be recalled. By God's gift, the Word and the sacraments are set in the midst of the world, for the life of the world.[89]

Baptism comes to expression in Christian vocation
Principle 52

Christians profess baptismal faith as they engage in discipleship in the world. God calls Christians to use their various vocations and ministries to witness to the Gospel of Christ wherever they serve or work.

Background 52A

"As baptized people, we see our daily life as a place to carry out our vocation, our calling. All aspects of life, home and school, community and nation, daily work and leisure, citizenship and friendship, belong to God. All are places where God calls us to serve. God's Word and the church help us to discover ways to carry out our calling."[90]

Application 52B

Teaching about vocation and opportunities for witness and service play an important role in the preparation of adults for Baptism and in post-baptismal catechesis for both adults and children.

The Word of God leads Christians to lived prayer
Principle 53

Because of the living Word of God, Christian assemblies for worship are occasions for intercessory prayer. On the grounds of the Word and promise of God the Church prays, in the power of the Spirit and in the name of Jesus Christ, for all the great needs of the world.

Application 53A

Intercessory prayer is one of the ways that Christians exercise the priesthood of all the baptized. In the Sunday service, such prayer is appropriately led by a lay assisting minister. This prayer is also lived. Christians are called and empowered by the triune God to be a presence of faith, hope, and love in the midst of the needs of the community and the world.[90]

The Holy Communion strengthens us to witness and to work for justice
Principle 54

As a means of grace Holy Communion is that messianic banquet at which God bestows mercy and forgiveness, creates and strengthens faith for our daily work and ministry in the world, draws us to long for the day of God's manifest justice in all the world, and provides a sure and certain hope of the coming resurrection to eternal life.

Background 54A

Christian eschatology, the teaching that God has an intention and a goal for all the beloved created universe, belongs to the celebration of Holy Communion and to the catechesis of all communicants. This Supper forms the Church, as a community, to bear witness in the world. Our need to be nourished and sustained in this mission is one principal reason for the frequent celebration of the sacrament.

Application 54B

"When you have partaken of this sacrament, therefore, or desire to partake of it, you must in turn share the misfortunes of the fellowship, . . . Here your heart must go out in love and learn that this is a sacrament of love. As love and support are given to you, you in turn must render love and support to Christ in his needy ones. You must feel with sorrow all the dishonor done to Christ in his holy Word, all the misery of Christendom, all the unjust suffering of the innocent, with which the world is everywhere filled to overflowing. You must fight, work, pray, and—if you cannot do more—have heartfelt sympathy. . . . It is Christ's will, then, that we partake of it frequently, in order that we may remember him and exercise ourselves in this fellowship according to his example."[91]

Notes to Appendix C

1 Apology of the Augsburg Confession, Article xiii. Note: all citations of confessional material are from the *Book of Concord*, translated and edited by Theodore G. Tappert (Philadelphia: Fortress Press, 1959).

2 John 1:14-16.

3 The Small Catechism, The Creed, The Third Article.

4 Augsburg Confession, Article xiii.

5 Augsburg Confession, Article vii.

6 *Constitution, Bylaws, and Continuing Resolutions of the Evangelical Lutheran Church in America*, 1995, 4.02.

7 Augsburg Confession, Article v.

8 Augsburg Confession, Article vii.

9 *Constitution, Bylaws, and Continuing Resolutions of the Evangelical Lutheran Church in America*, 2.02.

10 *LBW* Ministers Edition (Minneapolis: Augsburg Publishing House, and Philadelphia: Board of Publication, Lutheran Church in America, 1978), 36-37.

11 *LBW* Ministers Edition, 25. See also Principle 41.

12 See *Baptism, Eucharist and Ministry. Faith and Order Paper No. 111*, (Geneva: World Council of Churches, 1982), Ministry, 8; Augsburg Confession, Article xiv; also *The Study of Ministry Report to the 1991 Assembly: Study Edition* (Chicago: ELCA Division for Ministry, 1991).

13 Luke 24:27.

14 *LBW* Ministers Edition, 27.

15 The Athanasian Creed is also a confession of the Church, but is rarely used in public worship.

16 Colossians 3:16.

17 Revelation 7:9.

18 Smalcald Articles, iii, 4.

19 The Large Catechism, A Brief Exhortation to Confession, 15.

20 Cf. *LBW* (Minneapolis: Augsburg Publishing House, and Philadelphia: Board of Publication, Lutheran Church in America, 1978), 121, 124.

21 Matthew 28:19-20.

22 Luke 12:50; Mark 10:38.

23 The Confirmation Ministry Task Force Report, ELCA, 1993, 4.

24 Romans 6:3.

25 The Large Catechism, Baptism, 53.

26 *Baptism, Eucharist and Ministry*, Baptism, 13.

27 The Large Catechism, Baptism, 47-63.

28 The Small Catechism, The Sacrament of Holy Baptism, part four, 12. See also Romans 6.

29 Titus 3:5.

30 The Large Catechism, Baptism, 75-90.

31 Smalcald Articles, iii, 4.

32 *LBW*, 201.

33 *Baptism, Eucharist and Ministry*, Baptism, 11–12.

34 *Occasional Services: A Companion to Lutheran Book of Worship* (Minneapolis: Augsburg Publishing House and Philadelphia: Board of Publication, Lutheran Church in America, 1982), 13-15.

35 *Statement on Sacramental Practices*, Evangelical Lutheran Church in Canada, 1991.

36 *Baptism, Eucharist and Ministry*, Baptism, 22.

37 *Occasional Services* (1982), 16-22.

38 *Occasional Services* (1982), 17-22.

39 2 Corinthians 13:13.

40 *Baptism, Eucharist and Ministry*, Baptism, 17.

41 Athanasian Creed.

42 Action of the Conference of Bishops, March 8-11, 1991, ELCA.

43 Acts 2:38.

44 Apostolic Tradition of Hippolytus, 21.

45 Martin Luther, "The Holy and Blessed Sacrament of Baptism," 1, in *Luther's Works* 35:29.

46 *The Sacrament of the Altar and Its Implications*, United Lutheran Church in America, 1960, c.5.

47 *LBW* Ministers Edition, 30; cf. Baptism, Eucharist and Ministry, Baptism, 23.

48 *LBW*, 122.

49 The Small Catechism, part four.

50 Martin Luther, "The Holy and Blessed Sacrament of Baptism," 1, *Luther's Works*, 35:29.

51 *LBW* Ministers Edition, 30.

52 *The Confirmation Ministry Task Force Report*, 9–10.

53 *The Confirmation Ministry Task Force Report*, 9–10.

54 *LBW* Ministers Edition, 152.

55 The Small Catechism, and Augsburg Confession xiii.2.

56 Matthew 26:26-29 and parallels; 1 Corinthians 11:23-24.

57 See, for example, Mark 6:30-52 and parallels, Luke 24:13-35.

58 Augsburg Confession, Article x.

59 Apology of the Augsburg Confession, Article xxiv.

60 *The Sacrament of the Altar and Its Implications*, United Lutheran Church in America, 1960.

61 Apology of the Augsburg Confession, Article xxiv.

62 "The Grace-full Use of the Means of Grace: Theses on Worship and Worship Practices," Lutheran members of the North American Academy of Liturgy, 1994, 28.

63 *A Statement on Communion Practices*, ELCA, 1989, ii.b.2. (Identical to 1978 statement of predecessor church bodies.)

64 "The Grace-full Use of the Means of Grace: Theses on Worship and Worship Practices," 27.

65 *A Statement on Communion Practices*, 1989, ii.a.2.

66 "A Report on the Study of Confirmation and First Communion by Lutheran Congregations," Joint Lutheran Commission on the Theology and Practice of Confirmation. (Philadelphia: Lutheran Church in America, 1969).

67 *A Statement on Communion Practices*, 1989, ii.a.2.

68 *Constitution, Bylaws, and Continuing Resolutions of the Evangelical Lutheran Church in America*, 8.16.

69 *A Statement on Communion Practices*, 1989, ii.a.6. See also churchwide continuing resolution 7.44.a96 on the "Table of Sources of Calls for Ordained Ministers."

70 *Constitution, Bylaws, and Continuing Resolutions of the Evangelical Lutheran Church in America*, 7.61.01.

71 *Baptism, Eucharist and Ministry*, Eucharist, 29.

72 See also Application 8a.

73 *LBW* Ministers Edition, 25.

74 The Small Catechism, Article vi. Formula of Concord, Solid Declaration vii., 68-69.

75 1 Corinthians 11:28-29.

76 1 Corinthians 11:22.

77 1 Corinthians 12.

78 Apology of the Augsburg Confession, Article xxiv., 76.

79 *A Statement on Communion Practices*, 1989, ii.c.3.

80 See Smalcald Articles, iii., 6.

81 *A Statement on Communion Practices*, 1989, ii.c.3.

82 *A Statement on Communion Practices*, 1989, ii.c.3.

83 *A Statement on Communion Practices*, 1989, ii.c.2.

84 *Occasional Services* (1982), 76-82.

85 *Occasional Services* (1982), 83-88.

86   *A Statement on Communion Practices*, 1989, ii.a.2.

87   *A Statement on Communion Practices*, 1989, ii.a.7.

88   John 6:51.

89   John 1:14; Matthew 28:19; John 10:10.

90   *The Confirmation Ministry Task Force Report*, 5; *Together for Ministry: Final Report and Recommendations of the Task Force on the Study of Ministry*, 1993, 15-16.

91   Martin Luther, "The Blessed Sacrament of the Holy and True Body of Christ, and the Brotherhoods," 9,12. *Luther's Works*, 35:54, 56-57.

Statement on Sacramental Practices

EVANGELICAL LUTHERAN CHURCH IN CANADA

© 1991 Evangelical Lutheran Church in Canada

1.0   Preface

1.1   This Statement on Sacramental Practices identifies theological foundations and practical principles for Baptism and Holy Communion.

1.2   This Statement is intended for the enrichment of the life and ministry of the whole church. It is commended to this church—its synods, seminaries, congregations and individual members—to affirm the importance of the sacraments in our common life and to guide our sacramental practices.

1.3   This Statement is intended to encourage continuation of the process of study and dialogue which led to its formulation.

1.4   This Statement is both representative of Lutheran tradition and indicative of the ELCIC's commitment to and participation in ecumenical ministries.

1.5   Although confirmation is traditionally related to both Baptism and Holy Communion, in this Statement confirmation ministry is not addressed.

2.0   Introduction

2.1   The Evangelical Lutheran Church in Canada, guided by Scripture and the Lutheran Confessions and acknowledging its roots, both theological and historical, in the one, holy, catholic and apostolic church, affirms its commitment to a faithful ministry of Word and Sacrament.

2.2   From the earliest period of the Christian era, the church has celebrated the incorporation of its people into the Christian community and has nourished them through a ministry of Word and Sacrament. It is in accord with apostolic tradition to baptize and to offer Holy Communion to God's people.

2.3   It is the practice in the Evangelical Lutheran Church in Canada to use the name Baptism for the sacrament of incorporation, and a variety of names for the sacramental meal—Eucharist, Holy Communion and the Lord's Supper being the most common. In this Statement the names are used interchangeably.

2.4   The sacraments of Baptism and the Lord's Supper are means of grace through which God's gracious, forgiving, and nurturing love is freely given to God's people. These sacraments are gifts of God's presence.

2.5   Baptism is the sacrament of initiation into life with Christ. Holy Communion is the sacrament that nurtures and strengthens us in this life. "It is taught among us that the sacraments were instituted not only to be signs by which people might be identified outwardly as Christians, but that they are signs and testimonies of God's will toward us for the purpose of awakening and strengthening our faith" (The Augsburg Confession, Article XIII).

3.0   Theological Foundations: Baptism

3.1   The Sacrament of Christian Baptism is grounded in the life, death, and resurrection of Jesus. The institution of Christian Baptism has its source in the Great Commission and in Jesus' own baptism. (Matt. 28:19-20; Matt. 3:13-17; Mk. 1:9-11; Lk. 3:21-22; John 1:29ff.)

3.2   In Baptism we die and rise with Christ. God acted in Christ to save us; God acts through Baptism to save us. The baptized are pardoned, cleansed and sanctified in Christ. (Rom. 6:3-5.)

3.3   In Baptism we are called into the Christian community and incorporated into the body of Christ, in which we are made a new creation, reconciled to God, and entrusted with the ministry of reconciliation. The community of the baptized is, therefore, the body of Christ, continuing God's mission in the world and sharing in the hope of the world to come. (1 Cor. 12:12ff.; 2 Cor. 5:14-21.)

3.4   In Baptism God seals us with the Holy Spirit, who nurtures our life of faith until we enter into the full possession of our inheritance. We are born anew, and marked with the cross of Christ forever. (2 Cor. 1:21-22; Eph. 1:13-14; John 3:1-8; Rom. 6:1-11.)

3.5 In Baptism we renounce the powers of darkness and dedicate ourselves to participating in the inbreaking reign of God.

3.6 A person is baptized once; Baptism is not repeated. Christians live and affirm their Baptism through daily repentance, receiving forgiveness and renewal in the Holy Spirit. Baptism is a daily dying to sin and rising to newness of life.

4.0 Practical Principles: Baptism

4.1 Baptism is administered with water in the name of the Father, Son and Holy Spirit.

4.2 In the baptismal celebration water is used generously. A variety of modes is used; pouring and immersion are rich symbols of the nature of Baptism.

4.3 Candidates for Baptism are those children born to members of the congregation, children for whom other congregational members assume the responsibility of nurture in the faith, and older children or adults who, following preparation and instruction, declare their faith in Jesus Christ and desire Baptism.

4.4 Baptism is preceded by a period of instruction. Such instruction in faith and life constitutes training in discipleship. When young children are baptized, the parents and sponsors are instructed; otherwise the baptismal candidates themselves are instructed. This training in discipleship continues for the life of the baptized.

4.5 The celebration of the Sacrament of Baptism ordinarily includes the following: presentation, thanksgiving, renunciation of sin and evil, profession of faith, baptism with water, laying on of hands and invocation of the Holy Spirit, signing with the cross and welcome into the congregation.

4.6 Baptism normally takes place within the corporate worship of the congregation and is administered by an ordained minister called by the congregation or by an ordained minister granted permission by the former (Constitution for Synods, Article VII, Section 8).

4.7 In cases of emergency, a person may be baptized by any Christian in the name of the Father, Son and Holy Spirit. Should sudden death preclude such a Baptism, we believe the grace of God will prevail.

4.8   When circumstances require Baptism outside of corporate worship, a public announcement of the Baptism is made at the service the Sunday following. Provision is also made for the use of the rite for Public Recognition of the Baptism at corporate worship (Occasional Services, pp. 17–22).

4.9   The congregation assumes a sponsoring role for all baptized persons within its local setting. Congregations are encouraged to select at least one sponsor from the congregation for each candidate for Baptism. The parents may select additional sponsors. It is assumed that all sponsors are involved in the faith and life of a Christian community. The primary role of sponsors is to provide spiritual nurture and encourage integration of the baptized into the community of believers.

4.10   Baptism is affirmed throughout the Christian's life in daily living and in worship. Regular services of the congregation provide opportunities for participation in confession and forgiveness, the celebration of Holy Communion, and the Baptism of others. The rite for Affirmation of Baptism may be used at any time; it is especially appropriate at confirmation, at times of membership reception and restoration, and during the seasons of Lent and Easter.

4.11   All Baptisms are entered into the permanent records of the congregation and certificates are issued at the time of the administration of the sacrament.

5.0   Theological Foundations: Holy Communion

5.1   The Lord's Supper was instituted by Jesus Christ himself (1 Cor. 11:23-25; Matt. 26:26-28).

5.2   In Holy Communion the crucified and risen Christ is present in word and action. This presence is a mystery.

5.3   Holy Communion is a means of grace through which the crucified and risen Christ awakens faith, saves, forgives, unites, gives life, comforts and strengthens God's people for the work to which they are called in the world.

5.4   Holy Communion is also a great and joyous thanksgiving (Eucharist) for everything accomplished by God in creation, redemption and sanctification. In the Eucharist, God's people give thanks for all of God's blessings.

5.5 Eucharistic celebrations incorporate the whole Christian church in every time and place. The whole church is involved in each local eucharistic celebration (1 Cor. 10:16-17).

5.6 In the Lord's Supper, by the power of the Holy Spirit, we remember and experience anew the creative and redemptive acts of God, receive the gift of the presence of Christ, and look forward in anticipation to our future with God.

5.7 Participation in the Lord's Supper empowers and compels us to imitate the example of our Lord who is both host and servant and to embody and reflect the unity which the Lord's Supper symbolizes. (Lk. 22:24-27; Jn. 13:1-20; 1 Cor. 10:17.)

5.8 In Baptism we are incorporated into the body of Christ, the church. In Holy Communion the church is nourished and strengthened. Therefore we speak of and practice communion of the baptized.

6.0 Practical Principles: Holy Communion

6.1 In the Eucharist, Christ gathers, teaches and nourishes the people of God. It is these gathered people of God who celebrate the Eucharist.

6.2 In accordance with traditional church practice and the Lutheran Confessions, an ordained minister, as one whose ministry originates within and is affirmed by the whole church, presides over the eucharistic celebration. Only one ordained minister presides.

6.3 Persons not ordained may be authorized by the synodical bishop to preside at the Lord's Supper in those situations where an ordained minister is not available for an extended period of time. Such exemptions are allowed for only a specific time, place, and person.

6.4 Our liturgical practice embodies the priesthood of all believers; therefore, properly trained lay persons serve in a variety of roles including the distribution of the elements.

6.5 As a participant in the worshipping community and as a symbol of the unity of the church, the presiding minister communes at each Eucharist. Such communion may be served by an assisting minister or be self-administered.

6.6 The Brief Order for Confession and Forgiveness may be used before the Eucharist. Opportunities for corporate and private confession and forgiveness preceding the Eucharist are especially appropriate during penitential seasons of the Church Year.

6.7 Holy Communion has two principal parts: the proclamation of the Word and the sharing of the sacramental meal. Surrounded by prayer, praise and thanksgiving, these two parts are so intimately connected as to form one unified act of worship.

6.8 According to the Lutheran Confessions, Holy Communion is offered every Sunday.

6.9 The Lord's Supper is God's meal for the baptized. Admission to the Supper is by Christ's invitation, offered through the church to the baptized.

6.10 As persons move to congregations where practices differ regarding age for first Communion, care needs to be taken that the difference in practice is resolved in a manner which promotes growth in faith and discipleship for all who are concerned.

6.11 Preparation for the sacrament does not make one worthy to receive the sacrament. However, personal preparation, which may include self-examination, private confession, prayer, fasting, reconciliation with others, and meditation, is encouraged.

6.12 Personal and corporate educational activities of a life-long nature are encouraged as a means of developing an awareness of and receptivity to the gifts of Word and Sacrament.

6.13 We are committed to eucharistic hospitality. Baptized persons of Lutheran and other Christian faith communities are welcomed to the Lord's Table.

6.14 Because of the universal nature of the church, Lutherans may participate in eucharistic services of other Christian churches. As a visitor, one should respect the practice of the host congregation.

6.15 Lutherans traditionally use bread and wine in the celebration of the Lord's Supper. In certain circumstances grape juice is used. (1 Cor. 11:23-26; Matt. 26:26-29; Mk. 14:22-25.)

6.16 Both elements are offered in Holy Communion. Communicants normally receive both bread and wine. Under certain circumstances the reception of only one element is acceptable.

6.17 Practices vary as to the use of one loaf of bread or wafers and as to the use of a chalice or individual glasses. A loaf of bread and the common cup are rich biblical symbols of the unity of the church.

6.18 Holy Communion, usually celebrated within a congregational setting, may also be celebrated in non-congregational settings where the baptized gather for worship. The presider is to be an ordained minister.

6.19 Congregations will provide Holy Communion for those persons who, for reasons of illness or confinement, are unable to attend public worship. As an extension of the congregation's celebration of the Eucharist, trained and designated lay members may distribute Holy Communion following the worship service. At other times, ordained persons may celebrate the sacrament with those unable to participate in public worship. (Occasional Services, pp. 76–88.)

6.20 The biblical words of institution declare God's action and invitation. They are set within the context of the Great Thanksgiving. A variety of eucharistic prayers is available and their use is encouraged. These prayers of thanksgiving lift up the gracious work of God in creation, redemption, and sanctification.

6.21 A sufficient quantity of bread and wine to serve the congregation is brought to the altar. Should more of either element be needed during distribution, a further prayer for the sanctification of the elements may be said.

6.22 The elements offered for the celebration of the Lord's Supper have been set aside for a special purpose. Leftover elements are consumed by those present, or disposed of in an appropriate manner.

6.23 A variety of practices is followed in the distribution and reception of the elements. The practice chosen should provide the image and experience of unity in the body of Christ. One post-Communion blessing, after all have been served, best expresses this unity. Either kneeling or standing is an acceptable posture for reception. Care needs to be taken to ensure that hospitality is extended to disabled persons.

6.24 In the distribution and reception of the elements, the practice of placing the bread in the communicant's hand is encouraged. The chalice is to be guided or received by the communicant.

6.25 The practice of intinction—the dipping of the bread into the wine—is an acceptable mode of reception.

Bibliography

Adams, William Seth. *Shaped By Images: One Who Presides*. New York: Church Hymnal Corporation, 1995.

Bushkofsky, Dennis, and Craig Satterlee. *The Christian Life*. Using *Evangelical Lutheran Worship*, vol. 2. Augsburg Fortress, 2008.

Cherwien, David. *Let the People Sing! A Keyboardist's Creative and Practical Guide to Engaging God's People in Meaningful Song*. St. Louis: Concordia, 1997.

Evangelical Lutheran Worship Hymns Audio Edition, vol. 1 & 2. Augsburg Fortress, 2006-2007.

Evangelical Lutheran Worship Liturgies Audio Edition, vol. 1, 2, & 3. Augsburg Fortress, 2006, 2010.

Evangelical Lutheran Worship: Simplified Keyboard Accompaniment Edition, Service Music and Hymns. Augsburg Fortress, 2007. *Liturgies*. Augsburg Fortress, 2011.

Evangelical Lutheran Worship: Guitar Accompaniment Edition, Service Music and Hymns. Augsburg Fortress, 2007.

Farlee, Robert Buckley, ed. *Leading the Church's Song*. Augsburg Fortress, 1998.

Galley, Howard. *Ceremonies of the Eucharist: A Guide to Celebration*. Cambridge: Cowley, 1989.

Hackett, Charles D., and Don E. Saliers. *The Lord Be With You: A Visual Handbook for Presiding in Christian Worship*. Cleveland: OSL, 1990.

Hovda, Robert W. *Strong, Loving, and Wise: Presiding in Liturgy*. Fifth edition. Collegeville: Liturgical, 1983.

Huffman, Walter C. *Prayer of the Faithful: Understanding and Creatively Leading Corporate Intercessory Prayer*. Revised edition. Augsburg Fortress, 1992.

Indexes to Evangelical Lutheran Worship. Augsburg Fortress, 2007.

Kavanagh, Aidan. *Elements of Rite: A Handbook of Liturgical Style*. New York: Pueblo, 1982.

Lathrop, Gordon W. *Central Things: Worship in Word and Sacrament*. Augsburg Fortress, 2005.

Lathrop, Gordon W. *The Pastor: A Spirituality*. Fortress Press, 2006.

Leonard, John K., and Nathan D. Mitchell. *The Postures of the Assembly During the Eucharistic Prayer*. Chicago: Liturgy Training Publications, 1994.

Luther, Donald J. *Ministers of Communion from the Assembly: A Worship Handbook*. Augsburg Fortress, 2001.

Mueller, Craig. *Preparing the Assembly's Worship: A Worship Handbook*. Augsburg Fortress, 2002.

Musicians Guide to Evangelical Lutheran Worship. Augsburg Fortress, 2007.

Parker, Alice. *Melodious Accord: Good Singing in Church*. Chicago: Liturgy Training Publications, 1991.

Pfatteicher, Philip H., and Carlos R. Messerli. *Manual on the Liturgy*. Augsburg, 1979.

Principles for Worship. Evangelical Lutheran Church in America. Augsburg Fortress, 2002.

Puglisi, James F., ed. *Liturgical Renewal as a Way to Christian Unity*. Collegeville: Liturgical, 2005.

Ramshaw, Gail. *A Three-Year Banquet: The Lectionary for the Assembly*. Augsburg Fortress, 2004.

Ramshaw, Gail, and Mons Teig. *Keeping Time: The Church's Years*. Using *Evangelical Lutheran Worship*, vol. 3. Augsburg Fortress, 2009.

Rimbo, Robert A. *Why Worship Matters*. Augsburg Fortress, 2004.

Satterlee, Craig A. *Presiding in the Assembly: A Worship Handbook*. Augsburg Fortress, 2003.

Spice, Gerald. *Acolytes and Servers: A Worship Handbook*. Augsburg Fortress, 2002.

Spice, Gerald. *Assisting Ministers and Readers: A Worship Handbook*. Augsburg Fortress, 2001.

Stauffer, S. Anita. *Altar Guild and Sacristy Handbook*. Augsburg Fortress, 2000.

Stevick, Daniel. *Crafting the Liturgy*. New York: Church Hymnal Corporation, 1990.

Stuhlmann, Byron. *Prayer Book Rubrics Expanded*. New York: Church Hymnal Corporation, 1987.

Sundays and Seasons. Annual worship planning resource. Augsburg Fortress.

Torvend, Samuel. *Daily Bread, Holy Meal: Opening the Gifts of Holy Communion*. Augsburg Fortress, 2004.

Van Dyk, Leanne, ed. *A More Profound Alleluia: Theology and Worship in Harmony*. Grand Rapids: Eerdmans, 2004

Van Loon, Ralph R., and S. Anita Stauffer. *Assisting Ministers Handbook*. Augsburg Fortress, 1990.

Wengert, Timothy J., ed. *Centripetal Worship: The Evangelical Heart of Lutheran Worship*. Augsburg Fortress, 2007.

Westermeyer, Paul. *Hymnal Companion to Evangelical Lutheran Worship*. Augsburg Fortress, 2010.

Westermeyer, Paul. *The Church Musician*. Rev. ed. Augsburg Fortress, 1997.

Willimon, William. *Preaching and Leading Worship*. Philadelphia: Westminster, 1984.

Worship and Culture in Dialogue. Geneva: Lutheran World Federation, 1994.

Index

ISBN 978-0-8066-7013-3

9 780806 670133

90000